THE

PASSIONS

OF THE SOUL

THE
PASSIONS
OF THE SOUL

RENÉ DESCARTES

An English Translation of

Les Passions de l'âme

Translated and Annotated by

Stephen Voss

Hackett Publishing Company
Indianapolis/Cambridge

René Descartes: 1596-1650

The Passions of the Soul was originally published in 1649.

Cover design by Listenberger Design & Associates
Interior design by Dan Kirklin

For further information, please address

Hackett Publishing Company
P.O. Box 44937
Indianapolis, Indiana 46204

Library of Congress Cataloging-in-Publication Data

Descartes, René, 1596-1650.
    The passions of the soul.

    Bibliography: p.
    1. Emotions—Early works to 1800. 2. Mind and body—
Early works to 1800. I. Voss, Stephen H., 1940–
II. Title.
B1858.E5V67   1988   128'.3   87-23818
ISBN 0-87220-036-1
ISBN 0-87220-035-3 (pbk.)

The paper used in this publication meets the minimum
requirements of American National Standard for Information
Sciences—Permanence of Paper for Printed Library Materials,
ANSI Z39.48-1984.

CONTENTS

Translator's Introduction   vii

Introduction by Geneviève Rodis-Lewis   xv

The Passions of the Soul

Preface   1

Part I   About the Passions in General, and Incidentally about the Entire Nature of Man   18

Part II   About the Number and Order of the Passions, and the Explanation of the Six Primitives   50

Part III   About the Particular Passions   102

Lexicon   136

Index to Lexicon   144

Bibliography   146

Index   156

Index Locorum   160

To Geneviève Rodis-Lewis

TRANSLATOR'S INTRODUCTION

René Descartes offers a vision of the universe, seen and unseen; of our essential nature and our links with the rest of that universe; and of the paths we can take in order to become masters of the parts of it that matter to us. One part of the universe that matters a great deal is our own emotional life, for much of our satisfaction in life finally depends on how well we master it. Descartes voiced his vision with unique power, grace, and clarity, and in ways we understand only incompletely much of it permeates our own more clouded view of things. My aim in presenting this volume is to convey Descartes's vision of our emotions to readers of English in the final years of the twentieth century, by providing a reading of his last publication, *Les passions de l'âme*.

Appearing 350 years after Descartes's *Discours de la méthode*, this book helps celebrate that anniversary, but such a celebration may call for justification. A third of a millenium has passed since the death of Descartes. His outlook is now widely viewed as fundamentally misguided, and his treatise on the passions is ignored in the English-speaking world.

If you have any wish to understand Descartes's vision, you cannot afford to ignore *The Passions of the Soul*. In her Introduction to this volume, Professor Geneviève Rodis-Lewis displays the place of this treatise in the Cartesian enterprise, and so I need not demonstrate the point here.

Is Descartes's vision itself misguided? That is indeed a question worth asking. However, the possibility constitutes no reason at all, under the circumstances, to ignore his thought altogether. In many ways we are all Cartesians—partly because Descartes voiced convictions shared by many non-Cartesians, partly because he voiced new ideas we have assimilated. So we have at least two tasks. The first is to become clear about what Descartes really believed. Those who study this treatise will discover—often, I think, to their surprise—that he believed a good number of things worth taking seriously .

Our second task is to determine which aspects of Descartes's outlook are acceptable and which are not. When aspects of Descartes's thought strike us as simplistic or naive or inhumane, the easy reaction is to throw it all out. However, we should resist this easy reaction, for there is a Descartes who is little known to us, a Descartes whose basic aims and best achievements are little understood in the English-speaking world. That Descartes is perhaps most accessible in the present treatise, for *The Passions of the Soul* presents the upshot of the Cartesian enterprise in the realm that Descartes came to care about more than any other—the technology of the emotions. His concerns in this realm were forged through correspondence with people he saw as friends more than as scholars and for whom he sought to provide counsel that was not only rational but useful in the exigencies of life.

We may come to this treatise expecting to find a "rationalist"—a philosopher using reason alone to demonstrate truths about the emotions and their use and misuse. In fact, we find instead a paradoxical figure. While Descartes is indeed a rationalist, he thinks pure reason is of the greatest value in metaphysics—and this is not a metaphysical work. Once reason establishes that our creator is a perfectly good and powerful God, we are licensed to seek knowledge, using all our knowledge-gaining faculties. In fact, "encouraged" would be closer to the truth than "licensed," for the main aim of the metaphysics is to ground the scientific enterprise, so that it may bear its manifold fruits. That is not all: in the realm of the emotions, reason by itself can do very little. If any principle is axiomatic in this treatise, it is the Principle of Habituation that is introduced in article 44, and yet this Principle is defended, in article 50, by experience and not by reason. If you expect to find geometrically pure reason at work here, it will be a salutary exercise to seek out the passages in which Descartes recommends a mixture of reason and experience for the understanding of the emotions.

Then again, we may come to this work expecting to find unbelievable psychology. This work in particular is likely to arouse such suspicions: first Descartes labels the emotions "passions of the soul," and then he proceeds to treat them "as a physicist," by seeking the causal laws that link them with occurrences in the body. So we may well expect to find the pages of this book soaked with a poisonous compound of soul-body dualism and quaintly obsolete brain physiology.

Here too the Descartes we find is a paradoxical figure. On the one hand, the miasma of that poisonous brew rises off of nearly every page. On the other hand, a massive proportion of Descartes's doctrines remains when the odor dissipates. For example, if what makes you choke is the Cartesian claim that the soul is a substance without location, color, shape, or size, you will find that little if anything in this treatise entails that thesis. Quite the contrary: Descartes says only what he has to about the characteristics of the soul, which thus tends to shrink to a "metaphysical point" (to use Leibniz's phrase). Further, Descartes does his best to explain psychological phenomena physiologically, lodging only what is essential within the soul. For example, "inner conflict," according to article 47, is not a struggle within the soul, but rather between the soul and the brain. The radical consequence, clearly intended by Descartes, is to render much of the phenomenon accessible to the physicist.

Of course, you will find physiology that is now unbelievable; you will find some that should not have been believed then. That too is relatively innocuous, however, for Descartes frequently emphasizes elsewhere that his contribution is to show that *some* physical account, along the general lines of the one he happens to give, will do. For example, must we explain an angry fellow's florid face as the work of the choleric part of the soul—or can its rubicundity be explained physiologically? Descartes offers *one* account of the latter variety. His lasting contribution is often to open the door to just that variety of explanation. Once he gives one, we may criticize it—but we criticize it because we know how to give a *better* explanation that is *also* physiological. We may be dying to speak of electrical impulses, large molecules, and semipermeable membranes and to turn our backs on "animal spirits" in the blood. If so, Descartes would count us as allies, not opponents, in his enterprise.

The philosophical position called functionalism is valuable just at this point: it helps us see that a particular explanation of some human phenomenon often contains both a story about the structure of causal paths and a story about the particular realizations of the events at the nodes of those paths—and that often the first story (the functional one) is more interesting conceptually than the second. If we appreciate the insight within functionalism, we should be better prepared to sort out Descartes's interesting mistakes from those that matter less. (And then we should offer Descartes thanks; he is one of the people who taught us functionalism.)

Finally, we may approach this book expecting to find a bloodless and inhuman geometer of the spirit, one who truly needed a Pascal to remind him that "the heart has its reasons, which reason cannot know." Again we find paradox and complexity just under the surface. It is true that the treatise is the work of a geometrical mind, and one thing that I hope fascinates you as it has me is to watch a clear-minded mathematician picking his way through the minefields of the emotions. He maintains even here the intellectual clarity which is sometimes his most impressive attribute.

Yet Descartes always meant his enterprise to make us "masters and possessors of nature"; he meant the tree of his philosophy to bear fruit, which would provide flesh-and-blood human beings with nourishment and enjoyment. Descartes's rational metaphysics is only the root structure of that tree, and we miss seeing his motivation if we spend our time underground. This treatise is an expression of Descartes's conviction that he could provide help for people subject to disruptive emotions—people like Huygens, whose wife had died, and his friend Elisabeth, who had lost her kingdom, and Descartes himself, as he contemplated the prospect of his own death. His conviction is that metaphysics and physics can ground a strategy for overthrowing the tyranny of the emotions and deriving value from each of them. That strategy will make use of diverse human resources: clear Cartesian reason, informed by his distinctive method; sensitive observation and experiment; active attention, so that truth once apprehended is assimilated; and a resolute determination to apply the truth in order to live as well as possible. This triply paradoxical figure is a Descartes worth taking seriously. Is there a chance that his method can help in our own struggle with the emotions? Can we understand the emotions if we approach them as physicists? Can the peculiar combination of Cartesian reason, imagination, and the senses make this realm accessible? If we understand Descartes's program, we begin to see that these three questions are ones that twentieth-century civilization lays on our laps; a third of a millenium has not made them obsolete. Perhaps you will agree with me that it's worthwhile to get a clear and ordered understanding of the interesting fruit that grew on Descartes's tree.

This book contains a reading of Descartes's treatise on the passions of the soul. The reading consists of three parts: an English translation, a collection of footnotes, and a lexicon.

The aim of the translation is to give people who read English the best possible idea of what Descartes intended as he wrote his treatise. A translation can go in two very different directions: it can convey the reader back to the author, or convey the author to the reader. For example, a translation might teach us to hear Descartes as he spoke in the seventeenth century, or teach him to speak to us in the twentieth. I chose the first option.

I would *like* to convey you to René Descartes's pineal gland and perch you so securely astride it that you will not be disturbed by the streams of animal spirits buffeting it from all directions, and let you peer across the void and discern the very *pensées* that Descartes meant to communicate as he wrote. There are many aspects of his original text that we might try to retain to that end—Descartes's use of uppercase letters for a certain kind of emphasis, his choice between nouns and pronouns and between active and passive voice, his consistency in using his philosophical vocabulary, the cadences and the classical grace of his sentences, and many, many more. This translation's unique flavor derives from an attempt to retain as much of that as is consistent with common translating sense. The task of the reader is now to make a very specific kind of imaginative leap, from the present text to Descartes's *pensées*; the translator's task has simply been to provide the text from which that leap could best be attempted.

The basis for the translation is the text of the original edition of Descartes's treatise, published in 1649. I conjecture that in a couple of dozen places in the text Elzevier's typesetter misconstrued Descartes's manuscript (which is lost) in ways that do not matter much, and I note them here, using the style of abbreviating references to Adam and Tannery that is noted below. I read *s'allongent* for *s'alongent* at 335.19, *ame* for *Ame* at 392.22, *aysement* for *aysément* at 366.27, *Amour* for *amour* at 471.7, *Courage* for *courage* at both 376.7 and 461.8, *Cruauté* for *cruanté* at 483.21, *defense* for *defence* at 359.4, *defiance* for *de fiance* at 482.21, *Devotion* for *devotion* at 454.21, *Escole* for *escole* at both 311.13 and 453.25, *Estime* for *estime* at 373.19, *Haine* for *Hayne* at 410.6, *Indignation* for *indignation* at 378.7, *Joye* for *joye* at 413.20, *lascheté* for *lacheté* at 445.23, *Mespris* for *mespris* at 374.8, *noms* for *nous* at 443.13, *palir* for *pallir* at 478.12, *Passions* for *passions* at 302.10, *poulx* for *pouls* at 334.5, *Reconnoissance* for *reconnoissance* at 483.21, and *se vanger* for *se venger* at 478.27.

There are times when this translation contains terms that are justified by Descartes's original text, even though no corresponding terms occurred in the original. For example, the context might have shown that a feminine pronoun was short for *l'ame*, and that pronoun might be rendered here by "the soul." I mark such terms by brackets. Since the original justifies these terms, they are indeed part of the translation, but the brackets themselves are signals to the reader, not parts of the translation. There is one exception to this rule: sometimes I have added bracketed numerals—[1], [2], etc.—to clauses of long sentences; then, both brackets and numerals are aids to the reader rather than parts of the translation.

The second element in this reading is the footnotes, which are also meant to help the reader make the mentioned leap. One kind of footnote interprets or clarifies passages, along lines suggested by Descartes's original text. Since they are not forced on us by that text, we must place them among the ancillary apparatus, rather than including them in the translation. Another kind of footnote refers the reader to other passages by Descartes—either in the *Passions* or elsewhere—that take up the current point and perhaps cast light on it. Yet a third kind of footnote provides a running outline of the treatise, pointing out the aim of each block of text and its place in the enterprise. Descartes imposes an order upon the elements of his text and clearly believes that those elements cannot be understood fully unless we understand their place in the whole. In a final kind of footnote, I raise in a preliminary way philosophical questions that certain passages themselves suggest. These notes too are part of the reading, for a person cannot understand a text philosophically without seeing which doubts, objections, and requests for clarification the text occasions.

The final element in the reading provided here is the Lexicon, which follows the translation. I summarize my readings of some French terms that are crucial for the theory of the treatise, some that involve ambiguity and related slippage of meaning, some my rendering of which calls for explanation, and some which Descartes uses in ways that are unfamiliar today. Descartes writes in an extremely self-conscious manner; he chooses words carefully, and, like a geometer, once he has chosen a symbol to express an important notion, he usually tries to use it consistently thereafter. If our aim is to reconstruct Descartes's notions, we must pay the same kind of attention to the English words by which we do it. Often the Lexicon lets the reader reconstruct Descartes's own language—one step toward reconstructing his thought.

The book contains further elements that are not part of the reading of Descartes's text. The Bibliography mentions editions and English translations of the treatise and secondary literature, particularly in English, that deals specifically with it. The Index keeps track of people and important subjects mentioned in the text, and the Index Locorum keeps track of specific Cartesian texts mentioned in the footnotes to the text. The title page and the end piece are copies of the ones in Henry le Gras's 1649 printing of the first edition, and I gratefully acknowledge the help of Bancroft Library at the University of California, Berkeley, in reproducing them. The line drawings are a selection from those in Charles Le Brun's work *Conférence sur l'expression générale et particulière* (commonly known as *Conférence sur l'expression des passions*), first published posthumously by Henry Testelin in Paris in 1696. As Chancellor of the Royal Academy of Painting and Sculpture during the reign of Louis XIV, Le Brun (1619-1690) taught a generation of French artists to depict the passions on the basis of the theory he found in Descartes's treatise. Study of these drawings can enhance both philosophical and historical understanding of Descartes's treatise, and I am therefore very grateful to Stephanie Ross, who first called my attention to the connection between Descartes's treatise and Le Brun's *Conférence* some years ago. See her article "Painting the Passions," noted in the Bibliography. The drawings, which are engravings after Le Brun's originals, are housed in the Cabinet des Dessins of the Louvre in Paris; copies appear in Hubert Damisch's presentation of Le Brun's work, in *Nouvelle Revue de Psychanalyse* 21 (1980), 93-131.

Both Professor Rodis-Lewis and I abbreviate references to works we refer to frequently. We use these conventions:

Alquié   Ferdinand Alquié, ed. *Oeuvres philosophiques de Descartes.* Paris: Éditions Garnier Frères, 1963, 1967, 1973. Three volumes. Where no volume number is given, the reference is to Volume III, which contains *Les Passions de l'âme.*

AT   Charles Adam and Paul Tannery, eds. *Oeuvres de Descartes.* New edition, coedited by Centre National de la Recherche Scientifique: Paris: Librarie J. Vrin, 1957-1968. Twelve volumes. Roman and arabic numerals specify volume and page numbers to this edition, identical with those in Adam and Tannery's original edition. When no volume number is given, the reference is to Volume XI, which contains *Les Passions de l'âme*. References to line numbers are given in this style: VI, 42.12. In references to articles of both the *Passions* and the *Principles of Philosophy*, "a." abbreviates "article." In references in Professor Rodis-Lewis's Introduction, the letters "AT" are omitted.

CSM   John Cottingham, Robert Stoothoff, and Dugald Murdoch, eds. *The Philosophical Writings of Descartes*. New York: Cambridge University Press, 1985. Two volumes.

Hall   René Descartes. *Treatise of Man*. French text with translation and commentary by Thomas Steele Hall. Cambridge, Mass.: Harvard University Press, 1972.

K   Anthony Kenny, trans. and ed. *Descartes: Philosophical Letters*. Oxford: Clarendon Press, 1970.

London   R. Des Cartes. *The passions of the soule in three books*. . . . Trans. anonymous. London: J. Martin and J. Ridley, 1650.

Olscamp   René Descartes. *Discourse on Method, Optics, Geometry, and Meteorology*. Trans., with an introduction, by Paul J. Olscamp. New York: The Bobbs-Merrill Company, Inc., 1961.

RL   René Descartes. *Les passions de l'âme*. Introduction and notes by Geneviève Rodis-Lewis. Second edition, with revisions: Paris: Librarie Philosophique J. Vrin, 1970.

Translations in the footnotes are usually those found in the English editions cited, but every now and then they are mine. I am also responsible for the translation of Professor Rodis-Lewis's Introduction, as well as for the bracketed phrases in it.

I gratefully acknowledge the help of many people. First I thank my teachers Charles Wood of San Bernardino, Arthur F. Holmes of Wheaton College, and Jaakko Hintikka, then of Stanford. Edwin Curley, Michael Stocker, and Amélie Rorty were encouraging from the start, and I received valuable help as well from Roger Ariew, Dan Dionne, Lois Rew, Marianina Olcott, Stephen Beall, Michael Schmidt, Geneviève Lasserre, John Morris, Karen Voss, Dennis Chaldecott, Jean Guedenet, Philip Davis, Linn B. Konrad, Charles Paul, and anonymous reviewers for Hackett. In a stroke of genuine good fortune for the readers of this book, Eileen O'Neill read the entire manuscript; thanks to her, the book is better in many places than it would have been. I am similarly grateful to Dan Kirklin for his skill and patience in editing the manuscript for the publisher. Every interpreter of Descartes's treatise must stand on the shoulders of two giants, Ferdinand Alquié and Geneviève Rodis-Lewis, whose introductions and notes in their editions are filled with wisdom. Klaus Hammacher has recently joined this short list; regrettably, I learned of the manifold merits of his edition too late to use it here. I have been blessed with the ideal publisher: Hackett Publishing Company cares about philosophical classics as only lovers of wisdom can, and Bill and Frances Hackett and Jay Hullett could not have been better people to work with.

I have dedicated this book to Geneviève Rodis-Lewis, who honors it with an Introduction, which is only the latest in a very long line of illuminating writings on the world of René Descartes. Her Introduction continues certain lines of thought that were begun in the Introduction to RL, weaves them with lines developed elsewhere, and takes up new lines of thought, both historical and philosophical, which offer stimulus and direction for further work. Professor Rodis-Lewis has long been and continues to be the most illuminating writer on Descartes's treatise on the passions. She has provided a model of scholarship in which intellectual rigor and imagination are united by that ἔρως which, as Plato says, is the wellspring of real philosophy.

INTRODUCTION

Published a few weeks before his death,[1] this work of Descartes is an important branch of the tree of philosophy described in the Letter-preface to the translator of the *Principles of Philosophy*, Abbé Picot. It is perhaps he who is the author of the two letters which, with the philosopher's replies, constitute the preface of the *Passions of the Soul*. On 6 November 1648, the prefatory author expressed regret over not having seen this treatise, which he was urging Descartes to publish, during the latter's visit to Paris;[2] and Descartes then revised and completed the first manuscript, which he had written during the winter of 1645-46 for Princess Elisabeth. It was a ground-breaking study concerning a modality specific to the union between soul and body [henceforth simply "the union"]—a domain which Elisabeth's first questions had led him to posit as the third primitive notion, irreducible either to pure thought or to corporeal mechanism (21 May and 28 June 1643). In 1645 she steered Descartes toward moral philosophy; soon tiring of the commentaries of *les Anciens*, he spontaneously mentioned the passions, the traditional obstacle to virtue (4 August: IV, 267: K 166), and in relation to true contentment, the deformations of anger and of "all the other passions" (1 September: IV, 283-286: K 168-170). She asked him their definition and description (13 September and 28 October: IV, 288-289 and 322). Descartes admitted the difficulty of enumerating them (6 October: IV, 313: K 179), and their enumeration was to be different indeed from the first lists

---

1. *Les Passions de l'âme*, printed in Amsterdam by Elzevier, was also published in Paris by H. Le Gras. On the different title pages and vignettes and the details of the Elzevier printing, see G. Rodis-Lewis, Introduction to *Les Passions de l'âme* (second edition: Paris: Flock, Mayenne, 1964; reissued with corrections in 1966 and 1970) (henceforth "G.R.L. Intr"), pp. 38-39 and notes. Copies were ready for distribution in December of 1649.

2. Descartes had left Paris on account of the Fronde. Adrien Baillet (*La vie de Monsieur Des-Cartes* [Horthemels, 1691] II, 394) says the author is Clerselier, but to C. Adam this is incompatible with the letter Descartes addressed to Clerselier on 23 April 1649; he suggests Picot. The beginning of this text [XI, 302] cites the Letter-preface to the translator of the *Principles*, who was Picot. References to Descartes's works are first to the Adam-Tannery edition, by volume and page number, and then to English translations; for full identification of all these editions, see the Translator's Introduction, above.

given in *L'Homme* and the *Principles*.³ Such is the origin of the "little treatise on the nature of the passions of the soul" which he proclaimed on 15 June 1646 to Chanut, who had interrogated him about moral philosophy, of which this was one of the "particular questions." The *Principles* had not dealt with "the nature of man," but, Descartes added, "physics . . . has been extremely useful for establishing certain foundations in moral philosophy" (IV, 442 and 441: K 196). Elisabeth pronounced herself satisfied with the "moral part" (25 April 1646: IV, 404). Yet Descartes claims that he has explained the passions *"en physicien"* [as a physicist] and not *"en philosophe moral"* [as a moral philosopher].⁴

In reality, articles 7-16, making up for the fact that *L'Homme* was never finished, present the essentials of mechanist physiology (part of the "physical" trunk of the tree). The generally positive function of the passions belongs to the primitive domain of the union between soul and body, which is not developed elsewhere. The moral applications issue both from the mechanistic "physics" and directly, as we shall see (in the case of generosity), from the metaphysical roots. Because of these complementary aspects, this treatise is unique among Descartes's works. Anyone who cares about his philosophy will be delighted with this new English translation, which is careful to render with precision the terminology specific to the author.⁵

When Descartes says he has not treated the passions *"en philosophe moral,"* he sets himself against those for whom that is the point of departure: the Stoics saw in *pathos*, passion, a *pathological* phenomenon, which the sage was required to quash in aspiring to *apatheia*—something Descartes had found in college to be "nothing but insensitivity or pride" or "despair" (Cato) or "parricide" (Brutus) (*Discourse on Method*, Part 1: VI, 8: CSM I, 114). In 1614, Volume IX of J. P. Camus's *Diversitez* appeared, "treating of the passions of the soul,"⁶ and his description presaged the two titles which the

---

3. *Treatise on Man* cites joy, liberality (a forerunner of magnanimity and then generosity), love, and sad or choleric humors, nourished by the agitation of the "animal spirits" (XI, 163-167: Hall 68-73); the end of the treatise anticipates the study, after the body is united with a rational soul, of "the internal movements of appetites and passions" (XI, 202: Hall 113). *Principles* IV, a. 190 cites joy, sadness, love, anger, and then fear and so on.

4. The last letter of the Preface, 14 August 1649. He adds *"ni en Orateur,"* for Aristotle discussed the passions in his *Rhetoric*. Magnanimity, in the *Nicomachean Ethics*, is a virtue. The scholastics enlarged upon the moral aspects of the passions.

5. An edition of this work alone, which is addressed to a wider public than Robert Stoothoff's edition of *The Passions of the Soul* in Volume I of J. Cottingham, R. Stoothoff, and D. Murdoch, trans., *The Philosophical Writings of Descartes* (New York: Cambridge University Press, 1985).

6. In 1614 Descartes passed from the second into the third year of philosophical study.

philosopher would use successively, giving these words their true sense. For the scholastics, Platonists, and neo-Stoics, "*anima*" and "*spiritus*" designate the soul, or breath, which "animates" the body: they distinguish the sensitive and vital functions from the intellectual part, which has its seat in the brain, the others being referred to the heart and the belly.[7] Physiological disruptions—rapid heartbeat, rise in temperature, and so on—are then *effects* of an agitation of the sensitive soul. According to Descartes, the mind submits to the action of the body before reacting: the *passions of the soul* are truly so called. Life and death depend on the state of the machine, which requires a certain organization in order to function:[8] life ends if "one of the principal parts of the body disintegrates" (*Passions*, a. 6), and this confers on the body a certain unity, and even indivisibility, the extensionless soul alone being properly indivisible (a. 30). That bodily organization gives a man his individual identity: a leg amputee is no less a man, if his body retains "all the dispositions needed to preserve this union."[9] "I can well understand a man

During the second year, he had studied mathematics and probably read, in Volume IV (1610) of the *Diversitez* of J. P. Camus, the chapter entitled "De l'excellence des mathématiques" (see our lecture to the colloquium celebrating the 350th anniversary of the *Discourse on Method* at the University of Paris-Sorbonne: "Descartes et les mathématiques au collège: sur une lecture possible de J. P. Camus," printed in N. Grimaldi and J. L. Marion, eds., *Descartes et sa méthode* [Paris: P.U.F., 1987]). Volume IX of the *Diversitez* is the only volume dedicated to a single theme. Its Dedication and Privilege read "*Traité des passions de l'âme.*" Anthony Levi (who in the case of Camus as well as Descartes always speaks of the "*Traité des Passions*") minimizes the importance of Camus, the Bishop of Belley, next to that of his friend St. Francis de Sales: *French Moralists: The Theory of the Passions, 1585 to 1649* (Oxford: Clarendon Press, 1964), pp. 112-135. On works after Camus, prior to Descartes—especially Coëffeteau (1620), Senault (1641; violently anti-Stoic), Cureau de La Chambre (1640; Descartes was quickly disappointed by his verbosity: to Mersenne, 28 January 1641: III, 296)—see Levi, pp. 142-152, 213-224, 248-256; G.R.L. Intr, p. 23 and Appendix, pp. 221-222; and our article (prepared for the Bolzano Colloquium on the passions, June 1986) "Les traités des passions dans la première moitié du XVIIe siècle et l'amour," published in *Topoi* (Boston and Bologna: Dordrecht, 1987).

7. This triplicity derives from Plato, *Republic* IV, 436a-441c. Both appetites, the concupiscible and the irascible, are generally located in the heart, something Descartes criticizes in a. 33. Only Francis de Sales, in his conversation with Camus (Levi, p. 131), speaks of the liver in the case of anger (or choler: *cholera*=bile). Descartes calls attention to the rush of bilious blood in anger: a. 199.

8. G. Rodis-Lewis, "Limitations of the Mechanical Model in the Cartesian Conception of the Organism," in Michael Hooker, ed., *Descartes: Critical and Interpretive Essays* (Baltimore: Johns Hopkins University Press, 1978), pp. 152-170.

9. To Mesland, 9 February 1645: IV, 166: K 157. This characterizes the normal state

without hands or feet or . . ."—but when Pascal adds "head," rather than "thought" (*Pensées*, no. 339, ed. Brunschvicg), he envisages thought, affirming itself before knowing the body, and not man, in which thought together with the body constitutes "as it were a single whole" (Meditation 6: IX, 64: CSM II, 56). The soul is united with the whole body (a. 30), and its "seat" (aa. 32, 33) is so called metaphorically: the soul "exercises its functions" by the mediation of the "little gland"[10] in the middle of the brain, and by its direction the gland orients the "animal spirits"[11] toward the nerves and then the muscles. So Descartes bestows a physical reality upon the traditional image of a circuit for the governance of the passions. As in a power station, messages are transmitted and received; they are programmed to preserve life but may get out of order, in our body just as in those of animal-machines.[12] Mind alone perceives the utility or danger of the passions, and its knowledge of the associative mechanism enables it to control them. The consciousness of the inclination of the will being followed by movement[13] is global, for our

---

of man, consistently with aa. 6 and 30 of the *Passions*—by contrast with the "miracle" of the eucharist, in which the soul of Christ directly informs the bread: see G. Lewis, *L'individualité selon Descartes* (Paris: Vrin, 1950). The soul is said to be the "form" of the body, as in Aristotle, but the "substantial" union presupposes the Cartesian duality of two distinct substances.

10. The figures in the *Treatise on Man* (redrawn by La Forge) show it very large and pointed on top, marked by the letter *H* (is it the condition of the unity of l'*H*omme?). Did this foster its common confusion with the hypophysis [the pituitary gland]? Descartes himself clearly distinguishes the latter (the "*pituitaire*," which he locates beneath the brain and not at its center: to Mersenne, 24 December 1640: III, 263: K 85) from the epiphysis, which he calls the *conarium* [or *conarion*] (to Meyssonnier, 29 January 1640: AT III, 19: K 69-70; to Mersenne, 21 April 1641: III, 361: K 100-101; also called "pineal" on account of its form). Certain ancient thinkers said it was very mobile, a view criticized by Galen (G. A. Lindeboom, *Descartes and Medicine* [Amsterdam: Rodopi, 1979], pp. 81-82). The *Passions* (aa. 31-35, 44) supplies no name for it.

11. Descartes gives up the "vital spirits" (responsible for inferior functions) and retains the traditional expression for these spirits (*Treatise on Man*: XI, 130ff.: Hall 20ff.). "They are only bodies" (a. 10), in no way spiritual or animate: "*esprit*" means "very fine wind" (a. 7; *Discourse*, Part 5: VI, 54: CSM I, 138), distilled by heat from the blood. For want of a scientific chemistry, Descartes integrates into his mechanism certain complex models echoing his rustic childhood—the fermentation of hay, or new wine (*Treatise on Man*: XI, 121 and 123: Hall 7 and 9; *Discourse*, Part 5: VI, 46: CSM I, 134).

12. Articles 137-138; to Newcastle, 12 November 1646: IV, 574-575: K 206-207. For images of skilful training see the citations from Francis de Sales in G.R.L. Intr, p. 31; Camus also makes frequent use of them.

13. This simple connection (a. 44) and the fact that the global volition is *followed* by

mind knows none of the details of the mechanism.

The utility of many passions was acknowledged by the adversaries of Stoicism. The Sixth Meditation and the *Principles* compare them to the internal senses—hunger, thirst, pleasure, pain.[14] And the teleology that characterizes the entire realm of the sensible (which has meaning by its relation to us, without instructing us about the object) becomes the principle of classification for the passions, according as their physical causes "are harmful or beneficial to us."[15] The immediate consequence is the introduction of a primitive passion: wonder (with the nuance of surprise) puts us on alert, *before* we know whether the object is good or bad; in this way it is an incomplete passion, with no commotion in the heart (a. 71). Through this addition, and Descartes's suppression of any passion contrary to desire (a. 87), we recover the number six for the primitive passions, which had also been the number of the passions of the concupiscible appetite, consisting of

a mechanism of whose details we are ignorant (to Arnauld, 29 July 1648: V, 221-222: K 235) might seem to authorize occasionalism. But in spite of the repetition of *"donner occasion"* in the *Treatise on Man*, Descartes asserts there that "the movements . . . and their ideas may be reciprocally caused by one another" (XI, 182: Hall 94; see to Elisabeth, 21 May 1643: III, 665: K 138). It would be incorrect to suppose that "two substances of different natures" cannot act upon one another (letter [to Clerselier] replacing the Fifth Replies in the translation of the *Meditations*: IX, 213: CSM II, 275-276). Such action is inexplicable, but experience, as the passions evince, suffices to show that it takes place (*Conversation with Burman* on Meditation 6: V, 163).

14. Recalling ancient opinions, Descartes says that pleasure and pain are *sensus* (translated by *"sentiment"*: IX, 59: CSM II, 52, or by internal *"sens"*: *Principles* IV, a. 190; this also distinguishes them from the passions). These sensations are distinct from "bodily inclinations toward joy, sadness, anger, and other similar passions" (IX, 59: CSM II, 52). All such sensations are indications of "suitability" or "unsuitability" to the body (*ibid.*); this term *"sentiment"* is taken up again, after the proof of the existence of bodies that are not similar to these sensations, which signify to us this utility or harmfulness (IX, 65: CSM II, 56). This is the new contribution of Descartes. (It is therefore not correct to say, as Malebranche does (*Recherche de la Vérité* III-1, ch. 1, section 3) that he confuses pleasure and joy: see a. 94.)

15. Article 52. Our first edition (completed in 1948; published at the beginning of 1955) followed P. Mesnard, who had neglected the phrase *"qui nous importent"* ("which matter to us"). Examining the treatise once again, we gave a detailed statement of the teleological principle on which the enumeration rests, at Royaumont, in October 1955: see the discussion with P. Mesnard in *Descartes. Cahiers de Royaumont*, Philosophie no. II (Paris: Éditions de minuit, 1957), pp. 212-213, 229, and 233. However, the correction had to be delayed until the second edition (1964; reeditions in 1966 and 1970): see p. 13 and notes. Other corrections appear at pp. 24-26, 34, and 38-39.

the group desire-aversion, along with love-hate and joy-sadness. The last four were also marked off from the first two by the Stoics "according to time."[16] St. Augustine subordinated the others to the pair love-hate. However, the Cartesian treatise denies the status of original to irascibility and the four passions (hope-despair, courage-fear) that were connected with it. The Early Writings defined anger in terms of sadness together with knowledge of the cause of the evil (X, 257); the second part of the treatise presents anger after sadness (a. 65) and insists upon the fact that the evil must be related to us (a. 199). Article 134 takes up the observation of the first Notebook comparing a child who cries to one who gets irritated (X, 217: CSM I, 4). There are two sorts of anger: one makes us turn red (and sometimes cry), the other makes us grow pale (a cold anger: aa. 200-202). The complexity of the phenomenon reveals the subtlety of concrete psychology, the proper domain of the union. The seventeenth is the century of internal analysis, with all its refinements.

From his very first lines, Descartes was interested in *affectus* (a word translated by "*passions*" in article 190 near the end of the *Principles*), but he held off enumerating them for lack of better knowledge of the movements of the soul.[17] The Notebook comments on the abrupt transition with a group of people from joy to consternation upon the announcement of some new evil (X, 217: CSM I, 4)—something that stimulated Descartes's appetite (X, 225)! Elisabeth was astonished when Descartes elaborated in article 105 that he lost his appetite through anger rather than sadness. In his reply of May 1646, the importance of which has not been sufficiently emphasized, the philosopher explains this fact by *association*, in earliest childhood, with insufficient food (whence the sadness-hunger linkage) or with harmful food—in this way accounting for individual differences (IV, 409: K 193). Now, the beginning of this letter makes explicit three points only implicit in the original manuscript: the first, concerning thicker blood held in reserve in the liver or spleen, calls for a study to get to the bottom of the formation of

16. Article 57; and Cicero, *Tusculan Disputations* III, xi, and IV, vi: pleasure, desire for present or future good; sadness, fear of present or future evil. Augustine subordinates them to love and hatred (*City of God* XIV, vii). The primacy of love is also affirmed by Senault, who nevertheless recovers the eleven passions (six of concupiscibility, five of irascibility) that had been reinstated by everyone but Vives (*infra*, n. 20).

17. Beginning of the *Compendium Musicae*: X, 89: the aim of music is to please, and to arouse within us various passions (*affectus*). On the difficulty of enumerating them, see X, 95, 111, and 140. On the "*flexanime*" music of the time, see G. Rodis-Lewis, "Musique et passions au XVIIe siècle: Monteverdi et Descartes," *XVIIe Siècle* 92 (1971), 81-98.

the body[18] (a study not sufficiently worked out even in 1649); the last explains how one can, with difficulty, succeed in dissociating a passion's physical characteristic, which is often joined to another one.[19] The central point enunciates the principle of association (IV, 408: K 192), which must therefore have been added to articles 50, 107, and 136, which repeat "the principle on which everything . . . is based." There flow according to the principle certain complex effects from earliest childhood, which mark an individual for life, because there has occurred no perception of their origin (to Arnauld, 20 July 1648: V, 220-221: K 234), but only confusedly felt sensation, even before birth (to Chanut, 1 February 1647: IV, 604-605: K 210-211; none of this letter's new ideas concerning love were integrated into the treatise during its revision). The next letter to Chanut gives the complementary example of an attraction for women with a squint in their eyes, resulting from a childhood love, which is dissipated upon consciousness of their "defect" (6 June 1647: V, 57: K 224).

Now Descartes had read in a text by Vives (the only one cited in the *Passions*)[20] the example of food that had become forever nauseating because it once tasted bad on account of illness (a. 107) or a distasteful accident (a. 50). Vives had also envisaged enticing a dog to a meal or whipping it to the sound of music, thereby training it either to come or to run away. Replying to Mersenne on musical taste, Descartes enunciated this link using the same example of a dog (18 March 1630: I, 133-134: K 8). The year before he had established, in dualism, the metaphysical foundation of mechanism; since this association is entirely physical, it appears in beast-machines, which display "movements" of fear, hope, or joy (to Newcastle, 23 November 1646: IV, 574: K 207; a. 138), but not the sensations which they cause in our soul. If it is possible to specify the genesis of the link, knowledge of this principle makes it possible to prise it apart: just as one trains an animal, one guides another person at first, so that he learns to guide himself—a decently ethical attitude.

The study of the passions *"en physicien"* thus paves the way for a

---

18. IV, 407-408: K 192. Descartes began applying himself to this study in January 1648: see to Elisabeth, 31 January 1648: V 112.

19. IV, 408-409: K 192-193: heat and dilation characterize love joined with joy, but since the dilation disappears when there is sadness, it is proper to joy. These relationships are found, without this justification, in aa. 102 and 107 (heat in love) and in a. 104 (dilated blood in joy).

20. Article 127: laughter is irresistable when hunger is sated. See G. Lewis, "Une source inexplorée du traité des *Passions*," *Revue philosophique de la France et de l'étranger* 138 (1948), 330-334; and G.R.L. Intr, pp. 24-29.

practical application: "treating of moral philosophy with precision . . ."[21] is not totally beyond reach in this special domain. Yet the complexity of situations precludes analysis before action: he who would verify that none of his food is poisoned would die of hunger: better to trust one's hunger (to "Hyperaspistes," August 1641: III, 422–423: K 110)—and one's passions. . . . Still, even though they are "all in their nature good" (a. 211), they do get out of order (just as thirst becomes harmful for someone with dropsy) and become dangerous even to their specific object, the preservation of the union: to moderate their excesses, one must join experience and reason (a. 138). On the other hand, they do not have as a natural object the good of the soul: to safeguard life, hatred may be more necessary than love (a. 137), but the reverse is true for our spiritual perfection (aa. 139–143, for the primitive passions other than wonder—the ways in which wonder is good or bad for gaining knowledge having been specified in aa. 75–76). This double aspect renders any mechanical remedy insufficient. And Descartes—the adversary of the Stoics when they condemn all passion—borrows practical counsel from them when they stress the risk of accelerating disorder: to strive to destroy by reason fallacious opinions that perturb the soul, but also to temporize when the disturbance is too violent.[22] Not knowing whether chance or destiny reigned, the *Discourse on Method* made "a virtue of necessity," by conforming our desires to what does not depend on us— "fortune" or "the order of the world" (Part 3: VI, 25–27: CSM I, 123–124). Articles 143–147 limit our desires to what depends on free will and reject the chimerical "fortune," referring "fate or immutable necessity" to the infallible decree of Providence.

This is the primary metaphysical foundation of moral philosophy: it teaches us to welcome whatever happens to us as coming from God: we love his perfection and even accept afflictions, because they are his will.[23] It will

---

21. Letter-preface to the translation of the *Principles*: IX-2, 17: CSM I, 188: Descartes adds here medicine and mechanics, which were said above (IX-2, 14: CSM I, 186) to constitute the three principal branches of philosophy, in conjunction with "the highest and most perfect moral philosophy, which presupposes a complete understanding of the other sciences." This is the "program" [*dessein*: IX-2, 1: CSM I, 179] envisaged by Descartes. He had told Chanut that he had been "more easily satisfied" in moral philosophy than in medicine, although he had spent much more time on the latter (15 June 1646: IV, 441: K 196). Nonetheless, it will be easier for medicine in time to become an exact science like mechanics.

22. G. Rodis-Lewis, *La morale stoïcienne* (Paris: P.U.F., 1970), pp. 100–104. The neo-Stoics had already transposed Destiny into Providence.

23. To Elisabeth, 15 September 1645: IV, 291–292: K 171. The second truth is the spiritual nature of the soul, which allows the hope of immortality; the third (taken up again in connection with the love of God at IV, 608: K 213) is the indefinite

be observed that our liberty does not appear among the truths essential for our conduct. When, on 1 February 1647, at the request of Christine of Sweden, Descartes thoroughly developed this theme of our love of God, he insisted on the union of *our* will to his, welcoming evils and death, but also the joys of this life. Previously he had spoken of "the infinity of his power, . . . the extension of his providence . . . , the infallibility of his decrees." A new touch is the temptation to "wish to be gods" (an "extravagance" and a "very great error").[24] The letter on the Supreme Good, after having said that "free will . . . renders us in a way like God and seems to exempt us from being subject to him," explains that in itself "its good use is the greatest of all our goods."[25] Might the exposition in the *Passions* of generosity—self-esteem for good use of free will—be an addition dating from the treatise's revision for publication?[26] The "general remedy for the passions" in article 211 (probably

---

immensity of the world, which liberates us from anthropocentrism; the fourth is solidarity with others, in which prudence and heroism attain an equilibrium ("one would be willing to lose his soul, if he could, in order to save others": IV, 293: K 173). Elisabeth then spoke of "generous souls," in the traditional sense, and in his reply Descartes contrasts "great souls" (possessing magnanimity) with "weak and servile" ones (6 October 1645: IV, 317: K 181).

24. IV, 608: K 213. The Latin letter to Mesland (9 February 1645?) already affirms "this positive power we possess to follow the worse even though we see the better": IV, 174: K 160. In 1637 Ovid's verse had been quoted with *"proboque"* (I see the better *"and I approve it"*): failure to follow it then characterizes "weak minds" (to Mersenne, 27 April? 1637: I, 366: K 32-33). The awareness of the absolute power of liberty, and the decision to use it *badly,* is what distinguishes strong minds, or libertines. When, in September, Descartes enunciates the essential truths of moral philosophy, he leaves out this risk, which is unsettling to generosity.

25. To Christine, 20 November 1647: V, 85: K 228: this letter on the Supreme Good is the only one directly addressed to the Queen of Sweden. On the same day, Descartes sent to Chanut, to give to her, the manuscript on the passions and some of his letters to Elisabeth. He told Elisabeth he was doing so; the idea was to interest Christine in his friend and her family.

26. These additions are impossible to identify with precision. On 23 April 1649 Descartes wrote to Clerselier that he had increased it by "a third" (based on what Clerselier had judged lacking in it: V, 353-354: K 253—which presupposes that Clerselier had read it in Paris). The last Letter of the Preface said that only a few things had been added, without change to the *"discours,"* that is, the general construction. Descartes probably explicated certain physiological descriptions at the beginning (Elisabeth had seen the manuscript of the *Treatise on Man*: to Elisabeth, 6 October 1646: IV, 310; and 25 January 1648: V, 112), and the principle of association (we observe in a. 50 the nuance "nor *perhaps* any thought"; on 9 February 1649 the complete denial of thought to animals was said not to be demonstrable, and the arguments for its absence were multiplied: to More: V, 276-277: K 243-244). On the

the end of the first manuscript) is very different from generosity, which, however, itself becomes a "remedy for all" their "disorders" (aa. 153, 161, 203): the two are juxtaposed in article 145, where the mention of generosity may have been added as the first remedy against vain desires, for it completes our submission to what does not depend on us, by making the most of what does depend on us (a. 146).

From the time of his Early Writings (the child who does not cry: X, 217: CSM I, 4), Descartes was aware that not everyone has from birth the same strength of soul (a. 48) or the same intelligence. Everyone does, however, have the same "power to judge well" (*Discourse on Method*, Part 1: VI, 2: CSM I, 111), and an identical will (Dedication of the *Principles* to Elisabeth: IX-2, 22: CSM I, 191). One must therefore know the good (a. 69) and apply oneself to it with all one's strength, with "a firm and constant resolution" to "use well" one's free will—"that is, never to lack the volition to undertake and execute all the things that [one] judges to be best, which is to follow virtue perfectly" (a. 153). The philosopher here unites his original definition of virtue as firmness of resolution[27] and his appeal to "judge well"; while the appeal is hardly ever realizable, "it suffices . . . to judge the best one can in order to do one's best" and to be "content."[28] For man, progress is a sign of his finitude and of his aspiration to what is "better" (Meditation 3: IX, 41: CSM II, 32). The metaphysics of liberty relies upon the physical mechanism of dispositions [*habitudes*] in order to become effective, guiding weak souls, by new linkages, to become masters of themselves (a. 50). We must have confidence in the most mediocre (a. 154) and help them transcend their bodily dispositions to achieve the conquest of the "*habitus*" which defines virtue.[29] Descartes breaks with the aristocratic conception of the noble soul (a. 161). His method develops within everyone the power of judging well

---

possible addition of developments concerning generosity, see G. Rodis-Lewis, "Le dernier fruit de la métaphysique cartésienne, la générosité," *Études philosophiques* 42, 1 (1987), pp. 43–54. In a. 54 there is a divergence between the title (generosity) and the text (magnanimity—a virtue according to the scholastics: see a. 161, where it is first a passion and then a "*habitude*").

27. In the notes, the first of which are very old, called "*Cartesius*": XI, 650; also in the Latin dedication of the *Principles* to Elisabeth: IX-2, 22: CSM I, 191. The letter to Elisabeth of 4 August 1645 emphasizes that no one else has defined virtue in this way (IV, 265: K 165).

28. *Discourse*, Part 3: VI, 28: CSM I, 125. This passage's continuity with a. 148 is worth noticing: contentment is a joyful satisfaction, measured to our limitations.

29. Articles 54 and 161—since Aristotle, the traditional definition. The letter to Elisabeth of 15 September 1645 praises the thesis of mental dispositions and links it with the thesis of bodily dispositions in the course of counseling the creation, by practice, of "a firm disposition [*habitude*]" (IV, 296: K 174).

(VI, 2: CSM I, 111), and generosity is accessible to everyone. Among the three wonders of the first Notebook there appears free will (X, 218: CSM I, 5). The impulse which arouses wonder within us makes of generosity a passion and a virtue. From metaphysical roots, through physiology and its action in the union with the soul, and through the soul's reaction to it, the treatise offers the most complete branch of the Cartesian philosophy and its ripest fruit. It spurs man on to apprehend more of the highest moral philosophy, across the centuries that may be needed to bring knowledge to perfection (Letter-preface to the *Principles*: IX-2, 14 and 20: CSM I, 186 and 189), even if it is never "complete" and finished.

Geneviève Rodis-Lewis

LES
PASSIONS
DE L'AME.

PAR

RENE' DESCARTES.

A PARIS,

Chez *Henry Le Gras* , au troisiéme Pilier
de la grand' Salle du Palais,à L couronnée.
M. DC. XLIX.
Avec Privilege Du Roy.

THE
PASSIONS
OF THE SOUL

PREFACE

FOREWORD

By one of the Author's friends[1]

What I've decided to do about the fact that this book has been sent to me by Monsieur Descartes, with permission to have it printed and to add any preface I might want to it, is just to set out here the same letters I wrote him earlier to get it[2] from him, since they contain a good many things I consider the public has an interest in being told.

FIRST LETTER[3]

To Monsieur
DESCARTES

Sir:

    I was very pleased to see you in Paris this past summer, because I thought   *15* that you had come there with the intention of staying, and that—having

---

1. The preface consists of this foreword and an exchange of four letters between an anonymous "friend" and Descartes. The friend has been variously identified as Clerselier (Baillet II, 394), Picot (AT XI, 294–297; RL 10–11 and 48, n. 1), and Descartes himself (Hiram Caton, "Descartes' Anonymous Writings: A Recapitulation," *Southern Journal of Philosophy* 20 [1982], 299–311). In any case, Descartes endorsed the preface's publication (see the last two letters), and it therefore must be counted a genuine part of his treatise. The style of the first and third letters, by the friend, is more stilted than Descartes's usual style, but that proves little: in my view they were at least written under Descartes's direction and were probably written by the philosopher himself. The first letter is valuable because of its accurate summary of Descartes's view of science and also because of its picture of his attitude about patronage.
2. Possibly the permission to have the book printed, probably the book.
3. The ostensible purpose of the first letter is to ask Descartes for a copy of his treatise on the passions and to encourage him to seek the public assistance he needs in

greater opportunity there than anywhere else to carry out the experiments
you've indicated you needed in order to finish the treatises you've promised
the public—you would not fail to keep your promise, and we would see
[those treatises] printed very soon. But you completely deprived me of that
joy when you returned to Holland. And I can't refrain from telling you here
that I am still upset with you for not being willing, before your departure, to
let me see the treatise on the Passions I was told you'd composed. Besides, in
a preface that was attached two years ago to the French version of your
Principes, after speaking succinctly of the parts of Philosophy which must
still be found before its principal fruits can be gathered, and saying that

> you do not so distrust your strength that you would not venture to undertake to
> explain them all, if you had the opportunity to carry out the experiments needed
> to support and justify your reasonings,

you add

> that this would require great expenditures of which a private person like yourself
> would be incapable unless he were assisted by the public, but that, not seeing that
> this assistance is to be expected, you think you must be content to study for your
> private instruction from now on, and that posterity will excuse you if you fail to
> work for it henceforth.[4]

Reflecting on the words I read there, I'm afraid that now you're in earnest in
wanting to begrudge the public the rest of your discoveries, and that we'll
never have anything more from you if we let you follow your inclination.
This is why I've decided to torment you a little with this letter and get
revenge for your refusing me your treatise on the Passions, by reproaching
you frankly for the negligence and other failings which I judge keep you
from realizing your talent as much as you might and as much as your duty
obligates you. I really cannot believe it is anything but your negligence, and
your paltry interest in being useful to the rest of mankind, that keeps you
from going on with your Physics.[5] For, though I understand very well that

order to do the experiments necessary for his scientific work. Descartes can best seek
that assistance, the writer says, if he publicizes the usefulness of physics (308.31-
310.24), the likelihood that he will make great progress in that field (310.25-318.25),
and the dependence of that progress upon expensive experiments (318.26-321.25).
The letter covers much of the same ground as Part 6 of the *Discourse on Method*,
under the pretext of replying to the reticence expressed there.
4. A pretty accurate quotation from AT IXB, 17: CSM I, 188.
5. The following reproaches develop Descartes's point in Part 6 of the *Discourse*: AT
VI, 74-75: CSM I, 149: one reason to publish one's results and speak of one's actions
and plans is to encourage the public to contribute to those plans. The accusation of
negligence is taken up again at 325.12 and 326.6.

it is impossible for you to complete it without many experiments, and that
these experiments ought to be carried out at public expense, because the   *15*
profit from them will accrue to [the public] and because a private person's
assets cannot cover them, still I do not believe that this is what is stopping
you. For you couldn't fail to obtain from those who dispose of the public
treasury everything you could wish for this purpose if you'd deign to make   *20*
them understand the matter as it is—as you could easily represent it if you
had the will. But your way of life has always been so opposed to this that
there is reason to be convinced that you would not be willing to accept any   *25*
assistance from others even if it were offered to you; and you nevertheless
maintain that posterity will excuse you for no longer being willing to work
on its behalf, on the grounds that you suppose that this assistance is necessary for you to do so and that you cannot obtain it. This leads me to think   *30*
not only that you are too negligent, but also that you perhaps lack the   **304**
courage to hope to accomplish what those who have read your writings
expect of you, and that you're nevertheless so vain as to want to convince
our successors that you've let them down through no fault of your own, but   *5*
because your virtue has not been acknowledged as it should have been and
you've been refused assistance with your projects. I can see that this ambition of yours is on target, because the people who see your writings in the
future will judge on the basis of what you published more than twelve years   *10*
ago[6] that you had already found out everything that's been seen from you up
to now, and that what remains for you to discover concerning Physics is less
difficult than what you've already explained about it, so that since then
you'd have been able to provide us with everything that can be expected
from human reasoning on behalf of medicine and the other practices of life if   *15*
you'd had the opportunity to carry out the requisite experiments—and even
that you have doubtless not failed to find out a great part of them, but that
righteous indignation against the ingratitude of men has kept you from   *20*
sharing your discoveries with them. So you think that from now on you
will be able to acquire as much reputation resting as you would doing a great
deal of work—perhaps even a little more, since good that's possessed is
commonly esteemed less than what's desired or lamented. But I want to   *25*
deprive you of the means of acquiring a reputation in this way without
deserving it. And though I do not doubt that you know what you'd have
had to do if you had wanted public assistance, I want to write it down here   *30*
nevertheless. In fact, I shall have this letter printed, so that you cannot claim
to be ignorant of it, and so that if you fail hereafter to give us satisfaction, **305**
you can no longer excuse yourself by reference to these times. Understand,
then, that in order to obtain something from the public, it is not enough to

6. Probably Parts 5 and 6 of the *Discourse on Method*.

have dropped a word in passing about it in the preface of a book, without
saying explicitly that you desire and expect it or expounding the reasons that
suffice to prove not only that you deserve it, but also that people have a
great interest indeed in granting it to you and should expect great gain from
doing so. We are used to seeing that all those who fancy they are worth
something make so much fuss about it, and demand what they claim so
pertinaciously, and promise so far beyond their capacity, that when someone
only speaks modestly of himself, and requests nothing from anyone, and
doesn't confidently promise anything, then no matter what proof he may
give elsewhere of what he can do, it is ignored and no thought is taken of
him.

You will say, perhaps, that your temper does not incline you to request
anything or to speak highly of yourself, because the one seems to be a mark
of servility and the other of pride. But I maintain that this temper must be
corrected, and that it springs from error and weakness rather than an
honorable decency and modesty. As for requests, the only ones a person has
reason to be somewhat ashamed of are the ones he makes for his own needs,
to those from whom he has no right to exact anything. So far is he from
having to be ashamed of requests that are conducive to the utility and gain of
those to whom he makes them that, on the contrary, he may derive glory
from them, especially when he has already given [those people] things worth
more than the ones he wants to obtain from them. As for speaking highly of
oneself, it's true that this is a pride ridiculous and blameworthy in the
extreme when one is saying false things about oneself, and even that it's a
contemptible vanity, though one may only be saying true things about
oneself, when it is done ostentatiously and without any good accruing to
anyone. But when these things are such that knowing them matters to
others, it is certain that they can be suppressed only by an unvirtuous
humility which is a species of cowardice and weakness. Now it matters
greatly to the public to be informed of what you have found in the sciences,
so that, rendering judgment on that basis about what you may yet find
there, it may be incited to contribute all it can to help you with it, as a work
whose aim is the general good of all mankind. And the things you have
already given, namely the important truths you've explained in your writings, are worth incomparably more than anything you could request for this
purpose.

You may also say that your works speak sufficiently for themselves
without your having to add on promises and boasts, which, being common
in Charlatans who want to deceive, seem inconsistent with decorum in a
man of honor who seeks only the truth. However, what makes Charlatans
blameworthy is not that the things they say about themselves are great and
good; it's just that they are false and that they cannot prove them. In

contrast, the things that I maintain you must say about yourself are so true
and so plainly proven by your writings that all the rules of decorum allow   *30*
you to assert them—while, because knowing them matters to others, [the   307
rules] of charity obligate you to.[7] For though what you've written does
speak for itself sufficiently in the view of those who examine it carefully and
are capable of understanding it, that is still not sufficient for the design I
want you to have, because not everyone is able to read it, and those who   *5*
manage public affairs can scarcely get the spare time for it. It may indeed
happen that one of the people who have read what you've written will
mention it to them; but no matter what they may be told about it, the little
fuss they know you make and the excessive modesty you've always   *10*
observed in speaking of yourself will keep them from taking much account
of it. Likewise, because all the highest terms imaginable are often used
around them to praise people who are quite average, they have no reason to   *15*
take the prodigious praises bestowed on you by those who know you as
perfectly accurate truths—whereas, when someone speaks about himself,
saying very extraordinary things, people listen more attentively to him,
especially when he is a man of high birth and known not to be of such a   *20*
temper or station as to want to play the Charlatan. Since he would make
himself an object of ridicule if he used hyperbole on such occasions, his
words are taken at face value, and those who are not willing to believe them
are at least engaged by their curiosity or their jealousy to investigate wheth-   *25*
er they are true. This is why—since it's quite certain, and since the public
has a great interest in knowing, that [1] there has never been anyone but you
alone (at least whose writings we possess) who has discovered the true
principles and recognized the first causes of everything brought forth in   *30*
nature; and that [2] as you've already given an account by these principles of
all the things in the world that are discernible, and observed most often, you   308
only need observations that are more specific in order to find in the same
way the explanations of everything that can be useful to men in this life, and   *5*
so to give us a quite perfect understanding of the nature of all the minerals,
the virtues of all the plants, the properties of the animals, and in general
everything capable of contributing to Medicine and the other arts; and
finally that [3] as these specific observations cannot all be made in a short   *10*
time without great expense, all the peoples of the earth would have to vie
with one another to contribute to them, as to the most important thing in
the world, in which all of them have an equal interest—since this is quite
certain, as I say, and is sufficiently provable by the writings you've already   *15*
had printed, you would have to say it so loudly, publish it so assiduously, and

7. For the rules of charity, see *Discourse*, Part 6: AT VI, 61 and 66: CSM I, 142 and
145.

put it so explicitly in all your books' titles that there could be no one
ignorant of it thereafter. In this way you would at least at first arouse in
20   many the wish to investigate what there is to it; and the more they inquired
into it and the more diligently they read your writings, the more clearly
they would understand that you had not boasted falsely.
25   And there are three points above all that I'd want you to get everyone to
understand rightly. The first is that there is an infinity of things to find out
in Physics which can be extremely useful to life; the second, that there is
excellent reason to expect the discovery of these things from you; and the
30   third, that the more opportunity you have to carry out a great number of
experiments, the more of them you'll be able to find out. It is appropriate for
309   people to be informed of the first point because the greater part of mankind
think nothing better can be found in the sciences than what was found by
5   the ancients, and many do not even understand what Physics is or what it
can be good for.[8] Now it is easy to prove that the excessive respect maintained for antiquity is an error which is extremely prejudicial to the advance-
ment of the sciences. For we see that the savage peoples of America—and
10   many others as well who inhabit places not so far away—have a lot fewer of
the comforts of life than we do, and yet have an origin as ancient as ours, so
that they have as much cause as we to say that they are content with the
15   wisdom of their forefathers, and believe no one can teach them anything
better than what's been known and practiced among them from the most
ancient times. This opinion is so prejudicial that, so long as it is not given up,
it's certain that no new capacity can be acquired. Thus experience shows us
20   that the peoples in whose minds it is most deeply rooted are those who have
remained the most ignorant and uncouth. And since it's still very common
among us, it can serve as a proof that we are a very long way from knowing
25   all we are capable of knowing. This can also be proven quite clearly by
many very useful inventions, like the use of the compass, the art of printing,
30   telescopes,[9] and the like, which, though they seem easy enough now to those
who understand them, have only been devised in the most recent times. But
310   nowhere is our need to acquire new learning more apparent than in things
that concern Medicine.[10] For though no one doubts that God has provided

8. As Geneviève Rodis-Lewis suggests (RL 48, n. 1), the writer's statement here and
Descartes's promise to send him the treatise on the passions "to do as you please with
it" (324.10-11) are strongly reminiscent of lines in the first and third paragraphs of
the prefatory letter that Descartes wrote to Picot, who translated the *Principles of
Philosophy* into French (AT IXB, 1-3: CSM I, 179-180).
9. *Lunettes d'approach*—"perspective glasses," according to the London translation.
As Charles Paul has observed in conversation, this passage shows the influence of
Francis Bacon, who is mentioned explicitly at 320 below.
10. In a famous passage in the 1647 Letter-preface to the French version of the

this Earth with all things necessary for men to be preserved in perfect health
to an extreme old age, and though there is nothing whatever so desirable as 5
the knowledge of these things, so that in olden times it was the principal
study of Kings and Sages, nevertheless experience shows that we are still so
far from having all of [that knowledge] that we're often bedridden with little
illnesses which all the most learned Physicians cannot understand, and only 10
aggravate by their remedies when they undertake to dispel them. The
deficiency of their art and the need to perfect it are so plain herein that it is
sufficient to tell those who do not understand what Physics is that it is the 15
science which ought to teach people to understand so perfectly the nature of
man, and all things capable of serving him as nourishment or as remedy, that
it would be easy for him to free himself from all sorts of sicknesses by its
means. For without speaking of its other uses, this alone is important enough 20
to compel the most unperceptive to back the enterprises of a man who has
already proven by the things he has discovered that there is excellent reason
to expect from him everything that still remains to be found in this science.

Above all, the world needs to know that you've proven this yourself. 25
And to this end it's necessary that you do a little violence to your temper,
and drive out the excessive modesty which so far has kept you from saying
all you're obligated to say about yourself and others. I do not want to set 30
you against the learned of the age on this account; the greater part of those 311
to whom this name is given, namely all who cultivate what is commonly
called belles lettres[11] and all who are learned in the Law, have no interest in
what I maintain you ought to say. Theologians and Physicians likewise have 5
none, except as Philosophers. For Theology in no way depends on Physics;
even Medicine doesn't, as it's practiced today by the most learned and
prudent in the art: they are content to follow the maxims or rules which 10
long experience has taught, and are not so scornful of human life as to rest
their judgments, on which it often depends, on the uncertain reasonings of
Scholastic Philosophy. There remain therefore only Philosophers, among

---

Principles, Descartes said, "the whole of philosophy is like a tree, of which the roots
are metaphysics, the trunk is physics, and the branches emerging from the trunk are
all the other sciences, which may be reduced to three principal ones, namely medicine, mechanics, and morals," adding, "just as it is not the roots or the trunk of a tree
from which one gathers the fruit, but only the ends of its branches, so the principal
utility of philosophy depends on those parts of it which can only be learned last of
all" (AT IXB, 14-15: CSM I, 186). Ten years earlier, in Part 6 of the *Discourse*, he
argued that medicine is the most important application of physics (AT VI, 61-63:
CSM I, 142-143); and he reemphasized the primacy of medicine within his work in
correspondence (to [the Marquess of Newcastle], October 1645: AT IV, 329: K 184;
to Chanut, 15 June 1646: AT IV, 441-442: K 196). That point is endorsed again here.
11. *Belles lettres*; in the London edition, "good literature."

15   whom all those with any intelligence are already on your side, and will be
      extremely pleased to see that you're presenting the truth in such a way that
      the malice of the Pedants cannot crush it. So it is only those Pedants who
      could take offense at what you have to say—and since they are the laughing-
20   stock, the object of scorn, of all of the most cultivated people, you shouldn't
      worry very much about pleasing them. Besides, your reputation has already
      made them as hostile to you as they can be. And whereas your modesty
25   now causes some of them not to be afraid to attack you, I'm sure that if
      you'd display your worth as much as you can and should, they would see
      themselves to be so far beneath you that there would not be one who was
      not ashamed to undertake that. Therefore I don't see that there's anything to
30   keep you from boldly publishing everything you judge might further your
      enterprise, and nothing seems to me to be more useful for that than what
312   you've already written in a letter addressed to the Rev. Father Dinet, which
      you had printed seven years ago, while he was Superior of the French
5   Jesuits. You said, in speaking of the *Essais* you'd published five or six years
      previously,

> There I explained, not one or two problems, but more than six hundred which
> had not thus been explained by anyone before me. In fact, although many people
> so far have inspected my writings critically and tried in every way to refute them,
10 > still no one as far as I know has been able to find anything in them which is not
> true. Let there be an enumeration of all the problems which have been solved by
> means of other Philosophies, in all the centuries in which they have flourished:
> they will perhaps be found to be neither so numerous nor so important. Indeed, I
15 > proclaim that there is not a single problem which has ever been given a solution
> by means of the principles peculiar to Peripatetic Philosophy that I cannot prove
> to be illegitimate and false. Let the attempt be made: let a few well-chosen ones be
20 > exhibited—certainly not all of them (I do not, of course, consider that work on
> this matter warrants spending much time on it): I shall stand by these promises,
> etc.[12]

      So, in spite of all your modesty, the power of truth constrained you to write
25   there that in your first *Essais*, which contain hardly anything but the

12. A rather carelessly copied quotation from Descartes's letter, in Latin, to Dinet, a
former teacher of his at the College of La Flèche (AT VII, 579–580: CSM II, 391).
Descartes had published the letter at the end of the Seventh Objections and Replies
to his *Meditations*, in the second edition of that work in 1642. The *Essais* mentioned
here are the *Dioptrics*, the *Meteorology*, and the *Geometry*, which Descartes attached
to the *Discourse on Method* as "essays in that method" (according to the full title of
the publication). The French summary following the Latin quotation is a good
indication that the present letter was meant for publication along with the text of the
Passions right from the start.

Dioptrique and the *Météores*, you'd already explained over six hundred problems in Philosophy which no one before you had been able to explain so well, and that even though many had looked askance at your writings and sought all sorts of means of refuting them, you nevertheless knew of no one who had yet been able to discover anything in them which wasn't true. To this you add that if anyone wants to count one by one the problems which all the other ways of philosophizing that have been in vogue since the world began have been able to solve, he will perhaps not find that they are so numerous or so notable. You assert besides that no one has ever been able to find the true solution of any problem through the principles peculiar to the Philosophy attributed to Aristotle, which is the only one now taught in the Schools, and you explicitly challenge all who are teaching to name one which has been so completely solved by means of [those principles] that you could point out no error in their solution. Now as these things were written to a Jesuit Superior and published more than seven years ago, there is no doubt that some of the most capable of this great body would have tried to refute them if they were not entirely true, or could even be disputed with some appearance of reason. For, in spite of the little fuss you make, everyone knows that your reputation is already so great, and that they have such an interest in maintaining that what they teach is not wrong, that they cannot say they've overlooked it.[13] But the learned all know well that there is nothing in Scholastic Physics which is not doubtful, and they also know that in such matters being doubtful is little better than being false, for a science must be certain and demonstrative. So they cannot find it unusual that you've asserted that their Physics does not contain the true solution of any problem, for that means nothing but that it does not contain the demonstration of any truth of which others are ignorant. And if one of them examines your writings in order to refute them, he finds, entirely to the contrary, that they contain nothing but demonstrations concerning matters everyone has previously been ignorant of. This is why I'm not astonished they keep silence, judicious and circumspect as they are. I am astonished, however, that you have not yet deigned to extract some advantage from their silence, for nothing you could wish for would better reveal how much your Physics differs from that of others. Now it's important that the difference between them be recognized, so that the low opinion which people who are employed in and most successful with public affairs usually have of Philosophy doesn't keep them from understanding the worth of your own. For they commonly make judgments about what will happen only on the basis of what they have already seen happen, and since they've never perceived

30
313

5

10

15

20

25

30
314

5

10

15

13. The antecedent of this pronoun is not clear; perhaps it refers to the letter to Dinet.

the public gathering any fruit from Scholastic Philosophy—apart from its having made great numbers of men into Pedants—they cannot imagine that better is to be expected from yours unless they're led to take into consider-

20 ation that as the latter is entirely true, and the former entirely false, their fruits must be entirely different.[14] Indeed, an excellent argument for proving that there is no truth in Scholastic Physics is to mention that it is instituted

25 to teach all the discoveries useful for life, and that nevertheless, although many [discoveries] have been made from time to time, they have never been made by means of that Physics, but only by chance and by practice. Mathematics alone has contributed to them, if any science has; it is, in

30 addition, of all the human sciences, the only one in which anyone has so far been able to find a few truths that cannot be put in doubt. I am well aware

315 that the Philosophers want to embrace [mathematics] as a part of their Physics, but since almost all of them are ignorant of it, and since it's true not that it is a part thereof, but on the contrary that the true Physics is a part of

5 Mathematics, this can do nothing for them. But the certainty that has already been recognized in Mathematics does a great deal for you. For your eminence in this science is so well established, and you have so completely triumphed over envy in it, that even those who are jealous over the esteem

10 in which you're held in the other sciences usually say you surpass everyone else in this one, so that in according you a commendation they know cannot be disputed, they may be less suspected of calumny when they try to

15 deprive you of others. And anyone can see that in what you've published in Geometry, you determine how far the human mind can go, and what solutions can be given to every sort of difficulty, to such an extent that you seem to have gathered the whole crop; the others who wrote before you

20 only plucked some ears that were not yet ripe, and all who come after can only be like gleaners gathering up the ones you were willing to leave for them. Besides, you've shown, by the quick and easy solution of all the

25 problems which those who have wanted to test you have proposed, that the Method you use to this end is so infallible that you never fail to find out by means of it everything the human mind can about the things you investi-

30 gate. So to make sure no one can doubt that you're capable of putting

316 Physics in its final perfection, you need only prove that it is nothing but a part of Mathematics. And you've already proved that very clearly in your *Principes*, when, in explaining all the qualities capable of being sensed,

5 without taking anything into consideration but sizes, shapes, and motions, you showed that this visible world, which is the entire object of Physics,

---

14. This contrast between Descartes's physics and that of the scholastics is based upon a passage in the Letter-preface to the *Principles* (AT IXB, 18-19: CSM I, 188-189), in which Descartes draws a similar contrast.

contains only a small portion of the infinite bodies,[15] whose properties or qualities may all be imagined to consist in these same things—while the object of Mathematics contains all of them.[16] The same thing can also be proved by the experience of every age. For though at all times many of the best minds have occupied themselves with research in Physics, it cannot be said that anyone has ever found anything in it (that is, attained any true knowledge concerning the nature of corporeal things) through any principle that does not belong to Mathematics, whereas an infinity of very useful things have already been found through those that do belong to it, namely almost everything that's known in Astronomy, Surgery, and all the Mechanical arts—in which, if anything else is present besides what belongs to this science, it is not derived from any other [science], but only from certain observations whose true causes are not known. No one can closely attend to this fact without being constrained to admit that it is by Mathematics alone that one can attain knowledge of the true Physics. And inasmuch as no one doubts that you excel in the former, there is nothing which is not to be expected from you in the latter. A few qualms still remain, however, since we can see that all of those who have acquired some reputation through Mathematics are not on that account capable of finding anything out in Physics, and even that some of them understand the things you've written about it less than many who have never learned any science before. But it may be replied to this that although no doubt it's those whose minds are best suited to apprehend the truths of Mathematics who understand your Physics most easily, since all the reasonings of the latter are drawn from the former, they don't always turn out to have the reputation of being wisest in Mathematics, because to acquire this reputation one must study the books of

15. *Des corps infinis.* The interpretation is not clear; it may be "the infinite range of bodies" or perhaps "the infinitely many bodies." In either case, it runs counter to Descartes's principle that one should speak of indefiniteness rather than infinity about the extended universe, since only God may be described as infinite (First Replies: AT VII, 112-113: CSM II, 81; *Principles* I, a. 26 and II, a. 34: AT VIII, 14-15 and 59-60: CSM I, 201-202 and 239; to Chanut, 6 June 1647: AT V, 51-52: K 221; to More, 5 February 1649: AT V, 274-275: K 242; to Clerselier, 23 April 1649: AT V, 355-356: K 254). However, see the letter to Plempius for Fromondus, 3 October 1637: AT I, 422: K 39.

16. We may imagine that all the characteristics of extended bodies consist in sizes, shapes, and motions. This description of the object of mathematics admits of two readings—perhaps it contains abstract objects, of which all the sizes, shapes, and motions of bodies are exemplifications; perhaps it contains those concrete exemplifications themselves. For the first reading, see the Fifth Meditation: AT VII, 64: CSM II, 44-45; for the second, see Rule 14 of the *Rules for the Direction of the Mind*: AT X, 438-452: CSM I, 56-65.

those who have already written about this science, which most do not do.
And frequently those who do study them try to obtain through labor what
the strength of their mind can't give them, overly fatigue and even injure
their imagination, and in the bargain acquire many prejudices. This keeps
them from apprehending the truths you write much more than it keeps
them from passing as great Mathematicians, because so few people apply
themselves to that science that often they are the only ones in an entire
country; even though sometimes others do, they still make a great fuss,
inasmuch as the little they know has cost them considerable trouble. Furthermore, it isn't hard to apprehend the truths another has found; for that it
suffices to have a mind free of all sorts of false prejudices, and to be willing to
devote enough attention to them. Neither is it very difficult to come upon a
few of them detached from the rest, as Thales, Pythagoras, and Archimedes
in the past and Gilbert, Kepler, Galileo, Harvey, and a few others in our
times have done.[17] Finally, one can without a great deal of trouble imagine a
body of Philosophy less monstrous and supported by more probable conjec-
tures than the one derived from Aristotle's writings; this too has been done
by a few in these times. But to frame one that contains only truths proven
by demonstrations as clear and as certain as those of Mathematics is a thing
so difficult and so rare that in the more than fifty centuries the world has
already lasted, it turns out that you alone have shown by your writings that
you can accomplish it. But just as when an Architect has laid all the
foundations and raised the main walls of some great edifice no one doubts
that he can carry his plan to completion, because they can see that he's
already done what was most difficult, so those who have read your book of
Principes attentively, taking into consideration how you laid the foundations
of all natural Philosophy there and how long the chains of truths are that
you deduced from them,[18] cannot doubt that the Method you use is sufficient for you to finish finding everything that can be found in Physics,
because the things you've already explained, namely the nature of the
magnet, fire, air, water, earth, and everything discernible in the heavens, do
not seem to be less difficult than those which may still be desired.

Still, it has to be added here that no matter how expert an Architect may
be in his art, it will be impossible for him to finish the edifice he has begun if
he lacks the materials that must be employed in it. In the same way, no

17. William Gilbert (1540-1603): British physicist and author of *De Magnete* (1600);
Johannes Kepler (1571-1630): German astronomer and mathematician; Galileo Galilei (1564-1642): Italian scientist and philosopher; William Harvey (1578-1657): British physician and anatomist, whose *De Motu Cordis* (1628) was read by Descartes in
1632. Descartes speaks of them all elsewhere; for Harvey, see note 10 in Part I below.
18. Cf. Letter-preface to the *Principles*: AT IXB, 20: CSM I, 189-190.

matter how perfect your Method might be, it cannot enable you to proceed with the explanation of natural causes[19] if you can't conduct the experiments[20] needed to determine their effects. This is the last of the three points which I believe need to be explained above all, because most men understand neither how necessary these experiments are nor how expensive they are. Those who undertake to discourse on nature without leaving their study or casting their eyes anywhere but on their books may well say how they'd have wanted to create the world if God had given them the command and the power to do so—that is, they may write of Chimeras which have as much conformity to the weakness of their mind as the wondrous beauty of this Universe has to the infinite power of its author—but, without a truly divine mind, they cannot in that way form an idea of things by themselves that is like the one God had in order to create them. And though your Method promises everything that can be hoped for from the human mind concerning the search for truth in the sciences, it does not promise to teach divination, but only the deduction from certain given things of all the truths which can be deduced from them; and in Physics these given things can only be experiments. Also, because these experiments are of two sorts—the first easy, depending only on reflection upon the things that are present of themselves to the senses, the rest more rare and difficult, not attainable without some study and expense—it may be noted that you've already put in your writings everything that seems capable of being deduced both from the easy experiments and also even from those among the rarer ones which you've been able to learn of from books. For in addition to the fact that in them you've explained the nature of all the qualities that move the senses and all the most common bodies on the earth, such as fire, air, water, and some others, you've also given an account therein of everything that's been observed to date in the heavens, all the properties of the magnet, and many observations in Chemistry. So there is no reason to expect anything more

319

5

10

15

20

25

30

320

5

19. *L'explication des causes naturelles*: on Descartes's usual account, one seeks to explain (*expliquer*) effects by their causes and on the other hand to prove (*prouver*) causes from their effects. See Parts 5 and 6 of the *Discourse*: AT VI, 45-60, 63-65, and 76: CSM I, 133-141, 143-144, and 150; to Vatier, 22 February 1638: AT I, 562-564: K 48-49; to Morin, 13 July 1638: AT II, 197-200: K 57-59. In spite of the use of *explication* here, the writer has in mind the "proof" of "natural causes"—that is, their discovery *a posteriori* from their "effects," namely the phenomena to which they give rise. For more on how to do this, see *Description of the Human Body*: AT XI, 242: CSM I, 317-318.

20. Here and at 303.13-14 and 320.8, the writer uses the phrase *avoir experiences* to mean to be able or to be in a position to carry out experiments. At 302.2 and 18-19, 304.16-17, 308.30-31, and 320.10-11, he uses the phrase *faire experiences* to mean to carry out experiments.

from you concerning Physics until you can conduct more experiments
10   whose causes you could seek. Now I am not astonished that you don't
undertake these experiments at your own expense, for I know that research
into the least of things costs a great deal; without mentioning the Alchemists
or all the other searchers into mysteries, who usually ruin themselves at this
15   occupation, I've heard it said that the lodestone alone led Gilbert to spend
more than fifty thousand crowns, although he was a man of very high
intelligence, as he showed in being the first to discover the principal properties of that stone. I've also seen the *Instauratio Magna* and the *Novus Atlas*
20   of Chancellor Bacon,[21] who seems to me to be, of all those who wrote before
you, the one with the best thoughts concerning the Method that should be
followed to guide Physics to its perfection; but all the income of two or
25   three of the most powerful Kings on earth would not suffice to carry out all
the things he needs for this end. And though I don't think you need as many
sorts of experiments as he imagines, since you can make up for many by
30   your ingenuity and by the knowledge of the truths you've already found,
still, considering that [1] the number of particular bodies left for you to
321   examine is nearly infinite; that [2] there is not one which doesn't have
enough different properties, and on which enough tests can't be conducted,
to employ all the available time and work of many men; that [3] according to
5   the rules of your Method you need to examine at the same time all the
things which have some affinity with one another, in order to observe their
differences better and to make enumerations that give you confidence; that
[4] in this way you may usefully avail yourself at a single time of more
10   different experiments than the work of a very large number of skillful men
could supply; and finally that [5] money would be needed for you to have
the use of these skillful men, since if some were willing to occupy them-
15   selves for nothing, they wouldn't sufficiently submit to following your
orders, and would only provide you occasion for wasting time: considering
all these things, as I say, it's easy for me to understand that you cannot
worthily complete the project you began in your *Principes*—that is, to
20   explain in particular all the minerals, the plants, the animals, and man,[22] in
the same way in which you've already explained all the elements of the earth

---

21. Francis Bacon (1561-1626): British philosopher. His major work, *Instauratio
Magna*, was published in London in 1620. His utopian work, *New Atlantis*, first
published in 1627, was republished in Latin as *Nova Atlantis* in 1643 in Holland,
where Descartes then resided. An edition published in 1648 has the same misspelling
of the title that appears here.
22. In *Principles* IV, a. 188 (AT VIII, 315: CSM I, 279), Descartes said he had hoped
to write a fifth part of that work, on plants and animals, and a sixth, on man. On
homme, here translated as "man," see Lexicon.

and everything observed in the heavens—if the public doesn't supply the
funds needed for this end; and that the more liberally they're supplied you
the better you'll be able to execute your project.   *25*

Now because these very things can also be understood very easily by
everyone, and are all so true that they cannot be put in doubt, I'm sure that
if you'd represent them in such a way that they came to be known by those   *30*
to whom God, having given them the power to govern the peoples of the
earth, has likewise given the command and mission to do their utmost to   *322*
advance the public good, there wouldn't be one who would not want to
contribute to a project so obviously useful to everyone. And though our
France, which is your native Country, is so powerful a State that it would   *5*
seem that you could obtain everything needed for this end from her alone,
nevertheless, because the other nations have no less an interest in it than she
does, I'm sure that many would be generous enough not to yield to her in
that capacity and that there would be none so barbarous as not to want to   *10*
have a part in it.[23]

Still, if everything I've written here is not enough to make you alter your
temper, please at least be so kind as to send me your treatise on the Passions,   *15*
and to approve my adding a preface with which it may be printed. I'll try to
write it in such a way that there will be nothing in it which you could
disapprove of, and which would not be so congenial to the feelings of every
person of intelligence and virtue that none of them, after having read it, will   *20*
fail to participate in the zeal I have for the growth of the sciences, and to be,
etc.

From Paris, November 6, 1648.

REPLY   *323*

To the Preceding Letter

Sir:

Among the abuses and reproaches I find in the long letter you've taken   *5*
the trouble to write to me, I notice so many things to my credit that if you
should have it printed, as you declare you want to do, I'd be afraid that
people would imagine that there is a greater understanding[24] between us

---

23. Descartes's friends had already secured for him a pension from the King of
France, which he never used. See AT XII, 458-469.
24. *Intelligence.* The London edition gives "combination." The word means something weaker than collusion, something stronger than concord or rapport—something like concurrence, but with the added hint of the conscious or the deliberate
which "understanding" conveys. This is Descartes's strongest hint about the kind of
authority the first letter should be taken to possess.

10   than there is, and that I had entreated you to put many things in it which
     decorum would not allow me to make known to the public myself. This is
     why I shall not pause here to reply to it point by point; I'll give you just two
15   reasons which, it seems to me, ought to keep you from publishing it. The
     first is that I do not think the plan I judge you had in writing it can be
     successful. The second is that I am in no way of the temper you imagine—
20   neither indignation nor distaste takes away my desire to do everything in
     my power to render service to the public, to which I consider myself greatly
     obligated because the writings I've already published have been favorably
     received by many. And up to now I've refused you what I've written about
25   the Passions only in order not to be obligated to show it to others who
324 wouldn't have profited from it. Inasmuch as I composed it only to be read
     by a Princess whose mind is so far above the ordinary that she effortlessly
5   understands what seems to be most difficult to our scholars, I paused therein
     to explain only what I thought was new.[25] And now, so that you don't
     doubt what I'm saying, I promise you to review this work on the Passions
     and to add what I judge to be necessary to render it more intelligible; and
10   that afterwards I'll send it to you to do as you please with it. For I am, etc.

     From Egmont, December 4, 1648.

SECOND LETTER

To Monsieur
15   ·   *Descartes*

Sir:
     You have made me wait so long for your treatise on the Passions that I'm
     beginning to lose hope, and to imagine that you promised it to me only to
20   keep me from publishing the letter I had previously written to you. For I
     have reason to believe that you'd be upset if the excuse you employ for not
     finishing your Physics were taken from you. And my plan was to take it

---

25. Elisabeth, Princess Palatine of Bohemia (1618-1680), daughter of Frederick V of
Bohemia and Elizabeth Stuart, daughter of Charles I of England. Since Elisabeth was
probably Descartes's most acute and persistent correspondent and since they were
indeed friends, the praise is for once very likely sincere. In dedicating his *Principles* to
her, Descartes had written in a similar vein, "I have never encountered anyone who
has understood everything contained in my writings so thoroughly and so well. For
many find them very obscure, even among the best and most learned minds" (AT
VIII, 3-4: CSM I, 192). On her role in the genesis of this treatise, see RL 5-12. The
word *docteurs*, here translated "scholars," meant one who had passed through a full
course of study and was qualified to teach a science; an accomplished scientist. This is
its only occurrence in the treatise.

from you with that letter, inasmuch as the reasons I urged in it are such that   325
it seems to me that no one with the least honor and virtue to recommend
him could read them without their inciting him to desire, as I do, that you
should obtain from the public what's needed for the experiments you say are   5
necessary for you; and I hoped it would readily fall into the hands of some
who'd have the power to render this desire efficacious, either because they
have access to those who dispose of the public treasury or because they   10
themselves dispose of it. Thus I resolved to proceed in such a way that
you'd have exercise in spite of yourself. For I know that you are so good-
hearted that you wouldn't want to fail to repay with interest what you'd be
given in this fashion, and that this would make you completely abandon the   15
negligence of which I cannot at present abstain from accusing you, even
though I am, etc.

    July 23, 1649.

REPLY

To the Second Letter

Sir: 20
    I am quite innocent of the artifice you want to believe I have employed to
keep the long letter you wrote me last year from being published. I have had
no need to employ it. For, in addition to the fact that I do not for a moment   25
believe that it's capable of producing the effect you are aiming for, I am not
so inclined to sloth that the fear of the work of weighing many experiments,
to which I would be obligated if I received from the public the opportunity
to carry them out, can prevail over the desire I have to instruct myself and   5
to set down in writing something useful to other men. I cannot excuse
myself so easily for the negligence you reproach me about. For I confess that
I've taken more time to review the little treatise I'm sending you than I had
previously taken to compose it, and that nevertheless I've added only a few   10
things to it and changed nothing in the discourse, which is so simple and so
brief that it will reveal that my purpose has not been to explain the Passions
as an Orator, or even as a moral Philosopher, but only as a Physicist.[26] So I   15
anticipate that this treatise will have no better fortune than my other
writings; and though its title may perhaps invite more people to read it, it   20
will still only be capable of satisfying those who take the trouble to examine
it carefully. Such as it is, I put it in your hands, etc.

    From Egmont, August 14, 1649.

---

26. *En Physicien.* An absolutely crucial thematic statement by the author about the
nature of his work. We shall refer to it in appropriate notes to the body of the
treatise.

THE
PASSIONS
OF THE SOUL

FIRST PART

ABOUT THE PASSIONS
IN GENERAL,

and Incidentally about the Entire
Nature of Man

Article 1.   That what is a Passion with respect to a subject
is always an Action in some other respect.[1]

The defectiveness of the sciences we inherit from the ancients is nowhere more apparent than in what they wrote about the Passions. For even though this is a topic about which knowledge has always been vigorously sought,

1. In the first six articles, Descartes begins his study by developing a general principle: the first step in coming to understand anything that goes on within people should be to determine whether to attribute it to the soul or to the body. Then, in aa. 7-16, 17-29, and 30-50, he successively considers the nature of the body, the soul, and their union, insofar as they must be understood if we are to understand the nature of the passions of the soul: see notes 8, 18, and 31 below, and see the passages cited in note 29 below.

Descartes can be seen here as consciously applying the second rule of the method he had urged in Part Two of the *Discourse on Method*: "to divide each of the difficulties I examined into as many parts as possible and as may be required in order to resolve them better" (AT VI, 18: CSM I, 120); or the earlier *Rules for the Direction of the Mind*, Rules 5 and 6: AT X, 379-387: CSM I, 20-24. He begins both the *Treatise on Man* and the *Description of the Human Body* with similar applications of this rule: see AT XI, 119-120: Hall 1; and AT XI, 223-226: CSM I, 314-315. Elsewhere he suggests that there are three options, not just two, for locating what takes place within people: see to Elisabeth, 21 May 1643: AT III, 665-666: K 138; *Principles of Philosophy* I, a. 48: AT VIII, 23: CSM I, 208-209.

and though it does not seem to be one of the most difficult—because, as everyone feels them in himself, one need not borrow any observation from *15* elsewhere to discover their nature—nevertheless what the Ancients taught about them is so little, and for the most part so little believable, that I cannot *328* hope to approach the truth unless I forsake the paths[2] they followed. For this reason I shall be obliged to write here as though I were treating a topic which no one before me had ever described. To begin with, I take into *5* consideration that whatever is done or happens afresh is generally called by the Philosophers a Passion with respect to the subject it happens to, and an Action with respect to what makes it happen. Thus, even though the agent *10* and the patient are often quite different, the Action and the Passion are always a single thing, which has these two names in accordance with the two different subjects it may be referred to.[3]

Article 2. That in order to understand the Passions of the *15* soul we need to distinguish its functions from those of the body.

Then I also take into consideration that we notice no subject that acts more immediately upon our soul than the body it is joined to, and that conse- *20* quently we ought to think that what is a Passion in the former is commonly an Action in the latter. So there is no better path for arriving at an under- standing of our Passions than to examine the difference between the soul and the body, in order to understand to which of the two each of the functions *25* within us should be attributed.

Article 3. What rule must be followed to achieve this end. *329*

One will find no great difficulty in doing that if one bears this in mind: everything we find by experience to be in us which we see can also be in *5* entirely inanimate bodies must be attributed to our body alone; on the other

---

2. *Chemins.* As Rodis-Lewis hints (RL 65, n. 2), Descartes uses this word to distinguish his method from false ones. See *Discourse*, Parts 1 and 3: AT VI, 3.5-7 and 28.2: CSM I, 112 and 124-125; to Reneri for Pollot, April or May 1638: AT II, 38; and a. 2 below: 328.23. *Pace* AT (which—see note at XI, 719-720—retains dozens of trivial inaccuracies), Descartes's first use of *anciens* in a. 1 is lowercase.
3. See to Hyperaspistes, August 1641: AT III, 428: K 115. What is an action in the body may not be a mode or modification of the body; a mode of the soul will qualify if it is caused when the body acts on the soul.

10 hand, everything in us which we conceive entirely incapable of belonging to
a body must be attributed to our soul.[4]

Article 4.   That the heat and movement of the members proceed from the body, and thoughts from the soul.[5]

15 Thus, because we do not conceive the body to think in any way, we do
right to believe that every kind of thought within us belongs to the soul.
And because we have no doubt that there are inanimate bodies which can
20 move in as many different ways as ours, or more, and which have as much
heat, or more (experience shows this in [the case of] flame, which in itself has
much more heat and motion than any of our members), we must believe
25 that all the heat and all the movements which are in us, insofar as[6] they do
not depend on thought, belong to the body alone.

330   Article 5.   That it is an error to believe that the soul imparts motion and heat to the body.

5 By means of this we shall avoid an error many have fallen into, a very
serious one—so much so that I consider it the main reason why no one has

4. Here "attribute" translates *attribuer*, and "belong," below, translates *appartenir*.
When a person "attributes" a function to a thing, that person might be maintaining
either that it is a mode of that thing, present in it, or that it is caused by that thing.
That distinction must be kept in mind in the course of reading and assessing the
argument in aa. 3–6.
5. Articles 4–6 concern a central question about "the entire nature of man" (327.5–6):
the explanation of life. Heat and movement mark off living bodies from dead ones,
but since heat and movement are also found in inanimate bodies, they belong to and
must be attributed to the body alone, and do not proceed from or depend on the soul.
In this respect, life differs from thought. See to Regius, June 1642: AT III, 566: K 133;
to More, 5 February 1649: AT V, 275–279: K 243–245. The serious error which
Descartes identifies in a. 5 is considered in the Second Meditation: AT VII, 26: CSM
II, 17–18; and is criticized in *Description of the Human Body*: AT XI, 224–226: CSM
I, 314–315. When we learn (a. 29) that the passions are caused by movements within
the body, we also discover one reason why the error is a serious one: thinking that
those bodily movements depend on the soul would forestall explaining the passions as
a physicist (Preface, 326).
6. Descartes maintains a definite contrast between the phrase *en tant que*, which
means "insofar as," and the phrase *autant que*, which means "inasmuch as." For
example, his use of the former idiom here leaves open the possibility that the heat and
movement within us may not always belong to the body alone—namely when they
depend on thought. See however note 63 in Part II.

yet been able to explain the Passions correctly, and the other things belonging to the soul. [The error] consists in this: on seeing that all dead bodies   *10*
become devoid of heat and then movement, people have imagined that it
was the absence of the soul that made the movements and the heat cease.
And so they have groundlessly believed that our natural heat and all the
movements of our body depended on the soul—whereas people ought to   *15*
think, on the contrary, that the soul departs when someone dies only because
that heat ceases and the organs used to move the body disintegrate.

Article 6.   What the difference is between a living body and   *20*
a dead body.

Therefore, so that we may avoid this error, let us consider that death never
occurs through the fault of the soul, but only because one of the principal
parts of the body disintegrates. And let us judge that the body of a living   *25*
man differs from that of a dead man as much as a watch or other automaton   331
(that is, other self-moving machine), when it is wound and contains the
bodily principle of the movements for which it is constructed, along with   *5*
everything required for its action, [differs from] the same watch or other
machine when it is broken and the principle of its movement ceases to act.[7]

Article 7.   Brief explanation of the parts of the body and
some of its functions.[8]   *10*

To render this more intelligible, I shall explain here in a few words all about
the way in which the machine of our body is composed. There is no one

7. The "principle" of the body's functions is thermodynamic (a. 8). And heat is itself
explainable in terms of movement (see e.g. *The World*, ch. 2: AT XI, 7-10: CSM I,
83-84; *Meteorology*, Discourse 1: AT VI, 235-236: Olscamp 266; to Mersenne, 9
January 1639: AT II, 485; *Principles* IV, aa. 80, 92, and 198: AT VIII, 249, 255-256,
321-323: partially at CSM I, 284-285). Therefore it is accurate to describe the human
body as a "machine" and to compare it to various automata (as Descartes does e.g. in
Treatise on Man: AT XI, 120 and 130-132: Hall 2-5 and 21-22; in the Sixth
Meditation: AT VII, 84-85: CSM II, 58-59; and here in aa. 6, 7, 13, 16, and 34).
8. In articles 7-16 Descartes sketches the functions of the human body insofar as they
can help us understand the passions of the soul, following the procedure recommended in a. 2. The sketch is filled out in *Treatise on Man* and *Description of the Human
Body*, written respectively in 1632-1633 and 1648 but published posthumously, and
also in *Discourse*, Part V, and *Dioptrics*. Articles 7-10 are anticipated in to [the
Marquess of Newcastle], April 1645?: AT IV, 188-192.

15   who does not know by now that we have in us a heart, a brain, a stomach,
muscles, nerves, arteries, veins, and similar things. It is known, too, that food
that is eaten descends into the stomach and bowels, whence its juice, flowing
20   into the liver and all of the veins, mingles with the blood they contain and
thereby increases its quantity. Those who have heard even a little about
Medicine know moreover the way the heart is composed, and how all the
venous blood can easily flow from the vena cava into its right side, and pass
25   from there into the lungs by the vessel that is named the arterial vein, then
return from the lungs into the left side of the heart by the vessel named the
venous artery, and finally pass from there into the great artery, whose
332   branches spread out through the whole body.[9] Likewise, all those whom the
authority of the Ancients has not entirely blinded, and who have been
willing to open their eyes enough to examine Harvey's opinion concerning
5   the circulation of the blood, do not doubt that all the body's veins and
arteries are like streams through which the blood ceaselessly flows with
great rapidity, making its way from the right chamber of the heart by the
10   arterial vein, whose branches are dispersed all through the lungs and joined
with those of the venous artery, by which it passes from the lungs into the
left side of the heart; then from there it goes into the great artery, whose
branches, dispersed through all the rest of the body, are joined to the vena
15   cava's branches, which carry the same blood anew into the right chamber of
the heart: thus these two chambers are like sluices through each of which all
the blood passes on every circuit it makes in the body.[10] Further, it is known
20   that all the movements of the members depend on muscles, and that these
muscles are opposed to one another in such a way that when one of them
contracts it draws toward itself the part of the body it is attached to, which
at the same time extends the muscle opposed to it. Then, if this latter
25   happens to contract at another time, it extends the former, and draws back
toward itself the part they are attached to. Finally, it is known that all these
movements of the muscles, as well as all the senses, depend on nerves, which
30   are like little filaments or little tubes which all come from the brain and
which contain, just as it does, a certain very fine air or wind, called the
animal spirits.

9. The "arterial vein" is the pulmonary artery, the "venous artery" is the set of four
pulmonary veins, and the "great artery" is the aorta.
10. Descartes praised Harvey's discovery of the circulation of the blood, but wrongly
defended his own thermodynamic explanation of the heartbeat against Harvey's
nonthermodynamic account, e.g. in *Discourse*, Part 5: AT VI, 46-55: CSM I, 134-
139; *Description of the Human Body*: AT XI, 231-244: partially in CSM I, 316-319.
See also the passages cited in note 12 below and in note 46 in Part II. Concerning
Harvey, see note 17 in the Preface, above.

Article 8.   What the principle of all these functions is.   333

But the way in which these animal spirits and nerves contribute to the
movements and senses is not commonly known, nor the bodily Principle   5
that makes them act. This is why, although I have already described it
somewhat in other writings,[11] I shall nevertheless say briefly here that while
we live there is a continual heat in our heart, which is a species of fire that   10
the venous blood maintains in it, and that this fire is the bodily principle of
all the movements of our members.

Article 9.   How the movement of the heart takes place.

Its first effect is to expand the blood with which the chambers of the heart   15
are filled; this causes that blood, which needs a larger place to occupy, to pass
forcefully from the right chamber into the arterial vein and from the left into
the great artery.[12] Then, as this expansion ceases, blood immediately enters   20
the right chamber of the heart afresh from the vena cava, and the left from
the venous artery. For there are little membranes at the openings of these
four vessels, so disposed that they prevent blood from entering the heart   334
except by the latter two, and from leaving it except by the former two. The
new blood that has entered the heart is immediately rarefied there in the
same way as that which preceded it. And it is this alone in which the pulse   5
or beating of the heart and arteries consists; so this beating recurs as often as
blood enters the heart afresh. It is also this alone that gives the blood its
motion, and makes it flow ceaselessly with great rapidity in all the arteries
and veins, by means of which it carries the heat it acquires in the heart to all   10
the other parts of the body, and serves as their sustenance.

Article 10.   How the animal spirits are produced in the   15
         brain.

But what matters more here is that all of the liveliest and finest parts of the
blood that the heat has rarefied in the heart ceaselessly enter the cavities of
the brain in great numbers. And the reason they go there rather than   20

---

11. *Discourse*, Part 5: AT VI, 49-55: CSM I, 135-139; *Dioptrics*, Discourse 4: AT VI,
109-114: Olscamp 87-90.
12. For dilation as the active phase of the heartbeat, see *Treatise on Man*: AT XI,
124-125: Hall 13-15; to Plempius for Fromondus, 3 October 1637: AT I, 416: French
translation, Alquié I, 789. Cf. also a. 126, etc., below.

anywhere else is that all the blood leaving the heart by the great artery flows
toward that place in a straight line, and, since they cannot all enter it,
25   because there are only very narrow passages, only the most agitated and the
finest of its parts get there, while the rest spread out into all the other places
in the body. Now these very fine parts of the blood compose the animal
335   spirits. And to this end the only change they need to undergo in the brain is
to be separated there from the other parts of the blood that are not so fine.
5   For what I name spirits here are nothing but bodies; their only property is
that they are bodies which are very small and which move very rapidly—
just like the parts of the flame that emanates from a torch.[13] So they do not
10   stop anywhere, and to the extent that some of them enter the brain's cavities,
others leave through the pores in its substance; these pores guide them into
nerves and thence into muscles, by means of which they move the body in
all the different ways in which it can be moved.

15   ## Article 11.   How the movements of muscles take place.

For the sole cause of all the members' movements is that some muscles
contract and those opposing them become extended, as has already been said.
20   And the sole cause making one muscle contract, rather than the opposing
one, is that a slightly greater number of spirits come toward it from the
brain than toward the other. Not that the spirits coming immediately from
25   the brain suffice by themselves to move these muscles—but they make all
the other spirits already in the two muscles leave one of them extremely
rapidly and pass into the other, whence the one they leave becomes longer
336   and slacker, and the one they enter, rapidly becoming swollen with them,
contracts and pulls the member it is attached to. This is easy to understand,
5   provided one knows that there are only very few animal spirits continually
coming from the brain toward each muscle but that a great quantity of
others are always enclosed in the same muscle, moving very rapidly in it—
10   sometimes merely whirling about where they are, when they find no open
passages by which to leave it, and sometimes flowing into the opposing
muscle. For there are little openings in each of these muscles through which
these spirits can flow from one into the other, so disposed that when the
15   spirits coming from the brain toward one of them have even a little more
force than those going toward the other, they open all the openings through

13. The animal spirits are corporeal components of the blood; they are "spirits" as
wine is, not as ghosts are, more spiritous than spiritual (see a. 15). They are therefore
an appropriate resource for someone who wishes to treat the passions as a physicist
(326), and, as we shall see, they play a central role in Descartes's treatment.

which the other muscle's spirits can pass into the first, and at the same time
close all those through which its spirits can pass into the other one. By this   20
means all the spirits heretofore contained in these two muscles collect very
rapidly in one of them, swelling and contracting it, while the other becomes
extended and relaxed.

Article 12.   How objects outside us act upon the sense   25
               organs.

We still need to understand here the causes that keep the spirits from always
flowing in the same way from the brain into the muscles, and at times make   337
more of them come toward some than toward others. For, in addition to the
action of the soul, which as I shall relate below[14] is truly one of these causes
within us, two others besides, which depend only on the body, need to be   5
noted. The first consists in the diversity of the movements excited in the
sense organs by their objects, which I have already explained fully enough in
the *Dioptrique*.[15] But, so that those who see this work may need to have   10
read no others, I shall repeat here that there are three things to consider in
the nerves, namely, their pith or internal substance, which extends in the
form of little filaments from the brain, where it originates, to the ends of   15
the other members these filaments are attached to; then the membranes
which surround them and which, being continuous with the ones that
envelop the brain, compose little tubes in which the little filaments are   20
enclosed; then finally the animal spirits, which, carried by these same tubes
from the brain to the muscles, cause the filaments therein to remain completely free and extended, in such a way that the least thing that moves the
part of the body where the end of any of them is attached thereby makes the   25
part of the brain it comes from move, in the same way in which, when we
pull one end of a cord, we make the other move.

Article 13.   That this action of objects outside of us can   338
               guide spirits into the muscles in various ways.

And I explained in the *Dioptrique*[16] how all the objects of vision are   5
communicated to us in this way alone: by the mediation of transparent
bodies between them and us, they locally move the little filaments of the

14. Articles 18, 31, 34 (centrally), and 43.
15. Discourse 4: AT VI, 109-114: Olscamp 87-90.
16. Discourses 5 and 6: AT VI, 128-147: Olscamp 100-113.

10   optic nerves at the back of our eyes and then the parts of the brain these
      nerves come from—I said that they move them in as many different ways as
      there are diversities they make us see in things, and that it is not the
      movements occurring in the eye, but those occurring in the brain, that
15   immediately represent those objects to the soul. From this example it is easy
      to understand that sounds, odors, tastes, heat, pain, hunger, thirst, and in
      general all the objects both of our other external senses and of our internal
20   appetites also excite some movement in our nerves, which passes to the brain
      by means of them. In addition to the fact that these various movements of
      the brain make our soul have various sensations, they can also, apart from
      [the soul], make the spirits take their course toward certain muscles rather
25   than others, and so [make them] move our members. I will prove this here
      by only one example. If someone were suddenly to thrust his hand near our
339   eyes as if to strike us, even though we might know that he is our friend, that
      he is doing this only in jest, and that he will be very careful not to injure us,
5   it would nevertheless be hard for us to keep from closing them. This shows
      that it is not by the mediation of our soul that they close, since it is against
      our volition—which is its only or at least its principal action—but that it is
10   because the machine of our body is so composed that the movement of that
      hand toward our eyes excites another movement in our brain, which guides
      animal spirits into the muscles that make the eyelids lower.

15   Article 14.   That the diversity existing among the spirits can
                     also diversify their course.

      The other cause serving to guide animal spirits into muscles in various ways
      is the unequal agitation of these spirits and the diversity of their parts. For
20   when some of their parts are larger and more agitated than the rest, they pass
      further in a straight line into the brain's cavities and pores, and are thereby
25   guided into other muscles than they would be if they had less force.

340   Article 15.   What the causes of their diversity are.

      And this inequality may originate from the varieties of stuff they are
5   composed of, as we see in those who have drunk a lot of wine: the wine's
      vapors, suddenly entering the blood, rise from the heart to the brain, where
      they turn into spirits which, being stronger and more numerous than those
10   commonly there, are capable of moving the body in many unusual ways.

This inequality of the spirits may also originate from the diverse dispositions of the heart, liver, stomach, spleen, and all the other parts that contribute to their production. In this connection we must observe above all certain little [15] nerves set into the upper part of the heart,[17] which serve to enlarge and contract the openings to its hollows, so that the blood as it expands more or less there produces spirits of diverse dispositions. We must also observe that even though the blood entering the heart arrives from all the other places in [20] the body, it nevertheless often happens to be driven there from some parts more than others, because the nerves and muscles corresponding to the former parts press or agitate it more, and that according to the diversity of [25] the parts most of it comes from, it expands in different ways in the heart, and then produces spirits having differing qualities. So, for example, [blood] that comes from the lower part of the liver, where the gall is, expands in the heart [341] in a different way from that which comes from the spleen, and the latter otherwise from that which comes from the veins of the arms or legs, and finally this latter entirely otherwise from alimentary juice, when, having [5] just left the stomach and bowels, it passes rapidly through the liver to the heart.

Article 16. How all the members can be moved by the objects of the senses and by the spirits with no [10] help from the soul.

Finally it must be noticed that the machine of our body is composed in such a way that all the changes taking place in the motion of the spirits can make them open some of the brain's pores more than others, and conversely that [15] when one of these pores is open even slightly more than usual, through the action of the nerves serving the senses, this changes something in the motion of the spirits, and causes them to be led into the muscles serving to move the [20] body in the manner in which it is commonly moved on the occasion of such an action. Thus all the movements we make without our will contributing (as often happens when we breathe, walk, eat, and in short do all the actions [25] common to us and beasts) depend only on the arrangement of our members, and on the course which the spirits excited by the heat of the heart follow [342] naturally in the brain, nerves, and muscles—in the same way in which a watch's movement is produced by the sheer force of its spring and the shape [5] of its wheels.

17. *La baze du coeur*: the broad upper part, not the bottom, of the heart.

Article 17.   What the functions of the soul are.[18]

After having thus taken into consideration all the functions that belong to
the body alone, it is easy to understand that there remains nothing in us that
we should attribute to our soul but our thoughts, which are principally of
two genera—the first, namely, are the actions of the soul; the others are its
passions. The ones I call its actions are all of our volitions, because we find
by experience[19] that they come directly from our soul and seem to depend
only on it; as, on the other hand, all the sorts of cases of perception or
knowledge to be found in us can generally be called its passions, because it is
often not our soul that makes them such as they are, and because it always
receives them from things that are represented by them.

Article 18.   About volition.

Again, our volitions are of two sorts. For the first are actions of the soul
which have their terminus[20] in the soul itself, as when we will to love God
or in general to apply our thought to some object that is not material. The
others are actions which have their terminus in our body, as when, from the
mere fact that we have the volition to take a walk, it follows that our legs
move and we walk.

18. Articles 17–29 sketch the functions of the soul insofar as that will help provide an
understanding of the passions. Cf. again note 1. As Descartes had argued in Meditations 2 and 6 (AT VII, 25–29, 78, 85–86: CSM II, 17–19, 54, 59), it is precisely our
thoughts (*pensées*)—in Descartes's consciously extended sense of that term—that can
be attributed to our soul. The sketch here is a development of a passage in a letter to
Elisabeth, 6 October 1645: AT IV, 310–311: K 177–178; it culminates, at aa. 27–29, in
a definition of the passions of the soul.
19. *Nous experimentons que*: we find by experience that; we experience it to be true
that. In this sense, we experience our own causality and can thereby distinguish our
soul's actions from its passions. See Third Replies to the *Meditations*: AT VII, 191:
CSM II, 134; Fifth Replies: AT VII, 377–378: CSM II, 259–260; *Principles* I, aa. 39
and 41: AT VIII, 19–20: CSM I, 205–206; to Mersenne, 28 January 1641: AT III, 295:
K 93; to Regius, May 1641: AT III, 372: K 102; to Hyperaspistes, August 1641: AT
III, 432: K 118; and aa. 153, 158, and 159 below.
20. *Se terminer*. Not "come to an end," but "have as an end, have their issue." We
might even interpret "have as their intentional object," amplifying note 23 below.
Here I simply give a neutral reproduction of the Latin that stood behind this unusual
usage (the verb's only occurrences are in this article). For more, see Alquié 966–967,
n. 3.

Article 19.   About Perception.   10

Our perceptions are also of two sorts, and the first have the soul as cause, the others the body. Those which have the soul as cause are the perceptions of our volitions, and of all the imaginations or other thoughts that depend on   15
them. For it is certain that we could not will anything unless we perceived by the same means that we willed it. And though with respect to our soul it is an action to will something, it can be said that it is also a passion within it   20
to perceive that it wills. Nevertheless, because this perception and this volition are really only a single thing,[21] the denomination is always made by the loftier one, and so it is not usually named a passion, but an action only.   25

Article 20.   About imaginations and other thoughts that are   344
formed by the soul.

When our soul applies itself to imagine something which does not exist—as   5
to represent to itself an enchanted palace or a chimera—and also when it applies itself to attend to something which is solely intelligible and not imaginable—for example to attend to its own nature—the perceptions it has of these things depend principally upon the volition that makes it perceive   10
them. That is why they are usually regarded as actions rather than passions.

Article 21.   About imaginations that have only the body as   15
cause.

Among perceptions caused by the body, most depend on the nerves, but there are also some that do not depend on them, which are named imaginations, like those I just spoke of, but from which they differ in that our will is   20
not employed in forming them—which disqualifies them from being num-
bered among the actions of the soul. And they only arise because the spirits, agitated in various ways and coming upon traces of various impressions   25
which have preceded them in the brain, haphazardly take their course   345
through certain of its pores rather than others. Such are the illusions of our dreams and likewise the waking reveries we often have, when our thought

21. Descartes suggests elsewhere as well that a thought and one's perception of that thought are identical: to Mersenne, 28 January 1641: AT III, 295: K 93; Third Objections and Replies: AT VII, 173-175: CSM II, 122-124; to Regius, May 1641: AT III, 372: K 102-103.

5   wanders carelessly without applying itself to anything of its own accord.
     Now even though some of these imaginations are passions of the soul, taking
     this word in its most fitting and particular sense, and though they can all be
10   so named if it is taken in a more general sense, yet since they do not have so
     noteworthy and determinate a cause as the perceptions the soul receives by
     the mediation of the nerves, and since they seem to be only their shadow
15   and picture, before we can distinguish them rightly it will be necessary to
     consider the difference among these other ones.[22]

Article 22.   About the difference existing among the other perceptions.

     All the perceptions I have not yet explained come to the soul by the
20   mediation of the nerves, and there exists this difference among them: we
     refer some of them to objects outside us which strike our senses, others to
     our body or some of its parts, and finally others to our soul.[23]

22. In order to locate those imaginations that are passions in the narrow sense,
Descartes will first make the necessary distinction among perceptions that depend on
the nerves (aa. 22–25); it will then emerge (a. 26) that there are both imaginations
and neural perceptions which qualify as passions of the soul.

23. *Nous les rapportons*: "we refer them" to external objects, to our body, and to our
soul. Descartes uses the reflexive verb similarly, as at 350.16: our perceptions *se
rapportent*—"have reference"—to various objects. He provides some materials for an
account of the *content* or *intentionality* of passions in his use of these verbs and also
(note 14, Part II) in his talk of the passions as "representing" things to us and in his
talk of the "objects" of passions.

   Descartes holds that we refer all our neural perceptions to some object (a. 22), and
he regards it as a definitional truth that we refer the passions of the soul to our soul
(aa. 27, 29). Since not all passions are neural perceptions, the possibility remains that
some passions are *not* referred to the soul; see notes 22 and 26, and note 3 in Part II.
When we refer a perception to some external object, we have the opinion that it is
caused by that object, in such a way that we think we see or feel it (a. 23); when we
refer a perception to an external object or to a part of our body, we judge that the
action that is making us feel some quality of that object is in that object (a. 24); when
we refer a perception to our soul, however, we commonly know no proximate cause
of that perception, and we feel its effects as in the soul itself (a. 25; to Elisabeth, 6
October 1645: AT IV, 311: K 178).

   I propose this hypothesis about Descartes's conception of referring: we "refer" our
perception to an object just in case we spontaneously judge that the action causing
our perception is within that object. See Alquié 970, note 2.

   Part II opens with an enumeration of the principal passions, based (a. 52) on the
thesis that every sort of passion is normally caused, in part, by a judgment that some

Article 23.   About perceptions we refer to objects outside us. 346

Those we refer to things outside us, namely to the objects of our senses, are   5
caused (at least when our opinion is not false) by those objects, which,
exciting movements in the organs of the external senses, excite some in the
brain too by the mediation of the nerves, which make the soul feel them.[24]   10
So, when we see the light of a torch and hear the sound of a bell, the sound
and the light are two different actions, which, solely by exciting two
different movements in some of our nerves and thereby in the brain, impart   15
to the soul two different sensations, which we refer to the subjects we
suppose to be their causes in such a way that we think that we see the torch
itself and hear the bell, and not that we only feel the movements proceeding   20
from them.

---

object is good or bad for us or at least matters to us in some way or other. (Thus note
the descriptions of the six primitive passions in aa. 53, 56, 57, and 61, but note also the
possibility of exceptions to the thesis, which is suggested in Part III, note 29.) We
normally feel a passion only when we first judge that something is related to us in
some such way. When we do feel the resulting passion, it is then understandable that
we should spontaneously judge that that very passion is brought about by the fact
that that object stands in that relation to us.

   Now given the above hypothesis, to say that we make that spontaneous judgment
about our passion is to say that we refer it to ourselves (and, of course, to the object
which our judgment also concerns). But Descartes also holds that we are identical
with our souls (see the texts from the *Meditations* cited in note 18 above). It is
perhaps by such a line of thought that he might have concluded that, in general, we
refer the passions of the soul to our souls themselves. Here is a simple example.
Normally one of the causes of my love for X is my judgment that X is good for *me*
(see a. 56). So I spontaneously judge that X's being good for me is the cause of the
passion of love I now feel. In that way I "refer" my passion to myself. The apparent
ubiquity of a word like "me," within our spontaneous judgments about the causes of
our passions, may thus have led Descartes to the generalization that all the passions of
the soul are referred to the soul itself. See notes 20 and 25, notes 6 and 14 in Part II,
and notes 2 and 17 in Part III.
24. The final clause is ambiguous in French. It may mean either that the nerves or
that the brain movements make the soul feel either its own perceptions or the
movements of the organs or the objects. But, given the context (a. 24) and a parallel
passage (*Dioptrics*, Discourse 4: AT VI, 112-114: Olscamp 89-90), it probably means
that the brain movements make the soul feel the objects. As the rest of a. 23 explains,
the object the soul feels is not the torch or bell itself, but the movements which
proceed from it—these being identical with the "actions" (aa. 23, 24) which, by the
mediation of nerve and brain movements, give rise to these perceptions. As the Sixth
Meditation explains more fully, while the senses indeed convey some truth to the
mind, they cannot be counted on to inform it of the essential nature of external
objects (AT VII, 78-83: CSM II, 54-58).

Article 24.   About perceptions we refer to our body.

25   The perceptions we refer to our body or some of its parts are those we have
      of hunger, thirst, and our other natural appetites, to which may be added
347   pain, heat, and the other affections that we feel as in our members and not as
      in objects outside us. So we may feel at the same time, and by the mediation
5   of the same nerves, the coolness of our hand and the heat of the flame it
      approaches, or, on the contrary, the heat of the hand and the cold of the air it
      is exposed to—there being no difference between the actions making us feel
10   the warmth or coolness in our hand and those making us feel that which is
      outside us except that, [now supposing that] one of these actions succeeds the
      other, we judge that the first is already in us and that the succeeding [action]
      is not there yet but in the object causing it.[25]

Article 25.   About perceptions we refer to our soul.

      The perceptions that are referred to the soul alone are those whose effects
20   are felt as in the soul itself, and of which no proximate cause to which they
      may be referred is commonly known. Such are the sensations of joy, anger,
      and others like them, which are sometimes excited in us by objects that
25   move our nerves and sometimes also by other causes.[26] Now even though all
      of our perceptions—those which are referred to objects outside us no less
      than those which are referred to various affections of our body—are truly
348   passions with respect to our soul when this word is taken in its most general
      sense, nevertheless it is usually restricted to mean those only which have
      reference to the soul itself. And it is only these last which I have undertaken
5   to explain here under the name of passions of the soul.

25. If we feel cold hand and warm air simultaneously, the actions causing our
perceptions—movements in the air and hand— are identical. Perceptions referred to
the external world differ from perceptions referred to our body not because different
kinds of actions generate them but because we make different judgments about their
causes; that is shown by the case in which we feel cold hand and warm air one after
the other: in this case, similar actions produce perceptions about which we make
different causal judgments. Recall the hypothesis suggested in note 23.
26. These other causes are discussed in aa. 21, 26, 51, 93, and 94; cf. to Elisabeth, 6
October 1645: AT IV, 309-313: K 177-179.

Article 26.   That the imaginations that depend only on the
          haphazard movements of spirits may be passions
          as truly as the perceptions that depend on the
          nerves.

It remains here to observe that all the things the soul perceives by the   *10*
mediation of nerves may also be represented to it by the haphazard course of
spirits, the only difference being that impressions entering the brain through
the nerves are usually more lively and more definite than those the spirits   *15*
excite there—which led me to say in art. 21 that the latter are like the
shadow or picture of the former. It must also be observed that this picture
sometimes happens to be so similar to the thing it represents that one can   *20*
thereby be deceived, in connection with the perceptions which have reference to objects outside us, or those which have reference to some of the parts
of our body, but that one cannot be [deceived] in the same manner in
connection with the passions, inasmuch as they are so close and internal to   *25*
our soul that it is impossible it should feel them without their truly being
such as it feels them.[27] So, often when we are sleeping, and even sometimes
when awake, we imagine certain things so forcefully that we think we see   **349**
them before ourselves or feel them within our body, although they are not
there at all. But even though we be asleep and dreaming, we cannot feel sad,   *5*
or moved by any other passion, unless it be quite true that the soul has that
passion within itself.[28]

Article 27.   The Definition of the Passions of the soul.

After having considered wherein the passions of the soul differ from all its   *10*
other thoughts, it seems to me that they may generally be defined thus:

27. A pervasive Cartesian conviction is that what is far away can deceive, while what
is close at hand can give security. That is true not only of epistemic security (in
addition to the present passage, see Meditations 1 and 3: AT VII, 18 and 37: CSM II,
12-13 and 26; and a. 1 above), but also of emotional security (see *Discourse*, Part 3:
AT VI, 25-27: CSM I, 123-124; and aa. 147-148 below).
28. The word "feel" (*sentir*) here must be read so that "we feel sad" means that we
think we are sad, and not that we are sad, for the latter reading would render this
sentence's argument pointless. Descartes invites a similar confusion in the passage
from the Third Meditation cited in note 27. Yet the point—defended centrally in
Meditation 2: AT VII, 28-29: CSM II, 19— is clear: I can perhaps be deceived about
the cause of my thoughts, ideas, or passions, but not about their existence or specific
nature.

15 perceptions or sensations or excitations of the soul which are referred to it in
particular and which are caused, maintained, and strengthened by some
movement of the spirits.

Article 28.   Explanation of the first part of this definition.

20 They may be named perceptions when this word is used generally to mean
all the thoughts that are not actions of the soul, or volitions, but not when it
is used only to mean cases of plain knowledge. For experience shows that
25 those who are most agitated by their passions are not those who know them
350 best, and that [the passions] are numbered among the perceptions which the
close bond between the soul and the body renders confused and obscure.[29]
They may also be named sensations, because they are received into the soul
5 in the same manner as the objects of the external senses, and are not known
otherwise by it. But they may still better be named excitations of the soul,
not only because this name may be attributed to all the changes that take
10 place within it, that is, to all the different thoughts that come to it, but in
particular because, among all the sorts of thoughts it can have, there are no
others which agitate it and shake it so strongly as these passions do.

15 ## Article 29.   Explanation of its other part.

I add that they have reference to the soul in particular, in order to distinguish
them from other sensations—of which some, like odors, sounds, and colors,
are referred to external objects, and others, like hunger, thirst, and pain, to
20 our body. I also add that they are caused, maintained, and strengthened by
some movement of the spirits, in order to distinguish them from our volitions, which can be named excitations of the soul which have reference to it,
25 but which are caused by it itself, and also in order to explain their last and

29. Although my thoughts about the nature of my present passions must be true (a.
26), I am typically ignorant of their proximate cause (a. 25); in general I may not
know them, and they are themselves not cases of plain knowledge (*connoissances
evidentes*). They qualify as perceptions and as representations (a. 17), but they
always remain confused and obscure. See Sixth Meditation: AT VII, 78-84: CSM II,
54-58; *Principles* I, a. 66, and IV, a. 190: AT VIII, 32 and 317-318: CSM I, 216 and
281; to Elisabeth, 28 June 1643 and 1 and 15 September 1645: AT III, 690-695, and
IV, 283-287 and 294-295: K 140-143, 168-170, and 173; to Chanut, 1 February 1647:
AT IV, 602-603: K 209; to Christine, 20 November 1647: AT V, 84-85: K 227-228;
and aa. 138 and 211 below.

most proximate cause, which distinguishes them anew from other sensations.[30]

Article 30. That the soul is jointly united to all the parts of the body.[31]

351

But in order to understand all these things more perfectly, it is necessary to know that the soul is truly joined to the whole body, and that one cannot properly say that it is in any one of its parts to the exclusion of the others, because [the body] is one, and in a way indivisible, in proportion to[32] the disposition of its organs, which are all so related to one another that when any of them is removed this renders the whole body defective; and because [the soul] is of a nature which has no relation to extension, or to the dimensions[33] or other properties of the stuff the body is composed of, but only to the whole collection of its organs—as becomes apparent from the fact that one cannot in any way conceive of a half or a third of a soul, or of what extension it occupies, and from the fact that [the soul] does not become smaller from some part of the body being cut off, but separates from it entirely when the collection of its organs is dissolved.[34]

5

10

15

20

30. According to aa. 12, 23, and 24, the "last and most proximate cause" of the perceptions we refer to the external world or to our body is an activity of the nerves, in which the spirits have only a bit part to play (described at *Treatise on Man*: AT XI, 174-177: Hall 83-87; and aa. 32, 35 below). By contrast, the last and most proximate cause of the passions is "some particular agitation of the spirits," as Descartes had said to Elisabeth, 6 October 1645: AT IV, 311: K 178.

31. In aa. 30-50 Descartes discusses the phenomena that are due to the union of soul and body, insofar as that is useful for understanding the passions—once again following the procedure recommended in a. 2 (see note 1). It must be said, though, that a more accurate statement of Descartes's procedure in Part I than is offered in a. 2 is actually provided at the beginning of an entirely different work—the *Treatise on Man*: "I must first separately describe for you the body; then, also separately, the soul; and finally I must show you how these two natures would have to be joined and united to constitute men resembling us" (AT XI, 119-120: Hall 1).

32. *A raison de*: "in proportion to," not "because of." The latter, inaccurate rendering would entail an explanation of the body's unity in terms of its own structure; this rendering leaves room for (without entailing) an explanation in terms of the soul's more basic unity, described in the second half of this article—an explanation along the lines of the one in to Mesland, 9 February 1645: AT IV, 166-167: K 156-157; and 1645 or 1646: AT IV, 346.

33. See *Rules for the Direction of the Mind*, Rule 14: AT X, 447-452: CSM I, 62-65.

34. Descartes relies heavily on the principle of the simplicity or indivisibility of the soul in the Sixth Meditation: AT VII, 85-89: CSM II, 59-61—both to defend the

Article 31.   That there is a little gland in the brain in which the soul exercises its functions in a more particular way than in the other parts.[35]

25

It is also necessary to know that, even though the soul is joined to the whole
352 body, there is nevertheless one part in [the body] in which [the soul] exercises
its functions in a more particular way than in all the others. It is commonly
believed that this part is the brain, or perhaps the heart—the brain because
5 the sense organs are related thereto, and the heart because the passions are
felt as if therein. But in examining the matter carefully, I seem to have
plainly ascertained that the part of the body in which the soul immediately
10 exercises its functions is in no way the heart; it is not the whole brain either,
but only the innermost of its parts—a certain extremely small gland, situated
in the middle of its substance, and so suspended above the duct by which the
15 spirits of its anterior cavities are in communication with those of the poste-
rior that its slightest movements can greatly alter the course of these spirits,
and conversely the slightest changes taking place in the course of the spirits
20 can greatly alter the movements of this gland.

Article 32.   How it is known that this gland is the principal seat of the soul.

25 The reason which convinces me that in all the body the soul can have no
other place than this gland in which to exercise its functions immediately is
353 that I observe that the other parts of our brain are all double, just as we have
two eyes, two hands, two ears, and, in short, all the organs of our external

---

goodness of God and to argue that the soul is really distinct from the body, which is
divisible. In the Synopsis to the *Meditations*, he sketches a traditional proof for the
soul's immortality, which is based on this principle, but says that such a proof is
beyond the scope of that work (AT VII, 12-14: CSM II, 9-10; cf. to Mersenne, 24
December 1640: AT III, 265-266: K 87; Second Replies: AT VII, 153-154: CSM II,
108-109). Descartes also uses the principle in arguing that the pineal gland must be
the seat of the soul, in the passages cited in note 35, from the letters to Mersenne of
30 July and 24 December 1640; he offers a related argument in the letter to Plempius
mentioned in note 46 in Part II. The principle is used below at aa. 47 and 68.
35. The pineal gland. See *Treatise on Man, passim*; to Meyssonnier, 29 January 1640:
AT III, 19-20: K 69-70; and the letters to Mersenne of 1 April, 30 July, and 24
December 1640, and 21 April 1641: AT III, 47-49, 123-124, 263-265, and 361-362: K
71-72, 75, 85-86, and 100-101. This correspondence defends the thesis of a. 32, that
the gland is the seat of the soul. See also *Rules for the Direction of the Mind*, Rule 12:
AT X, 414-415: CSM I, 41-42; Sixth Meditation: AT VII, 86-88: CSM II, 59-61.

senses are double; and that, inasmuch as we only have a single and simple thought of a given thing at a given time, there must necessarily be some 5 place where the two images coming through the two eyes, or the two other impressions coming from a single object through the double organs of other senses, can coalesce into one before they reach the soul, so that they do not 10 represent two objects to it instead of one. And we can easily understand these images or other impressions to unite in this gland by the mediation of the spirits filling the brain's cavities, but there is no place else in the body 15 where they can thus be united unless it is done in this gland.

Article 33. That the seat of the passions is not in the heart.

As for the opinion of those who think the soul receives its passions in the 20 heart, it is not worth considering. For it is founded only on the fact that the passions make [us] feel some alteration there, and it is easy to observe that this alteration is felt as in the heart only by the mediation of a little nerve 25 descending to it from the brain, just as pain is felt as in the foot by the mediation of the nerves of the foot, and the stars are perceived as in the sky 354 by the mediation of their light and the optic nerves. So it is no more necessary that our soul exercise its functions immediately in the heart to feel its passions there than it is necessary that it be in the sky to see the stars 5 there.[36]

Article 34. How the soul and the body act on one another.

Therefore let us understand here that the soul has its principal seat in the little gland in the middle of the brain, whence it radiates into all the rest of 10 the body by the mediation of spirits, nerves, and even blood, which, participating in the impressions of the spirits, can carry them through the arteries into all the members. We recall what was said above about the machine of our body. [1] Our little nerve-filaments are so distributed in all of [the body's] 15

36. The passions themselves are mainly felt as in the heart; see also aa. 31 and 36. However, the effects of the passions are felt as in the soul: see a. 25 and to Elisabeth, 6 October 1645: AT IV, 311: K 178. (What are these effects? Perhaps the volitions to which the passions dispose the soul, according to a. 52.) But the soul exercises its functions immediately in the pineal gland (for "only the brain can act directly upon the mind"—to Regius, May 1641: AT III, 373: K 103); and therefore Descartes, breaking with tradition much more cleanly than he had in the letter just cited, declares that the pineal gland and not the heart is the principal seat of the passions.

parts that, on the occasion of different movements excited in them by objects capable of being sensed, they open the pores of the brain differentially, which

20   makes the animal spirits contained in its cavities enter the muscles differen-tially, whereby they can move the members in all the different ways in

25   which they are capable of being moved.[37] Furthermore, [2] all the other causes capable of moving the spirits in different ways are sufficient to lead them into different muscles. And let us add here that the little gland which is

355   the principal seat of the soul is suspended among the cavities containing these spirits in such a way that it can be moved by them in as many different ways as there are differences capable of being sensed in objects, but that it

5   can also be moved diversely by the soul, which is of such a nature that it receives into itself as many different impressions—that is, has as many different perceptions—as there are different movements which take place in this gland. Thus also, conversely, the machine of the body is so composed

10   that, merely because this gland is moved diversely by the soul or any other cause there may be, it drives the spirits that surround it toward the brain's pores, which guide [the spirits] through the nerves into the muscles, by means of which it makes them move the members.

15   ## Article 35.   Example of the way impressions of objects unite in the gland in the middle of the brain.

So, for example, if we see some animal coming toward us, the light re-

20   flected from its body casts two images of it, one in each of our eyes,[38] and by the mediation of the optic nerves these two images form two other [images] of it on the inner surface of the brain, facing its hollows. Then, by the

25   mediation of the spirits with which its cavities are filled, these images radiate from there toward the little gland which these spirits surround, in such a way that the motion that composes each point of one of the images

356   approaches the same point of the gland which that motion approaches that forms the point of the other image representing the same part of this animal. By this means the two images in the brain compose only a single [image] of it

5   on the gland, which, acting immediately on the soul, makes it see the animal's shape.

37. Points [1] and [2] were discussed above in aa. 12-16. I propose this clarification of some of the obscure phrases here. "Carry them": carry the impressions, not the spirits; "they open the pores": the nerve-filaments do so; "they can move the mem-bers": the filaments, or conceivably the spirits, can move them.
38. For more detail see *Dioptrics*, Discourse 5: AT VI, 114-129: Olscamp 91-100.

Article 36.   Example of the way the Passions are excited in the soul.

Furthermore, if that shape is very unusual and very frightful, that is, if it *10* bears a close resemblance to things that have previously been harmful to the body, this excites the passion of apprehension in the soul, and thereupon that of boldness or that of fear and terror, according to the differing temperament *15* of the body or the strength of the soul, and according to whether one has previously secured oneself by defense or by flight against the harmful things to which the present impression bears a resemblance. For in some men this *20* so predisposes the brain that the spirits reflected from the image thus formed on the gland turn to flow in part into the nerves serving to turn the back and move the legs for running away, and in part into those which so enlarge or contract the heart's orifices, or those which so agitate the other parts from *25* which blood is sent to [the heart], that this blood, being rarefied there in an unusual manner, sends spirits to the brain suitable to maintain and streng- *357* then the passion of fear—that is, suitable to hold open or reopen the pores of the brain that guide them into the same nerves. Simply in virtue of entering *5* these pores, these spirits excite a particular movement in this gland which is instituted by nature to make the soul feel this passion. And because these pores correspond principally to the little nerves that serve to contract or enlarge the heart's orifices, this makes the soul feel it principally as in the *10* heart.

Article 37.   How it becomes apparent that they are all caused by some movement of the spirits.

And because something like that occurs with all the other passions—namely *15* that they are caused principally by the spirits contained in the brain's cavities, insofar as they proceed toward the nerves that serve to enlarge or contract the heart's orifices or in various ways to drive the blood in other *20* parts toward [the heart] or in any other way there may be to maintain the same passion—it can be understood clearly why I have put above in their definition that they are caused by some particular[39] movement of the spirits. *25*

39. *Particulier.* This word had not appeared in aa. 27 or 29, although Descartes did use it in the letter to Elisabeth, 6 October 1645: AT IV, 311: K 178. This clause in the definition will play a theoretical role later, at aa. 170, 194, and 207.

358   Article 38.   Example of the movements of the body that
                       accompany the passions and do not depend on
                       the soul.

5   Furthermore, just as the course these spirits take toward the nerves of the
        heart suffices to impart the movement to the gland by which fear is put in
        the soul, so too, simply in virtue of the fact that certain spirits proceed at the
10   same time toward the nerves that move the legs to flee, they cause another
        movement in the same gland by means of which the soul feels and perceives
        this flight—which can in this way be excited in the body merely by the
        disposition of the organs without the soul contributing to it.

15   Article 39.   How the same cause can excite different passions
                       in different men.

        The same impression that the presence of a frightful object forms on the
20   gland which causes fear in some men may excite courage and boldness in
        others. The reason for this is that all brains are not disposed in the same
        manner, and that the same movement of the gland which in some excites
25   fear, in others makes the spirits enter the brain's pores that guide part of them
359   into the nerves that move the hands for self-defense, and part of them into
        those that agitate the blood and drive it toward the heart in the manner
        needed to produce spirits suitable to continue this defense and sustain the
        volition for it.[40]

5   Article 40.   What the principal effect of the passions is.

        For it is necessary to notice that the principal effect of all the passions in men
10   is that they incite and dispose their soul to will the things for which they

40. Character, insofar as it is displayed by diversity in the passions, is explained
physiologically here. On bodily tendencies toward passions, see also Sixth Meditation: AT VII, 74: CSM II, 52; and a. 51 below. A more theoretically elaborate
physiological explanation, of diversity in the effects as well as in the causes of the
passions, appears at a. 136. On the other hand, a. 161 allows as well for psychological
explanation of diversity in the passions, in terms of dispositions (*habitudes*) of the
soul; and the strength of one's soul is said, at aa. 36, 48-50, 133, 164, and 170, to have a
bearing on one's passions. The passions are explained by reference to both kinds of
tendencies throughout Parts II and III.

prepare their body, so that the sensation of fear incites it to will to flee, that of boldness to will to do battle, and so on for the rest.

Article 41. What the power of the soul is with respect to the body.

But the will is by its nature free in such a way that it can never be 15
constrained; and of the two sorts of thoughts I have distinguished in the
soul, of which the first are its actions—namely its volitions—and the others
its passions—taking this word in its most general sense, which comprises all 20
sorts of perceptions—the former are absolutely in its power and can only
indirectly be altered by the body, whereas the latter depend absolutely on 25
the actions that produce them and can only indirectly be altered by the soul,
except when [the soul] is itself their cause.[41] And the whole action of the soul 360
consists in this: merely by willing something, it makes the little gland to
which it is closely joined move in the way required to produce the effect 5
corresponding to this volition.

Article 42. How we find in our memory the things we will to remember.

Thus when the soul wills to remember something, this volition makes the 10
gland, inclining successively to different sides, drive the spirits toward different places in the brain, until they come upon the one where the traces are
which the object we will to remember has left there. These traces are 15
nothing but this: the pores of the brain through which the spirits have
previously made their way because of the presence of this object have
thereby acquired a greater facility than the others for being opened again in 20
the same way by spirits approaching them. So these spirits, coming upon
these pores, enter into them more easily than into others—whereby they
excite a particular movement in the gland, which represents the same object 25

41. Only our thoughts are absolutely in our power—and even some of them are not:
Discourse, Part 3: AT VI, 25-27: CSM I, 123-124; to Reneri for Pollot, April or May
1638: AT II, 36-37: K 51-52; to Mersenne, 3 December 1640: AT III, 248-249: K 84-
85; to Elisabeth, 1 September 1645: AT IV, 281-282: K 167-168; to Christine, 20
November 1647: AT V, 82-83: K 226. The case of perceptions caused by the soul
itself is discussed at aa. 19-20, 91-93, and 147-148; see notes 76 and 78 in Part II.

to the soul and makes it understand that this is the one it willed to remember.[42]

361   ## Article 43.   How the soul can imagine, be attentive, and move the body.

5   Thus when we will to imagine something we have never seen, this volition has the power to make the gland move in the way required to drive the spirits toward the pores of the brain by whose opening that thing may be
10   represented. Thus, when we will to fix our attention to consider a single object for some time, this volition keeps the gland inclined to the same side during that time. Thus, finally, when we will to walk or move our body in some other manner, this volition makes the gland drive the spirits toward the
15   muscles conducive to this effect.

Article 44.   That each volition is naturally joined to some movement of the gland, but that by artifice or habituation one can join it to others.

20   Yet it is not always the volition to excite some movement or some other effect in us which enables us to excite it; this varies rather according as nature or habituation has diversely joined each movement of the gland to
25   each thought.[43] So, for example, if someone wills to dispose his eyes to look

42. Cf. *Treatise on Man*: AT XI, 177-179: Hall 87-90.
43. The usefulness of this principle is emphasized at aa. 50, 107, and 211; and at a. 136 Descartes marks it off as "the principle on which everything I have written about [the passions] is based." It is further invoked in to Elisabeth, May 1646: AT IV, 407-409: K 192-193; to Chanut, 1 February 1647: AT IV, 603-606: K 210-211; and to Elisabeth, 8 July 1647: AT V, 65-66.
     There is a fixed and a variable aspect to the explanation of the passions of the soul. First, certain movements in the brain cause certain passions according to "the institution of Nature," and nothing can change that. This is a special case of the general rule about the mind-body union that is defended in Meditation 6: AT VII, 86: CSM II, 59-60. Secondly, other movements in the brain can come to be joined with certain passions—and thoughts generally—through a habit that is instituted either by accident or intentionally. I shall speak of this as Descartes's Principle of Habituation.
     These two metaphysical principles provide the basis for the study of the passions "as a physicist" (326). And that study in turn provides the basis for moral philosophy.

at an extremely distant object, this volition makes the pupil of [the eyes]   362
dilate; and if he wills to dispose them to look at an extremely close object,
this volition makes it contract. But if he thinks only of dilating the pupil, he
may well have the volition but he will not thereby dilate it, inasmuch as   5
nature has not joined the movement of the gland that serves to drive the
spirits toward the optic nerve in the manner needed to dilate or contract the
pupil with the volition to dilate or contract it, but rather with [the volition]
to look at distant or close objects.[44] And when in speaking we think only of   10
the meaning of what we will to say, this makes us move the tongue and lips
much more rapidly and much better than if we were to think of moving
them in all the ways required for uttering the same words. For the disposi-   15
tion we have acquired in learning to speak has made us join the action of the
soul which by the mediation of the gland can move the tongue and lips with   20
the sense of the words that follow from these movements, rather than with
the movements themselves.

Article 45.   What the power of the soul is with respect to its passions.

Our passions cannot likewise be directly excited or displaced by the action of   25
our will, but they can be indirectly by the representation of things which
are usually joined with the passions we will to have and opposed to the ones   363
we will to reject. Thus, in order to excite boldness and displace fear in
oneself, it is not sufficient to have the volition to do so—one must apply
oneself to attend to reasons, objects, or precedents that convince [one] that   5
the peril is not great, that there is always more security in defense than in
flight, that one will have glory and joy from having conquered, whereas one
can expect only regret and shame from having fled, and similar things.

Since the fixed laws governing the union were instituted by a good creator, the
passions will in general tend to occur when they are apt to benefit us, and each of
them has some good use. And the possibilities for habituation allowed by the second
principle form the basis of therapy or remedy for disorders of the passions. Such
therapy is analogous to the technological applications of physics that are possible in
the external world, under the head of "mechanics," and to those applications that are
possible in our own bodies, under the head of "medicine." See aa. 50, 107, 136, and 211
for particular applications.

44. "The detail of the corporeal mechanism subordinated to the will escapes us . . .
and appears as a *fact*" (RL 98, n. 1). See *Dioptrics*, Discourse 3: AT VI, 105-108:
Olscamp 84-86; for [Arnauld], 29 July 1648: AT V, 221-222: K 235; and aa. 18 and 41
above.

10   Article 46.   What the reason is on account of which the
                       soul cannot completely control its passions.

        There is one particular reason why the soul cannot readily alter or check its
15   passions, which led me to put in their definition above that they are not only
        caused but also maintained and strengthened by some particular movement
        of the spirits.[45] This reason is that they are almost all accompanied by some
20   excitation taking place in the heart, and consequently also throughout the
        blood and the spirits, so that until this excitation has ceased they remain
        present to our thought, in the same way as objects capable of being sensed
25   are present to it while they are acting upon our sense organs. And as the
        soul, in becoming extremely attentive to something else, can keep from
364   hearing a little noise or feeling a little pain, but cannot in the same way keep
        from hearing thunder or feeling the fire burning the hand, so it can easily
5   overcome the lesser passions, but not the most vigorous and the strongest,
        until after the excitation of the blood and spirits has abated. The most the
        will can do while this excitation is in its full strength is not to consent to its
        effects and to restrain many of the movements to which it disposes the body.
10   For example, if anger makes the hand rise in order to strike, the will can
        ordinarily restrain it; if fear incites the legs to flee, the will can stop them;
        and so on with the rest.[46]

        Article 47.   What the struggles consist in that people
15   customarily imagine between the lower part of
                       the soul and the higher.

20   And all the struggles that people customarily imagine between the lower
        part of the soul, which is called sensitive, and the higher, which is rational, or
        between the natural appetites and the will, consist only in the opposition
        between the movements which the body by its spirits and the soul by its
        will tend to excite simultaneously in the gland. For there is only a single soul
25   in us, and this soul has within itself no diversity of parts; the very one that is
        sensitive is rational, and all its appetites are volitions.[47] The error which has

45. See article 27 as modified in a. 37.
46. This metaphysical principle sets the limits on the therapeutic advice given below
in a. 211.
47. The adversary here is twofold: first, theories like Plato's, which allow conflicts
between reason and desire, or similar agencies, within the soul; secondly, theories like
the scholastic ones based on Aristotle, which assign to the soul activity beyond
volitions guided by reason, such as the "vegetative" activity of sustaining life or the
"locomotive" activity of sustaining movement. Descartes's premise is that the soul has

been committed in having it play different characters, usually opposed to one another, arises only from the fact that its functions have not been rightly 365 distinguished from those of the body, to which alone must be attributed everything to be found in us that is opposed to our reason. So no struggle 5 whatever occurs here, except as follows: as the little gland in the middle of the brain is capable of being driven from one side by the soul and from the other by the animal spirits, which, as I have said above,[48] are only bodies, it often happens that these two impulses are in opposition and the stronger one 10 prevents the other from taking effect. Now one can distinguish two sorts of movements excited by the spirits in the gland: the first represent to the soul objects that move the senses or impressions that are met within the brain, and they make no great difference to its will; the others do make some such 15 difference to it—namely those which cause the passions or the movements of the body that accompany them. As for the former [movements], even though they often prevent the actions of the soul or are prevented by them, yet because they are not in direct opposition we notice no struggle here. We 20 notice [a struggle] only between the latter [movements] and the volitions that oppose them—for example, between the impetus by which the spirits impel the gland to cause in the soul the desire for some thing and that by which 25 the soul repels [the gland] by the volition it has to shun that very thing. And what makes this struggle become noticeable for the most part is that, the will not having the power to excite the passions directly, as has already been

---

no diversity of parts, and its corollary is that no "power" (*puissance*: 366.10-11) in the soul exists to sustain activity that might conflict with reason-guided volition. The reasoning suggests that a *puissance* is more a substantival agency than an adjectival function or faculty; observe that in a. 68 Descartes seems to allow for *facultez* what he denies here for *puissances*. But his intentions here are, I think, disappointingly hazy. In any case, what looks like conflict within the soul is either conflict between soul and body or vacillation in the soul. The word *personage*, translated "character" in the next line, appears in the treatise only here; it means a role or character in a play.

The anti-Platonic argument encounters apparent opposition even in other writings by Descartes—for example, *Principles* IV, a. 190: AT VIII, 317-318: CSM I, 281, which contrasts some appetites with volitions; a. 13 above, which seems to allow for action of the soul other than volition; a. 48 just below, which seems to allow for internal conflict; and passages in the *Passions*, like those at 338.18-19 and 346.25-26, which seem to allow for appetites that are not volitions. How is the soul affected when the spirits' tendency to arouse desire is more forceful than the will's contrary tendency to repel the gland's movements? For a different statement of the anti-scholastic position, see to Regius, May 1641: AT III, 371: K 102; and of course see aa. 4-6 above.

48. Article 10.

366 said,[49] it is constrained to employ artifice and apply itself to attend successively to different things. If the first of these happens to have the strength to
change the course of the spirits for a moment, it may happen that the one
5   following does not have it and that they immediately revert, because the
previous disposition in the nerves, heart, and blood is unchanged—which
makes the soul feel driven almost at the same time to desire and not to desire
10   the same thing. This is what has given people occasion to imagine two
powers within [the soul] which struggle against one another. All the same, a
certain struggle can still be conceived, in that often the same cause which
excites some passion in the soul also excites certain movements in the body,
15   to which the soul does not contribute and which it stops or tries to stop as
soon as it perceives them, as we experience when what excites fear also
makes the spirits enter the muscles that move the legs to flee, and our
20   volition to be bold stops them.

Article 48.   How to tell the strength or weakness of souls;
and what the misfortune of the weakest is.

25   Now it is by the outcome of these struggles that everyone can tell the
strength or weakness of his soul. For there is no doubt that those in whom
the will can naturally conquer the passions most easily and stop the accom-
367 panying movements of the body have the strongest souls. However, there
are some who cannot test their strength,[50] because they never make their
will do battle with its proper weapons, but only with the ones which some
5   passions supply it in order to resist other [passions]. What I call its proper
weapons are firm and decisive judgments concerning the knowledge of good
and evil, which it has resolved to follow in conducting the actions of its life.
10   And the weakest souls of all are those whose will does not decide in this way
to follow certain judgments, but continually allows itself to be carried away
by present passions, which, often being opposed to one another, draw [the
15   will] by turns to their side, and, getting it to struggle against itself, put the
soul in the most deplorable condition it can be in. Thus, when fear represents death as an extreme evil avoidable only by flight, if ambition from the
20   other side represents the infamy of this flight as an evil worse than death,
then these two passions agitate the will in different ways; obeying now the

49. Article 45.
50. I.e., the strength of their souls.

one and now the other, it is in continual opposition to itself, and so renders the soul enslaved and unhappy.

Article 49. That strength of the soul does not suffice without knowledge of the truth.[51]

25

It is true that there are very few men so weak and irresolute that they will nothing but what their passion dictates to them. The greater part have decisive judgments which they follow in regulating a part of their actions. And though these judgments are often false, and even founded on passions by which the will has previously allowed itself to be conquered or seduced, yet, because it continues to follow them when the passion that caused them is absent, they can be regarded as its proper weapons, and souls can be thought to be stronger or weaker to the extent that they are more or less able to follow these judgments and resist the present passions opposed to them. But there is still a great difference between resolutions that proceed from some false opinion and those that rest on knowledge of the truth alone, since we are sure never to have either regret or repentance if we follow the latter, whereas we always have them upon following the former, when we discover the error therein.

368

5

10

15

Article 50. That there is no soul so weak that it cannot, when well guided, acquire an absolute power over its passions.

20

And here it is useful to know that—as has already been said above[52]—although each movement of the gland seems to have been joined by nature to each of our thoughts from the beginning of our life, one can nevertheless join them to others by habituation. Experience shows this in the case of words, which excite movements in the gland which according to the institution of nature represent only their sound to the soul when they are uttered vocally, or the shape of their letters when they are written, but which

25

369

5

51. On the place of knowledge of the truth in gaining contentment, see to Elisabeth, 4 August 1645: especially AT IV, 266-267: K 166; 15 September 1645: AT IV, 290-296: K 171-174. See note 73 in Part II.
52. Article 44. For other discussions of this linguistic case of the Principle of Habituation (note 43), see *The World*: AT XI, 4: CSM I, 81; and *Dioptrics*, Discourse 4: AT VI, 112-113: Olscamp 89-90.

nevertheless, by the disposition acquired in thinking of what they mean
upon having heard their sound or seen their letters, usually make one
10   apprehend this meaning rather than the shape of their letters or the sound of
their syllables. It is also useful to know that although the movements—both
of the gland and of the spirits and brain—which represent certain objects to
15   the soul are naturally joined with those [movements] which excite certain
passions in it, they can nevertheless by habituation be separated from them
and joined with other quite different ones; and even that this disposition can
be acquired by a single action and does not require long practice. Thus when
20   someone unexpectedly comes upon something very foul in food he is eating
with relish, the surprise of this encounter can so change the disposition of
the brain that he will no longer be able to see any such food afterwards
25   without abhorrence, whereas previously he used to eat it with pleasure. And
the same thing can be observed in beasts, for even though they have no
reason and perhaps[53] no thought either, all the movements of the spirits and
the gland that excite the passions in us still exist in them, and serve in them
30   to maintain and strengthen, not the passions as in us, but the nerve and
370   muscle movements that usually accompany them. So when a dog sees a
partridge it is naturally inclined to run toward it, and when it hears a gun
5   fired the noise naturally incites it to run away. But nevertheless setters are
commonly trained so that the sight of a partridge makes them stop, and the
noise they hear afterwards, when [the bird] is fired on, makes them run up to
it. Now these things are useful to know in order to give everyone the
10   courage to study the regulation of his passions. For since with a little skill
one can change the movements of the brain in animals bereft of reason, it is

53. Descartes distinguishes at least seven questions in comparing higher animals with
people: Do animals have life, souls, sensation, passions, thought, reason, the use of
language? His discussions are complex: often we cannot predict his answer to one
from his answer to another, and at times he appears to give conflicting answers to the
same question. His discussions often illuminate his understanding of these seven
phenomena, and hence of course their application to humans, even more than they
illuminate his view of animals.

See *Discourse*, Parts 1 and 5: AT VI, 2 and 56–59: CSM I, 112 and 140–141; Fourth
Replies: AT VII, 229–231: CSM II, 161–162; Fifth Replies: AT VII, 356: CSM II,
246; Sixth Replies: AT VII, 426: CSM II, 287–288; to Plempius for Fromondus, 3
October 1637: AT I, 414–416: K 36–37; to Reneri for Pollot, April or May 1638: AT
II, 39–41: K 53–54; to Regius, May 1641: AT III, 369–370: French translation, Alquié
II, 330–331; to Buitendijck, 1643: AT IV, 64–65: K 146; to [the Marquess of Newcas-
tle], 23 November 1646: AT IV, 573–576: K 206–208; to More, 5 February 1649: AT
V, 275–279: K 243–245; and a. 138 below (where "subhuman" is glossed "without
reason").

plain that one can do it even better in men, and that even those who have the weakest souls could acquire a quite absolute dominion over all their passions if one employed enough skill in training and guiding them.[54]

15

---

54. "Them" *(les)* probably refers to the people, not the passions. What is striking here is that Descartes evidently envisages people coming to regulate their passions by being trained by others, Pavlov style. Similarly, the impersonal pronoun "one" *(on)* in the title of a. 44 carries no implication that the person doing the habituating is the person being habituated. Cf. the early letter to Mersenne, 18 March 1630: AT I, 133–134: K 7–8.

THE
PASSIONS
OF THE SOUL

SECOND PART

5

About the Number and Order of the Passions,
and the Explanation of the Six Primitives

Article 51. What the first causes of the passions are.[1]

10 We know, from what has been said above,[2] that the last and most proximate cause of the passions of the soul is nothing other than the agitation with which the spirits move the little gland in the middle of the brain. But this is

1. Thus far Descartes has educed the facts about soul, body, and their union which will help him construct a theory of the passions. The first stage in the construction is to *enumerate* the passions, now viewed as elements of a problem to be solved; more fully, to enumerate them in order and to review the passions once the enumeration is complete. For accounts of this stage in Descartes's method, see *Rules for the Direction of the Mind*, Rules 5-7: AT X, 379-392: CSM I, 20-28; *Discourse on Method*, Part 2, on Rule 4: AT VI, 19: CSM I, 120. As he was composing the *Passions*, Descartes wrote to Elisabeth about his difficulty in carrying out this step: 6 October and 3 November 1645: AT IV, 313 and 332: K 179 and 185. The diffidence he expressed there reflected the fact that he had come to take this task seriously in a way in which he had not during prior theoretical discussions of the passions: *Treatise on Man*: AT XI, 163-167: Hall 68-73; *Principles* IV, a. 190: AT VIII, 316-318: CSM I, 280-281.

The enumeration is carried out in aa. 51-69. In aa. 51-52, Descartes recalls the theory from Part I that provides the basis for carrying out the enumeration; in aa. 53-67 he enumerates; and in aa. 68-69 he discusses the array that has resulted, carrying out a *review* of it. Cf. also a. 210 below.

2. Articles 29 and 33-39. As Alquié observes (975-976, n. 1), Descartes enunciates a "physiological" rather than an "intellectual" theory of the causation of the passions.

insufficient for them to be distinguished one from another; it is necessary to
seek their sources and investigate their first causes. Now though they may   *15*
sometimes be caused by the action of the soul, which decides to conceive of
this or that object, and also by the temperament of the body alone or by
impressions haphazardly encountered in the brain, as happens when one feels   372
sad or joyful without being able to say why, still it is apparent from what has
been said that all of them can be excited as well by objects which move the   *5*
senses, and that these objects are their most common and principal causes--
from which it follows that, in order to find them all, it is sufficient to take
into consideration all the effects of these objects.[3]

Article 52.   What their use is, and how they can be   *10*
enumerated.

Moreover, I note that objects which move the senses do not excite different
passions in us in proportion to all of their diversities, but only in proportion   *15*
to the different ways they can harm or profit us or, generally, be important
to us; and that the use of all the passions consists in this alone: they dispose
the soul to will the things nature tells us are useful and to persist in this   *20*

Roughly, the causal sequence is

    action of external object, representation, bodily change, then passion,

rather than

    action of external object, representation, passion, then bodily change.

The "last and most proximate cause" of the passions is the movement of the pineal
gland by the spirits—a physical transaction. Further back we find the passions' "most
common and principal causes"—perceived external objects that somehow matter to
us. Typically, the action of the object generates, in perception, a particular representation of it; that in turn arouses the bodily changes whose culmination is the last and
most proximate cause of a passion.

3. Since some passions are caused by intentional acts of conception (a. 45) and others
by fortuitous brain events (aa. 21, 26; see note 30 below), there are times when the
"first cause" of a passion is not an object that moves the senses. In order for Descartes
to succeed, in aa. 51-52, in providing the basis for an enumeration of all of the
principal passions, however, these objects must be their "most common and principal
causes," at least to this extent: for every occurrence of a passion without such an
object as its cause, (i) there must be some grounds, apart from this question of causal
history, for classing it as a *passion*; and (ii) there must be some such grounds for
classing it as a *kind* of passion—anger, joy, or the like—such that there do occur
passions of that kind which *are* caused by objects that move the senses.

volition, just as the same agitation of spirits that usually causes them disposes
the body to the movements conducive to the execution of those things. This
is why, in order to enumerate them, one needs only to investigate, in order,
25   in how many different ways that are important to us our senses can be
moved by their objects.[4] I shall effect the enumeration of all the principal
passions[5] here according to the order in which they may thus be found.

373   *The order and enumeration*
of the Passions.

Article 53.   Wonder.

5   When the first encounter with some object surprises us, and we judge it to
be new, or very different from what we knew in the past or what we
10   supposed it was going to be, this makes us wonder and be astonished at it.
And since this can happen before we know in the least whether this object is
suitable to us or not, it seems to me that Wonder is the first of all the
15   passions. It has no opposite, because if the object presented has nothing in it
that surprises us, we are not in the least moved by it and regard it without
passion.[6]

20   ### Article 54.   Esteem and Scorn, Generosity or Pride, and
Humility or Servility.

Esteem or Scorn is joined to Wonder according as it is the greatness of an
object or its smallness we are wondering at. And we can thus esteem or
374   scorn our own selves, whence come the passions and then the dispositions of
Magnanimity or Pride, and Humility or Servility.[7]

4. Objects arouse passions in us differentially as they matter to us. Given the claims of
Part II thus far, we can enumerate all the passions by reference to all the ways in
which perceivable objects can matter to us. The phrases *par ordre*—"in order"—and
mettre par ordre in a. 57 are neutral between two enumerative procedures: listing the
passions by some intrinsic order or listing them by some imposed order. Both
procedures are sanctioned by the *Rules*.
5. See the amplification of this notion at a. 68.
6. Things can matter to us apart from being useful or harmful to us—when they
surprise us by being new or different. Even in this case, however, the passion is
normally aroused by a judgment about a thing's relationship to us (see notes 23 in
Part I and 2 in Part II).
7. Concerning both the change of name from "generosity" to "magnanimity" and the
notion of a disposition (*habitude*) related to a passion, see a. 161.

Article 55.   Veneration and Disdain.

But when we esteem or scorn other objects which we regard as free causes, capable of doing good or evil, then Veneration arises from Esteem, and Disdain from simple Scorn.

5

Article 56.   Love and Hatred.

10

Now all the preceding passions may be excited in us without our perceiving in any way whether the object causing them is good or bad. But when a thing is represented to us as good from our point of view, that is, as being suitable to us, this makes us have Love for it, and when it is represented to us as bad or harmful, this excites us to Hatred.

15

Article 57.   Desire.

20

All the other passions originate from the same consideration of good and evil, but to put them in order I distinguish times from one another, and, considering that [these passions] incline us much more to face the future than the present or the past, I begin with Desire. For it is plain that it always faces the future—not only when one desires to acquire a good one does not yet have or avoid an evil one judges might occur, but also when one wishes only the preservation of a good or the absence of an evil, which is all this passion can extend to.[8]

375

5

Article 58.   Hope, Apprehension, Jealousy, Confidence, and Despair.

10

It is sufficient to think that acquisition of a good or escape from an evil is possible, in order to be incited to desire it. But when one takes into consideration as well whether the likelihood of obtaining what one desires is great or small, what represents to us that it is great excites Hope in us, and what represents to us that it is small excites Apprehension, of which Jealousy is a species. When Hope is extreme, it changes its nature and is named Confidence or Assurance, as, on the other hand, extreme Apprehension becomes Despair.

15

20

8. Desire is identified with the genus of passions incited by thoughts about the future. Even the passions mentioned in aa. 58 and 59 qualify .

Article 59.   Irresolution, Courage, Boldness, Emulation, Cowardice, and Terror.

And we can thus hope and be apprehensive even though the outcome of what we are awaiting in no way depends on us. But when it is represented to us as depending on us, there may be difficulty in the choice of means or in the execution. Irresolution, which disposes us to deliberate and take counsel, arises from the former. Courage, or Boldness, of which Emulation is a species, sets itself against[9] the latter. And Cowardice is opposed to Courage, as Fear or Terror is to Boldness.

Article 60.   Remorse.

And if one has decided upon some action before Irresolution has been displaced, that gives rise to Remorse of conscience, which does not face time to come like the preceding passions, but the present or the past.[10]

Article 61.   Joy and Sadness.

The consideration of present good excites Joy in us, that of evil Sadness, when it is a good or evil which is represented to us as belonging to us.

Article 62.   Mockery, Envy, Pity.

But when it is represented to us as belonging to other men, we may deem them deserving or undeserving of it. When we deem them deserving of it, that excites no other passion but Joy in us, to the extent that it is a good for us to see that things are happening as they should. There is just this difference: the Joy arising from good is serious, while that arising from evil is accompanied by Laughter and Mockery. But if we deem them undeserving of it, the good excites Envy and the evil Pity, which are species of sadness. And it should be noted that the same passions which have reference to present goods or evils may often likewise be referred to those yet to come, insofar as one's opinion that they are going to occur represents them as present.

---

9. *S'oppose* is obscure, but this reading, due to Alquié (1002, n. 2), makes sense: one feels bold when setting one's face against some difficulty in acquiring a good.
10. Article 177 makes clear what the order of enumeration does not: remorse is a species of sadness.

Article 63.   Self-satisfaction and Repentance.   *15*

We may also take into consideration the cause of good or evil, whether
present or past. And the good done by us ourselves gives us an inner   *20*
satisfaction which is the sweetest of all the passions, whereas the evil excites
Repentance, which is the most bitter.

Article 64.   Approval and Gratitude.

But the good done by others causes us to have Approval for them, even   *25*
though it may not have been done for us; if it was for us, we join Gratitude   378
to the Approval.

Article 65.   Indignation and Anger.

In just the same way, the evil done by others which is not referred to us only   *5*
makes us have Indignation for them; when it is referred to us, it stirs up
Anger as well.

Article 66.   Vainglory and Shame.   *10*

Moreover, the good that is or has been in us that is referred to the opinion
others may have of it excites Vainglory in us; the evil, Shame.

Article 67.   Distaste, Regret, and Lightheartedness.   *15*

And sometimes continuance of the good causes Weariness or Distaste, while
that of the evil diminishes the Sadness. Finally Regret, which is a species of
Sadness, arises from past good, and Lightheartedness, which is a species of   *20*
Joy, arises from past evil.

Article 68.   Why this enumeration of the Passions differs   379
from the one commonly accepted.

Such is the order which seems to me to be the best for enumerating the   *5*
Passions. In this I know well that I am departing from the opinion of all
those who have written about it before. But this is not without excellent

10
reason. For they obtain their enumeration by distinguishing two appetites in the sensitive part of the soul, of which they name one the *Concupiscent* and the other the *Irascible*. And because I discern no distinction of parts in the soul, as I have said above,[11] this seems to me to mean nothing except that it
15
has two faculties, one of desiring and the other of being vexed. And because it has in the same way the faculties of wondering, loving, hoping, fearing, and thus of receiving each of the other passions into itself, or of doing the actions these passions impel it to, I fail to see why they wanted to refer all of
20
them to concupiscence or anger. Moreover, their enumeration does not include all the principal passions, as I believe this one does. I speak only of the principal ones, because many other more particular ones could be distin-
25
guished besides, and their number is indefinite.

380
Article 69.   That there are only six primitive Passions.

But the number of those which are simple and primitive is not very large.
5
For by carrying out a review[12] of all those I have enumerated, one can discover with ease that only six of them are of this kind—namely Wonder, Love, Hatred, Desire, Joy, and Sadness—and that all the others are composed
10
of some of these six or are species of them. This is why, so that their multiplicity may not perplex readers, I shall treat the six primitives separately here, and show later in what way all the others originate from them.

15
Article 70.   About Wonder. Its definition and its cause.[13]

Wonder is a sudden surprise of the soul which makes it tend to consider
20
attentively those objects which seem to it rare and extraordinary. So it is

11. Articles 30 and 47. The adversaries here are the same as those in a. 47; see note 47 in Part I.
12. On a review as part of the Cartesian method, see the passages from the *Rules* and the *Discourse* cited in note 1. The status of certain passions as primitive is established during the stage of review—after the passions are enumerated, but before they are defined.
13. The enumeration has set the terms for the solution of the problem. Descartes turns now to provide a scientific theory of the passions, making the tasks of defining them and describing their causes central. Elisabeth had asked him in letters of 13 and 30 September 1645 to do this—"I would still like to see you define the passions, in order to understand them well . . . ;" "In order to profit from the particular truths you speak of [in his letter to her of 15 September: AT IV, 294: K 173] it is necessary to have an accurate understanding of all these passions . . ." (AT IV, 289 and 303).

caused first by the impression in one's brain that represents the object as rare and consequently worthy of being accorded great consideration, and then by the motion of spirits disposed by this impression to advance with great force 25 upon the place in the brain where it is, to strengthen and preserve it there— 381 as they are also disposed by it to flow from there into the muscles for keeping the sense organs in the same position they are in, so that if it has 5 been formed by them it will still be maintained by them.

Article 71. That in this passion no change takes place in the heart or the blood.

And this passion has the following peculiarity: it is not observed to be 10 accompanied, as the other passions are, by any change taking place in the heart and in the blood. The reason for this is that, not having good or evil as its object, but only knowledge of the thing wondered at,[14] it has no relation 15 to the heart and blood, which all the good of the body depends on, but only

---

The rest of the treatise is devoted to the systematic attempt to discover the nature of the passions, *en physicien* (326): in the rest of Part II, he investigates the "primitive passions" (a. 69), and in Part III he investigates the remaining "principal passions" (a. 68). At the same time, Descartes persistently asks the salient moral questions (given the point made in note 43 in Part I): (i) how each passion is useful and (ii) how its disorders can be set right. So the subject of the rest of the treatise is the nature and use of the principal passions.

Descartes's investigation of the nature of the primitive passions occupies aa. 70–73 and 79–136; his investigation of their use occupies aa. 74–78 and 137–148. The former investigation falls approximately into three parts (with one significant complication, deriving from the exception mentioned in note 32 below). First, he examines the nature of the passions themselves, as excitations of the soul (aa. 70–95); then their physiological causes (aa. 96–111); finally their physiological expressions (aa. 112–136). The upshot is an account that ranges extremely widely over specific aspects of the passions, upon which other theories usually focus much more selectively .

14. Descartes speaks of the "objects" (*objets*) of passions elsewhere at 390.3 and 10–11, 391.17, 404.2, 461.17–18, 462.1, 470.16, 486.12 and 29–30, and 487.7–8. Such passages contain materials for an account of the intentionality of passions, since they portray the passions as directed toward objects. So do those passages that speak of the passions as "representing" objects to the soul—aa. 48, 89, 90, 138–140, 166, and 211. Indeed, every perception is said to represent something (a. 17). I propose this hypothesis about Descartes's conception in this treatise: one of our perceptions represents a thing just in case we refer it to that thing. Still, Descartes's uses of *representer* and its cognates are sufficiently heterogeneous as to render the task of extracting a theory discouraging. See notes 23 and 29 in Part I, and 2 and 26 in Part II.

to the brain, where the organs of the senses are that contribute to this knowledge.

Article 72.   What the strength of Wonder consists in.

This does not keep it from having considerable strength because of the surprise, that is, the sudden and unexpected arrival of the impression that alters the motion of the spirits. This surprise is proper and peculiar to this passion, so when it is found in others—as it usually is found in and augments almost all of them—that is because wonder is joined with them. And its strength depends on two things, namely on the novelty and on the movement it causes being at its full strength from the start. For it is certain that such a movement has a greater effect than those which, being weak at first and growing only gradually, can easily be diverted. It is also certain that novel objects of the senses affect the brain in certain parts not usually affected, and that, these parts being more tender or less firm than those a frequent agitation has hardened, this increases the effect of the movements they excite there. This will not be found unbelievable if one considers that a similar cause brings it about that, the soles of our feet being accustomed to a fairly harsh contact by the weight of the body they bear, we feel this contact but very little when we walk, whereas a much lighter and gentler [contact] when they are tickled is almost unbearable to us, just because it is unusual to us.

Article 73.   What Astonishment is.

And this surprise has so much power to make the spirits in the cavities of the brain make their way from there, toward the place where the impression of the object wondered at is, that it sometimes drives all of them there, and so occupies them in preserving that impression that none of them pass from there into the muscles, or even get diverted in any way from the first traces they followed in the brain. This makes the entire body remain immobile like a statue, and renders one incapable either of perceiving anything of the object but the face first presented or, consequently, of acquiring a more specific knowledge of it. This is what is commonly called being astonished. And Astonishment is an excess of wonder which can never be anything but bad.

Article 74. Wherein all the passions are serviceable, and wherein they are harmful.

Now it is easy to understand from what has been said above[15] that the utility of all the passions consists only in their strengthening thoughts which it is good that [the soul] preserve and which could otherwise easily be effaced from it, and causing them to endure in the soul. So too all the evil they can cause consists either in their strengthening and preserving those thoughts more than necessary or in their strengthening and preserving others it is not good to dwell upon.

Article 75. Wherein Wonder in particular is serviceable.

And it can be said in particular of Wonder that it is useful in making us learn and retain in our memory things we have previously been ignorant of. For we wonder only at what appears rare and extraordinary to us. And nothing can appear so to us except through our having been ignorant of it or through its being different from things we have known, for it is in virtue of this difference that it is called extraordinary. Now even though something which has been unknown to us may be newly present to our understanding or our senses, we do not on that account retain it in our memory unless the idea we have of it is strengthened in our brain by some passion, or alternatively by the application of our understanding, which our will fixes in a particular [state of] attention and reflection.[16] And the other passions can serve to make one notice things which appear good or evil, but we just have wonder for ones which appear rare only. Accordingly, we see that those who have no natural inclination to this passion are ordinarily very ignorant.

Article 76. Wherein it can be harmful, and how a deficiency of it can be supplemented and an excess of it corrected.

But it happens much more often that one wonders too much and is astonished, in perceiving things worth considering only a little or not at all, than that one wonders too little. This can entirely eradicate or pervert the use of

15. Compare aa. 40 and 52.
16. A persistent theme, as Descartes seeks remedies for the disorders of the passions, is the application of attention, characterized at a. 43.

10   reason. That is why, although it is good to be born with some inclination to this passion, since it disposes us to the acquisition of the sciences, we should still try afterwards to emancipate ourselves from it as much as possible. For it is easy to supplement a deficiency of it by a particular [state of] reflection

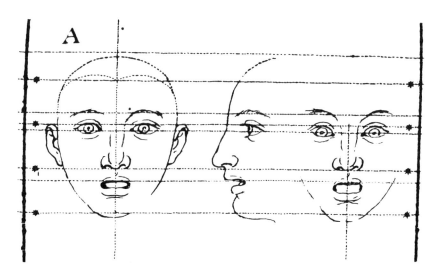

L'admiration—Wonder

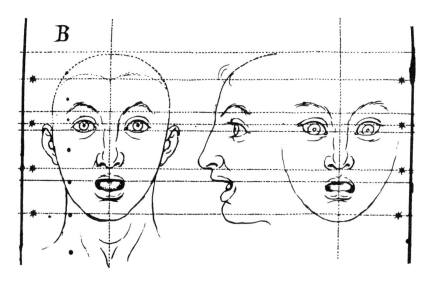

L'estonnement—Astonishment

and attention to which our will can always bind our understanding when   *15*
we judge that the thing presented is worth the trouble. But to prevent
excessive wonder there is no remedy but to acquire the knowledge of many
things, and to apply oneself to the consideration of all those which may seem   *20*
most rare and unusual.[17]

Article 77.   That it is neither the most stupid nor the most astute who are most inclined toward Wonder.

Furthermore, though it is only the dull and stupid who do not have any   *25*
constitutional inclination toward Wonder, this is not to say that those who   *386*
have the most intelligence are always the most inclined to it. For it[18] is
mainly those who, even though they have a good deal of common sense, still   *5*
do not have a high opinion of their competence [who are most inclined
toward wonder].

Article 78.   That its excess may pass into habit when one fails to correct it.

And though this passion seems to diminish with use, because the more one   *10*
encounters rare things one wonders at, the more one routinely ceases wondering at them and comes to think that any that may be presented thereafter
will be ordinary, nevertheless, when it is excessive and makes one fix one's   *15*
attention solely upon the first image of presented objects without acquiring
any other knowledge of them, it leaves behind a habit which disposes the
soul to dwell in the same way upon all other presented objects, provided
they appear the least bit new to it. This is what prolongs the sickness of the   *20*
blindly curious—that is, those who investigate rarities only to wonder at
them and not to understand them. For they gradually become so given to
wonder that things of no importance are no less capable of engaging them   *25*
than those whose investigation is more useful.

17. One result of Cartesian science should be the reduction of wonder at natural
phenomena. See e.g. *Rules for the Direction of the Mind*, Rule 9: AT X, 400-403:
CSM I, 33-34; *Meteorology*, First Discourse: AT VI, 231: Olscamp 263. Wonder is
recommended only beyond the realm physics can touch—at God and at oneself, in
respect of a quality that, in a way, makes us like God. See *Olympica*: AT X, 218:
CSM I, 5; Fourth Meditation: AT VII, 57: CSM II, 40; and a. 152 below.
18. The sentence's subject is ambiguous, but it probably concerns those who are
given to wonder rather than those who are most intelligent.

387   Article 79.   The definitions of Love and Hatred.

5   Love is an excitation of the soul, caused by the motion of the spirits, which
         incites it to join itself in volition to the objects that appear to be suitable to
         it.[19] And Hatred is an excitation, caused by the spirits, which incites the soul
         to will to be separated from the objects that are presented to it as harmful. I
10   say these excitations are caused by the spirits in order to distinguish Love
         and Hatred, which are passions and depend on the body, both from judg-
         ments which also incline the soul to join itself in volition with the things it
         deems good and to separate itself from those it deems bad, and from excita-
15   tions which these judgments excite by themselves in the soul.

         Article 80.   What it is to join or separate oneself in volition.

         Moreover, by the phrase "in volition" I do not intend here to speak of desire,
20   which is a passion by itself and has reference to the future, but of the
         consent by which we consider ourselves from the present as joined with
         what we love, in such a way that we imagine a whole of which we think
         ourselves to be only one part and the thing loved another.[20] So, on the other
25   hand, in hatred we consider ourselves alone as a whole, entirely separated
         from the thing for which we have the aversion.

388   Article 81.   About the distinction customarily made between
                        the Love of concupiscence and that of
                        benevolence.[21]

5   Now two sorts of Love are commonly distinguished, of which one is named
         the Love of benevolence—that is, that which incites us to will the good of

19. Context—the next sentence—shows that it is love, rather than the movement of
the spirits, which incites the soul in this way. With Kenny (e.g. at K 208), I translate
de volonté neutrally, by "in volition" and not by "willingly" or "will to ——," in order
to leave open the philosophical problem of what it amounts to in Descartes's theory
of love and hatred. Articles 79 and 80 do appear to equate *se separer de volonté*
("separate oneself in volition") with *vouloir estre separé* ("will to be separated"), but
Descartes does not make that equation elsewhere.
20. Beyond the *Passions*, Descartes's account of love is presented in to Elisabeth, 15
September 1645 (where it is intimately related to the fourth point in his "definitive
moral philosophy"—see note 71 below): AT IV, 292-294: K 172-173; to Elisabeth, 6
October 1645: AT IV, 308-309: K 176-177; to Chanut, 6 June 1647: AT V, 55-58: K
223-225; but especially in to Chanut, 1 February 1647: AT IV, 600-617: K 208-218.
This letter is sometimes known as "the letter on love." On self-love, a distinct
phenomenon, see note 38 in Part III.
21. For a somewhat different account of this distinction see to Chanut, 1 February

what we love; the other is named the Love of concupiscence—that is, that
which makes us desire the thing we love. But it seems to me that this
distinction concerns only the effects of Love and not its essence. For as soon   *10*
as we have joined ourselves in volition to some object, whatever its nature
may be, we have benevolence for it; that is, we also join to it in volition the
things we believe to be suitable to it—which is one of the principal effects of   *15*
Love. And if we judge it to be a good to possess it or to be associated with it
in some other manner than in volition, we desire it—which is likewise one of
the most common effects of love.

Article 82. How very different passions agree in that they participate in Love.   *20*

Nor is there any need to distinguish as many species of Love as there are
different objects which may be loved. For, e.g., although the passions an   *25*
ambitious person has for glory, an avaricious person for money, a drunkard   *389*
for wine, a brutish man for a woman he wants to violate, a man of honor for
his friend or his mistress, and a good father for his children may be very
different from one another, they are nevertheless similar in that they partici-   *5*
pate in Love. But the first four have Love only for the possession of the
objects their passion has reference to, and have none whatever for the objects
themselves, for which they have only desire mixed with other particular   *10*
passions. On the other hand, a good father's Love for his children is so pure[22]
that he desires to have nothing from them, and wills neither to possess them
otherwise than he does nor to be joined to them more closely than he
already is; instead, considering them each as another himself,[23] he seeks their   *15*
good as his own or with even greater solicitude, because, representing to
himself that he and they make up a whole of which he is not the best part,

---

1647: AT IV, 606: K 211. Articles 79 and 81 appear to entail that the volition to
which love incites a person is a special case of benevolence, namely the odd case in
which the object of one's "benevolence" is oneself.

22. Alquié says (1015, n. 1) that Descartes probably means that this father's love is
unmixed with other passions rather than that it is pure in a moral sense. All the same,
the phrase *pur amour* was also used at the time to speak of charity, a wholly
disinterested love of God or neighbor; J.-P. Camus, one author Descartes had read,
uses the phrase in the title of one of his works in this sense.

23. *Les considerant comme d'autres soy-mesme*: like *de volonté* above (see note 19),
this phrase poses a philosophical problem whose solution is not the task of the
translator. Accordingly, I translate it neutrally, if awkwardly. The same locution
appears in a. 90, at 395.21: *une personne, qu'on pense pouvoir devenir un autre soy-
mesme*.

he often prefers their interests to his, and is not afraid to lose himself in order
20   to save them. The affection people of honor have for their friends is of this
same nature, though it is rarely so perfect, and that which they have for
their mistress participates greatly in it, but also participates a little in the
other.

25   Article 83.   About the difference between simple Affection,
Friendship, and Devotion.[24]

390   It seems to me that distinctions within love may more reasonably be made in
terms of our esteem for what we love in comparison with ourselves. For
when we esteem the object of our Love less than ourselves, we have only a
5   simple Affection for it; when we esteem it equally with ourselves, this is
named Friendship; and when we esteem it more, the passion we have may
be named Devotion. So we may have affection for a flower, a bird, a horse;
10   but, unless our mind is extremely disordered, we can have Friendship only
for men. They are the object of this passion, in such a way that there is no
man so imperfect that we cannot have a quite perfect friendship for him
when we think ourselves loved by him, and have a truly noble and generous
15   soul, in accordance with what will be explained below in Arts. 154 and 156.
As for Devotion, its principal object is without doubt the supreme divinity,
to which we cannot fail to be devoted when we know it as we should. But
20   we may also have Devotion for our Prince, our country, our city, and even a
private man when we esteem him much more than ourselves. Now, the
difference between these three sorts of Love becomes apparent principally
through their effects, for inasmuch as in all of them we consider ourselves as
25   joined and united to the thing loved, we are always ready to abandon the
lesser part of the whole we compose with it in order to preserve the other.
Therefore in simple affection we always prefer ourselves to what we love,
30   while on the other hand in Devotion we so prefer the thing loved to
ourselves that we are not afraid to die to preserve it. We have often seen

24. The French word is *devotion*. The only occurrence of the cognate verb *devouer*
appears, in participial form, at 391.4; see the Lexicon for its similar force. Rodis-Lewis
says (RL 125, n. 1) of the noun: "This word has a strong sense here: in *dévotion*, one
is 'devoted' totally to the being one loves. Furetière's *Dictionnaire* (1690) cites, under
the heading '*devotion*', the ceremony of Antiquity in which 'a man sacrifices himself
for his country, as Decius did: from devotion he threw his body to the enemy and
was killed.' The end of article 83 evokes just these celebrated examples. Cf. a. 173."

examples of this in those who have exposed themselves to certain death in 391
defense of their Prince or their city, and sometimes even on behalf of private
people to whom they were devoted.

Article 84. That there are not so many species of Hatred as of Love. 5

But although Hatred is directly opposed to Love, it is not distinguished into
so many species, because we do not notice the difference between the evils 10
from which we are separated in volition so much as that between the goods
to which we are joined.

Article 85. About Delight and Abhorrence.

And I find only one distinction worth considering that is similar within 15
both of them. It consists in the fact that the objects of both Love and Hatred
can be represented to the soul either by the external senses or by the internal
ones[25] and its own reason. For we commonly call good or evil what our 20
internal senses or our reason makes us judge suitable or opposed to our
nature, but we call beautiful or ugly what is so represented to us by our
external senses—above all by that of sight, which by itself is more highly 25
regarded than all the others. Two species of Love arise hence, namely that 392
which one has for good things and that which one has for beautiful ones, to
the latter of which the name of Delight may be given so as not to confuse it
either with the former or with Desire, to which the name of Love is often 5
given. And two species of Hatred also arise hence in the same way, of which
one has reference to bad things and the other to those that are ugly; and this
latter may be called Abhorrence or Aversion to distinguish it. But what is 10
most worth noticing here is that these passions of Delight and Abhorrence
are usually more vigorous than the other species of Love and Hatred,
because what comes to the soul represented by the senses affects it more
forcibly than what is represented to it by its reason, and that nevertheless 15
they ordinarily have less truth: so of all the passions it is these which deceive
the most and which one must guard oneself against the most carefully.

---

25. Alquié asks (1018, n. 1) whether *les sens interieurs* are senses like smell and taste
or instead bodily sensations. In either case, the sense of sight remains central to our
aesthetic emotions. See to Mersenne, 18 March 1630: AT I, 132-133: K 7.

20   Article 86.   The Definition of Desire.

The passion of Desire is an agitation of the soul, caused by the spirits, which disposes it to will for the future the things it represents to itself to be
25   suitable. Thus we desire not only the presence of absent good but also the preservation of the present, and in addition the absence of evil, both what we already have and what we believe we might receive in time to come.

393   Article 87.   That this is a passion which has no opposite.[26]

I know well that usually within the Schools the passion that tends to the
5   search for the good, which alone is named Desire, is opposed to the one that tends to the avoidance of evil, which is named Aversion. But since there is no good whose privation is not an evil, nor any evil considered as a positive
10   thing whose privation is not a good, and since in seeking riches, for example, we necessarily avoid poverty, in avoiding sicknesses we seek health, and so on, it seems to me that it is always the same movement that inclines us to
15   the search for the good and at the same time to the avoidance of the evil that opposes it. I note only this difference, that the Desire we have when we tend toward some good is accompanied by Love and then by Hope and Joy, whereas the same Desire when we tend to withdraw from the evil opposed
20   to this good is accompanied by Hatred, Apprehension, and Sadness, which causes us to judge [that desire] opposed to itself. However, if we are willing to consider it when it has reference equally and at the same time to some
25   good in order to seek it and to the opposite evil in order to shun it, we can see very plainly that it is only one passion that does both.

394   Article 88.   What its different species are.

It would be more correct to distinguish Desire into as many different species
5   as there are different objects sought after. For Curiosity, for example, which

26. It is true that good and evil are opposed to one another and that the thought of seeking the one is distinct from the thought of fleeing the other. However, the directedness or intentionality of desire and aversion—toward good and evil, respectively—has misled *les Anciens* (a. 1) into thinking that these are two passions. They are not. The thought of good and the thought of evil cause the same movement of spirits (393.13) and hence in turn only a single passion (393.25-26). That passion causes one to tend toward the good and flee the evil. The thought of the good and the thought of the opposing evil do tend to cause different additional passions—on the one hand, love, hope, and joy; on the other, hatred, apprehension, and sadness.

is nothing but a Desire to understand, differs greatly from Desire for glory, and this from Desire for vengeance, and so on. But here it is enough to know that there are as many of them as there are species of Love or Hatred, and that the most noteworthy and the strongest are the ones arising from Delight and Abhorrence.

Article 89. What the Desire is that originates from Abhorrence.[27]

Now although, as has been said, it is but a single Desire that tends to the search for a good and the avoidance of the opposing evil, the Desire which arises from Delight is still very different from that which arises from Abhorrence. For the Delight and the Abhorrence, which are truly opposites, are not the good and the evil that serve as objects of these Desires, but only two excitations of the soul which dispose it to seek two very different things. To be specific, Abhorrence is instituted by Nature to represent to the soul a sudden and unexpected death, so that, though it is sometimes only the touch of a little worm or the rustling of a trembling leaf or its shadow which produces Abhorrence, one immediately feels as much excitation as if a very plain threat of death were being offered to the senses. This suddenly arouses the agitation that inclines the soul to employ all its powers to avoid such a present evil. And it is this species of Desire which is commonly called Avoidance or Aversion.

Article 90. What the one is that originates from Delight.

On the other hand, Delight is particularly instituted by Nature to represent the enjoyment of what delights as the greatest of all the goods that belong to man—making one desire this enjoyment very ardently. It is true that there are different sorts of Delights, and that the Desires arising from them are not all equally powerful. For the beauty of flowers, for example, only incites us to look at them, and that of fruits to eat them. But the principal one[28] is that

27. The thought of ugliness causes abhorrence, and that of beauty causes delight (a. 85), and these species of love and hatred generate desire (following the pattern given in a. 137 below). Here specific details emerge: abhorrence generates the thought of sudden death, and delight generates the thought of sexual union (a. 90); these thoughts give rise to equally specific movements of the spirits, sufficient to generate the specific desires they do generate. See note 29.

28. *Le principal.* Probably the principal delight, possibly the principal desire arising from delight. The phrase suggests a variety among the objects of delight not mirrored within abhorrence, in accord with a. 84.

20   which comes from the perfections one imagines in a person who one thinks
can become another oneself. For with the sexual difference which Nature
has placed in men, as in animals which lack reason, she has also placed certain

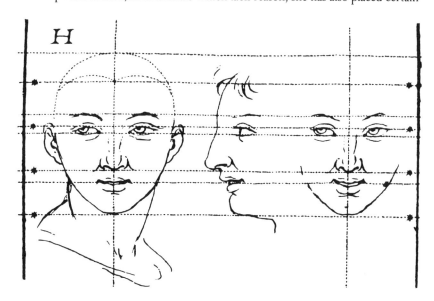

L'amour simple—Simple Love

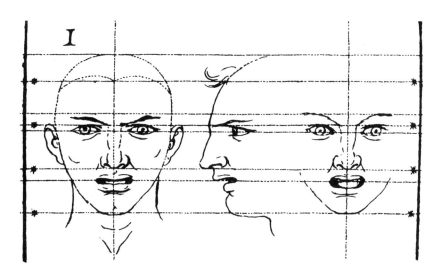

Le Desir—Desire

impressions in the brain which make one at a certain age and season consider 25
oneself as defective, and as though one were only half of a whole whose
other half has to be a person of the other sex—so that the acquisition of this
half is confusedly represented by Nature as the greatest of all imaginable 396
goods. And although one may see many people of this other sex, that does
not make one wish for many of them at the same time, inasmuch as Nature 5
does not make one imagine that one needs more than one half. But when
something is noticed in one of them which gives more delight than what is
noticed at the same time in the rest, this makes the soul feel for that one 10
alone all the inclination Nature gives [the soul] to seek the good which she
represents to it as the greatest that could be possessed. And the inclination or
Desire which originates in this way from Delight is called by the name of
Love more commonly than the Passion of Love which has been described 15
above. It likewise has effects which are more unusual; this it is which serves
as the principal subject matter for writers of Romances and Poets.[29]

Article 91.   The definition of Joy.   20

Joy is a delightful excitation of the soul, wherein consists the enjoyment it
has of the good which the impressions of the brain represent to it as its own.
I say that it is in this excitation that the enjoyment of the good consists, 25
because in reality the soul receives no other fruit from all the goods it
possesses, and while it is getting no Joy from them it can be said that it does
not enjoy them any more than if it did not possess them at all. I also add that 397
it is of the good which the impressions of the brain represent to it as its own,
in order not to confuse this joy, which is a passion, with the purely intellectual joy which comes into the soul by the action of the soul alone, and 5
which can be said to be a delightful excitation, excited in it by itself, wherein
consists the enjoyment it has of the good which its understanding represents

29. This account of sexual desire derives from Aristophanes' myth in Plato's *Sympo-
sium*. However, the myth is meant to explain love and not sexual desire, and
Descartes's aim here is to distinguish sexual desire from the species of love he calls
delight (*agréement*: a. 85). Delight is aroused by the thought of a person's perfections,
but, once this happens, the thought of *that* good generates the thought of *another*
good—the acquisition of that person, as an imagined half of a whole of which one is
the other half. For love inclines one to consider oneself as a half of a whole of which
one's beloved is the other half (aa. 79, 80), and, when one now represents the
acquisition of this half as a good that one does not yet possess, the result is likely to
be just the sort of desire which Descartes wishes to explain here.

to it as its own. It is true that while the soul is joined to the body, this
10   intellectual joy can hardly fail to be accompanied by the one that is a passion.
For as soon as our understanding perceives that we possess some good, even
though this good may be so different from everything which belongs to the
15   body that it is in no way whatever imaginable, imagination without fail
immediately forms some impression in the brain, from which follows the
movement of spirits that excites the passion of Joy.

20   ## Article 92.   The definition of Sadness.

Sadness is an unpleasant languor, wherein consists the distress which the soul
receives from the evil or defect which the impressions of the brain represent
25   to it as belonging to it. And there is also an intellectual Sadness, which is not
the passion but which hardly ever fails to be accompanied by it.

398   ## Article 93.   What the causes of these two Passions are.

Now, when intellectual Joy or Sadness excites that which is a passion in this
5   way, its cause is plain enough, and we see from their definitions that Joy
arises from one's opinion that one possesses some good, and Sadness from
one's opinion that one has some evil or defect. But it often happens that
10   someone feels sad or joyful without for all that being able to take distinct
notice of the good or evil which is its cause, namely when the good and the
evil form their impressions in the brain without the mediation of the soul—
sometimes because they belong only to the body, and sometimes also, though
15   they belong to the soul, because it does not consider them as good or evil but
under some other form, whose impression is joined with [the impression] of
good and evil in the brain.[30]

30. According to aa. 93 and 94, joy and sadness need not be indirectly caused by
thoughts; according to aa. 21, 26, and 51, the same is true of the passions generally.
While the pattern set out in a. 61—wherein joy and sadness are caused by the
thought of present good or evil—is common enough to allow these two passions to
take their place in a preliminary *enumeration,* it is not so ubiquitous as to form the
basis of a *definition.* In spite of the disclaimer, the "other form" under which good
and evil are said to be considered certainly appears to provide a kind of mediation.
What is more surprising is the suggestion here that a brain impression not associated
with a thought in the soul can play the same role a thought can in the generation of a
passion. See note 36, concerning Descartes's use of *idée* to speak of images in the
brain.

Article 94.   How these passions are excited by goods and   20
evils which only concern the body, and what
titillation and pain consist in.

So when one is in sound health and the weather is more serene than usual, one
feels a cheerfulness within oneself which does not come from any function of   25
the understanding, but only from impressions which the movement of spirits   399
forms in the brain; and one feels sad in the same way when the body is
indisposed, even though one may not know it is. Thus titillation of the senses
is so closely followed by Joy, and pain by Sadness, that most men do not   5
distinguish them. Nevertheless they differ so greatly that one can sometimes
suffer pains with Joy, and undergo titillations which displease. What makes
Joy usually follow titillation is that what we call a titillation or delightful   10
sensation always consists in the fact that objects of the senses are exciting some
movement in the nerves which would be capable of harming them, if they did
not have enough strength to withstand it or the body were not well disposed.   15
This produces an impression in the brain which, being instituted by Nature
to testify to this sound disposition and this strength, represents it to the soul as
a good which belongs to it, insofar as it is united with the body, and so excites   20
Joy within it. For nearly the same reason one naturally takes pleasure in
feeling moved to all sorts of Passions, even Sadness and Hatred, when these
passions are caused only by the unusual adventures one sees represented on a   25
stage or by other similar matters, which, not being able to harm us in any
way, seem to titillate our soul in affecting it. And what makes pain usually
produce Sadness is that the sensation we call pain always comes from some   30
action so vigorous that it injures the nerves, so that, being instituted by nature   400
to signify to the soul the damage the body receives by this action and its
weakness in not having been able to withstand it, [this sensation] represents
both of them to [the soul] as evils which are always unpleasant to it, except   5
when they bring about goods it esteems more than them.[31]

Article 95.   How they may also be excited by goods and
evils which the soul does not notice even though
they belong to it, such as the pleasure one takes   10
in running risks or recalling past evil.

Thus the pleasure young people often take in undertaking difficult things
and exposing themselves to great perils, even though they do not hope for   15

31. Pleasure (or titillation: *chatoüillement*) and pain (*douleur*) are based on similar
bodily mechanisms: *Treatise on Man*: AT XI, 143-144: Hall 36-38; *Principles* IV, a.
191: AT VIII, 318: CSM I, 282.

profit or glory from doing so, arises within them because the thought they have that what they are undertaking is difficult forms an impression in their brain, which—when joined with the one they could form if they were to
20   think it a good to feel so courageous, fortunate, skillful, or strong as to dare to run a risk—is the cause of their taking pleasure therein. And the contentment old people have when they recall evils they have suffered arises because
25   they represent to themselves that it is a good to have been able to survive notwithstanding.

401   ## Article 96.   What the movements of the blood and spirits are that cause the five preceding passions.[32]

5   The five passions I have begun to explain here are joined or opposed to one another in such a way that it is easier to consider them all at once than to treat each one separately, as Wonder has been treated. And their cause is not,
10   as its is, in the brain alone, but also in the heart, the spleen, the liver, and all the other parts of the body insofar as they contribute to the production of blood and then spirits. For though all the veins guide the blood they contain
15   toward the heart, it nevertheless sometimes happens that [the blood that] is in some [veins] is driven there with greater force than that which is in others, and it likewise happens that the openings through which it enters the heart or those through which it leaves are enlarged or contracted more at one time than at another.

32. In aa. 96–111 Descartes investigates some of the movements of the blood and spirits that help cause love, hate, desire, joy, and sadness. His method is instructive: it is sketched in to Elisabeth, May 1646: AT IV, 407–409: K 192–193, where he explains to her how he gained the results she has already seen in a first draft of the treatise.

First, the primitive passions other than wonder (a. 71 explains this exception) are caused by movements of the animal spirits which are affected in characteristic ways by the state of the heart and the blood (a. 96). Descartes begins their study by reviewing the bodily changes and sensations that have been experienced or observed to accompany these five passions and which must result from the movements of the blood and spirits he wishes to investigate (aa. 97–101). He then draws inferences about the movements themselves which characteristically help to cause each of those five passions (aa. 102–106). It becomes apparent that his investigation concerns those movements which have not been instituted by nature to cause those passions, for he concludes by attempting to discover the events early in life which, according to the Principle of Habituation (aa. 44 and 50), gave rise to the association just discovered between passions and movements of blood and spirits (aa. 107–111).

Article 97.   The principal experiences which are serviceable *20*
for understanding these movements in Love.

Now, in the course of considering the different alterations which experience
reveals in our body while our soul is agitated by different passions, I observe   **402**
in Love when it is by itself, that is, when it is not accompanied by any
strong Joy or Desire or Sadness, that the pulse beat is regular and much   *5*
greater and stronger than usual, that a mild warmth is felt in the chest, and
that digestion of food is carried out very rapidly in the stomach—so that this
Passion is beneficial to the health.

Article 98.   In Hatred.   *10*

On the other hand, I observe in Hatred that the pulse is irregular, fainter, and
often quicker; that chills are felt in the chest, interspersed with I know not
what sort of sharp and prickling heat; that the stomach ceases to do its part,   *15*
and is inclined to vomit and reject food that has been eaten, or at any rate to
corrupt it and convert it into bad humors.

Article 99.   In Joy.   *20*

In Joy [I observe] that the pulse is regular and quicker than usual, but not so
strong or so great as in Love; that a pleasant warmth is felt, not only in the   *25*
chest, but also spreading into all the external parts of the body with the   **403**
blood we see entering them in abundance; and that meanwhile the appetite is
sometimes lost because digestion is carried out less than usual.

Article 100.   In Sadness.   *5*

In Sadness [I observe] that the pulse is weak and slow; that one feels as it
were bonds around the heart, which constrict it, and pieces of ice, which
freeze it and communicate their coldness to the rest of the body; and that
meanwhile one sometimes still has a good appetite and feels that one's   *10*
stomach is not failing to do its task, provided there is no Hatred mingled
with the Sadness.

Article 101.   In Desire.   *15*

Finally I observe this in particular in Desire: it agitates the heart more
vigorously than any of the other Passions, and supplies the brain more

20   spirits; these, emerging from there into the muscles, render all the senses
      more acute and all the parts of the body more mobile.

Article 102.   The movement of the blood and the spirits in Love.

25   These observations and many others which would be too lengthy to write
404   down have led me to judge that when the understanding represents to itself
      some object of Love, the impression this thought forms in the brain guides
5   the animal spirits via the sixth pair of nerves toward the muscles around the
      intestines and stomach, in the manner required to make the alimentary juice
      that is turning into new blood pass swiftly, without stopping in the liver,
      toward the heart; and that, being driven there with greater force than [the
10   blood] in the other parts of the body, it enters [the heart] in greater abun-
      dance and excites a stronger heat there, because it is coarser[33] than that
      which has already been rarefied many times in passing and repassing
      through the heart. This makes it also send toward the brain spirits whose
15   parts are larger and more agitated than usual, and these spirits, strengthening
      the impression which the first thought of the lovable object has formed
      there, compel the soul to dwell upon that thought. And this is what the
      passion of Love consists in.

20   ### Article 103.   In Hatred.

      In Hatred, on the other hand, the first thought of the object arousing
25   aversion guides the spirits in the brain toward the muscles of the stomach
      and intestines in such a way that they keep the alimentary juice from
      mingling with the blood, by contracting all the openings through which [the
      juice] usually flows into it. [This thought] also guides them toward the little
405   nerves of the spleen, and the lower part of the liver where the receptacle[34]
      for bile is located, in such a way that the parts of the blood that are usually
      thrown back to these places emerge from them, and flow with what is in the
5   branches of the vena cava toward the heart. This causes many inequalities in
      its heat, since the blood which comes from the spleen is heated and rarefied
      only with difficulty, while, on the other hand, that which comes from the

---

33. *Plus grossier*: ambiguous between "thicker" and "coarser," but *grossier* at 421.20 in
a. 126 indicates the latter reading. The present article contains a particularly clear
account of the bodily causal sequence that generates a passion.
34. The gall bladder.

lower part of the liver, where gall is always present, ignites and expands very *10*
readily. And then the spirits going to the brain also have very unequal parts
and very extraordinary movements, whereby they strengthen the ideas of
Hatred that are imprinted there already, and dispose the soul to thoughts full *15*
of sharpness and bitterness.[35]

Article 104.   In Joy.

In Joy it is not so much the nerves of the spleen, liver, stomach, or intestines
which act as those in all the rest of the body, particularly the one around the *20*
heart's orifices—opening and enlarging these orifices, it enables the blood
which the other nerves drive from the veins toward the heart to enter and
leave it in greater quantity than usual. And because the blood entering the *25*
heart then has already passed and repassed through it many times, having
flowed from the arteries into the veins, it expands very easily and produces
spirits whose parts, being very equal and fine, are suitable to form and *406*
strengthen the brain impressions that give cheerful and tranquil thoughts to
the soul.

Article 105.   In Sadness. *5*

On the other hand, in Sadness the heart's openings are tightly contracted by
the little nerve that surrounds them, and the venous blood is not agitated at
all; therefore very little of it goes toward the heart. And meanwhile the
passages through which the alimentary juice flows from the stomach and *10*
intestines toward the liver remain open; therefore the appetite does not
diminish, except when Hatred, which is often joined to sadness, closes them.

Article 106.   In Desire. *15*

Finally, the Passion of Desire has this characteristic: one's volition to obtain
some good or flee some evil sends spirits suddenly from the brain toward all *20*
the parts of the body capable of contributing to the actions required for this
purpose, particularly toward the heart and the parts which supply most of
its blood, so that, in receiving a greater abundance than usual, it sends a

35. This physiological explanation of the observable "sharp and prickling" (*aspre &*
picquante: a. 98) heat related to hatred is augmented in the same terms at aa. 199 and
202.

407   greater quantity of spirits toward the brain, both to maintain and strengthen
the idea[36] of that volition there and to pass from there into all the sense
5   organs and all the muscles that can be employed to obtain what one desires.

Article 107.   What the cause of these movements is in Love.

And I deduce the reasons for all this from what has been said above:[37] that
10   there is such a connection between our soul and our body that when we
have once joined some bodily action with some thought, one of the two is
never present to us afterwards without the other also being present—as we
15   see in those who, with great aversion, have taken some potion while sick:
afterwards they cannot drink or eat anything approaching it in taste without
having the same aversion again; likewise, they cannot think of the aversion
20   for medicines without the same taste returning to them in thought. For it
seems to me that our soul's first passions, when it was originally joined to our
body, must have been due to the blood, or other juice entering the heart,
25   sometimes being a more suitable nourishment than the usual for maintaining

36. The word *idée* occurs only seven times in the treatise, at 319.15, 384.15, 405.13, 407.2, 417.19, 429.18, and 444.8. The first occurrence, in the Preface, seems consistent with what is often taken to be Descartes's official doctrine—that an idea is a modification of the soul rather than of the body; this doctrine is suggested e.g. in to Mersenne, 16 June 1641: AT III, 383: K 104: "I use the word 'idea' to mean everything which can be in our thought. . . ."

On the remaining occasions, however, Descartes seems to use the term to speak of a corporeal image in the brain. In a definition at the end of the Second Replies (AT VII, 160-161: CSM II, 113), he gives a fuller account, perhaps capable of reconciling the conflicting claims; its core is the stipulation that "I understand ['idea'] to mean the form of any given thought, immediate perception of which makes me aware of the thought. . . . I call . . . images in the corporeal imagination . . . 'ideas' only insofar as they give form to the mind itself, when it is directed towards that part of the brain." Here is a good sample of relevant passages beyond the *Passions*: *Rules for the Direction of the Mind*, Rule 12: AT X, 414-417: CSM I, 41-43; *Treatise on Man*: AT XI, 174-177: Hall 83-87; *Discourse*, Part 5: AT VI, 55: CSM I, 139; Third Replies: AT VII, 181 and 188: CSM II, 127-128 and 132; Fifth Replies: AT VII, 366: CSM II, 253; to Mersenne, July 1641: AT III, 392-397: K 105-108. A question: to what extent is this usage of "idea," to speak both of modifications of the soul and of modifications of the body, consistent with the doctrine of a. 2?

37. In aa. 44 and 50. The causes given in aa. 102-106 are themselves explained causally in aa. 107-111, with the aid of the Principle of Habituation, which was supported by experience in a. 50. See to Chanut, 1 February 1647: AT IV, 604-606: K 210-211, for another version of aa. 107-110.

the heat in it which is the principle of life. That caused the soul to join this nourishment to itself in volition, that is, to love it; and at the same time the spirits flowed from the brain toward the muscles capable of pressing or 408 agitating the parts from which it had come to the heart, in order to make them send it more. These parts were the stomach and intestines, whose 5 agitation increases the appetite, or the liver and lungs as well, which the diaphragm muscles are able to press. That is why this same movement of the spirits has accompanied the passion of Love ever since.

Article 108.   In Hatred. 10

Sometimes, on the other hand, there would come to the heart some extraneous juice which was not fit to maintain the heat, or could even have extinguished it; this caused the spirits rising from the heart to the brain to 15 excite the passion of Hatred in the soul. And at the same time too these spirits would go from the brain toward the nerves that were capable of driving blood from the spleen and the liver's little veins toward the heart, in 20 order to keep the harmful juice from entering it, and additionally toward those capable of driving this same juice back toward the intestines and stomach and sometimes also of forcing the stomach to vomit it. This is why these same movements usually accompany the passion of Hatred. And 25 anyone can see at a glance that there are a large number of good-sized veins or ducts in the liver through which alimentary juice can pass from the portal vein into the vena cava and from there to the heart without stopping in the liver at all, but that there are also an infinity of other smaller ones where it 409 can stop, which always contain blood in reserve, as the spleen also does. This blood, being coarser than that which is in the other parts of the body, can 5 better serve as nourishment for the fire in the heart when the stomach and intestines fail to supply it any.

Article 109.   In Joy.

Sometimes it also happened, as our life was just beginning, that the blood in 10 the veins was a suitable enough nourishment for maintaining the heat of the heart, and that they contained so much of it that it had no need to extract any sustenance from elsewhere. This excited the Passion of Joy in the soul, 15 and at the same time got the heart's orifices opened wider than usual and got the spirits that were flowing abundantly from the brain—not only in the nerves that serve to open these orifices, but also generally in all the others 20 that drive venous blood toward the heart—to keep any [venous blood] from coming there anew from the liver, spleen, intestines, and stomach. That is why these same movements accompany Joy.

410 Article 110. In Sadness.

5   Sometimes, on the other hand, the body happened to lack sustenance, and that must have been what made the soul feel its first Sadness, at least [the first] that was not joined with Hatred. The same thing also made the heart's orifices contract, because they were only receiving a little blood, and made a
10 very considerable portion of this blood come from the spleen, because it is, as it were, the last reservoir that serves to supply it to the heart when enough does not come from elsewhere. This is why the movements of the spirits and nerves that serve to contract the orifices of the heart in this way and to
15 guide blood to it from the spleen always accompany Sadness.

Article 111. In Desire.

Finally, the first Desires the soul had when it was newly joined to the body
20 must all have been to receive the things which were suitable to it[38] and to repel those which were harmful to it. It was for these same ends that the
411 spirits began from then on to move all the muscles and sense organs in all the ways they are capable of moving them. This is the reason why, when the soul desires anything, the whole body now becomes more agile and disposed
5   to move than it usually is otherwise. And when the body happens to be so disposed anyway, that renders the soul's desires stronger and more ardent.

Article 112. What the external signs of these Passions are.[39]

10 What I have set down here yields sufficient understanding of the cause of differences in pulse and all the other properties I have attributed to these passions above, without it being necessary for me to stop and explain them
15 further. But because I have only pointed out in each one what may be

38. Possibly the soul, probably the body.
39. In articles 112-136 Descartes studies the observable manifestations of the six primitive passions, and since these external signs are most evident when they manifest mixtures of passions, Descartes isolates the signs and not the passions in examining their relations. The data are provided by observation; their explanation is provided by the general physiology of aa. 7-16, augmented by the special account of the relation of physiology to passion developed in aa. 70-73 and 96-111.

observed in it when it is by itself, and what affords knowledge of the
movements of the blood and spirits that produce them, it still remains for me
to treat many external signs which usually accompany them, and which are
observed much better when lots of [passions] are commingled, as they   *20*
usually are, than when they are separate. Among these signs, the principal
ones are actions of the eyes and face, changes in color, trembling, languor,   *25*
fainting, laughter, tears, groans, and sighs.

Article 113.   About actions of the eyes and face.[40]   412

There is no Passion which is not manifested by some particular action of the
eyes. This is so obvious, in the case of some of them, that even the stupidest   *5*
servants can tell from their master's eye whether or not he is upset with
them. But although these actions of the eyes are easily perceived, and what
they mean is known, that does not make it easy to describe them, because   *10*
each of them is composed of many changes taking place in the movement
and shape of the eye, so singular and slight that there is no perceiving each of
them separately, even though what results from their conjunction may be   *15*
quite easy to recognize. Almost the same can be said of the actions of the
face which also accompany the passions, for even though they are more
extensive than those of the eyes, it is nevertheless hard to distinguish them;
they differ so little that there are men who have almost the same look when   *20*
they cry as others when they laugh. It is true that there are some that are
quite recognizable, like a wrinkled forehead in anger and certain movements
of the nose and lips in indignation and mockery, but they do not seem to be   *25*
natural so much as voluntary. And in general all the actions of both the face
and the eyes can be changed by the soul, when, willing to conceal its
passion, it forcefully imagines[41] one in opposition to it; thus one can use   413
them to dissimulate one's passions as well as to manifest them.

40. A strikingly sophisticated article—from Descartes's uncharacteristic recognition of
the awareness of another's passions through a nonanalytic awareness of *gestalts*, to his
recognition of variation in facial expression of passion (a lesson insufficiently learned
by the Cartesian court painter Charles Le Brun), to his new application of the fact
that intentional representation of things (a. 45) is valuable in the struggle against
imagination (a. 211) for control over the passions and their concomitants.
41. *Imagine fortement.* Here the phrase marks the voluntary exercise of imagination,
but as a. 26, 348.28–349.3, shows, it need not. (We already knew from a. 21 that
imagine by itself sometimes marks a voluntary action and sometimes a passion.)
Descartes's use of *action* in the present article reminds us that, when he speaks of the
actions of the body or its parts, he usually speaks nonteleologically; we must beware
of reading in the idea of intentional action. See notes 24 and 25 in Part I.

5   ## Article 114.   About changes in color.

One cannot so easily keep from flushing or turning pale when some passion
so disposes, because these changes, unlike the preceding ones, do not depend
10   on nerves and muscles, and because they come more directly from the heart,
which may be called the source of the passions insofar as it prepares the
blood and spirits to produce them. Now it is certain that the face's color
comes solely from the blood, which, as it flows continually from the heart
15   through the arteries into all the veins and from all the veins into the heart,
colors the face more or less, in proportion as it fills the little veins near its
surface.

Article 115.   How Joy makes one flush.

20   Thus Joy renders the color more vivid and rosy, because in opening the
heart's sluices, it makes blood flow more quickly into all the veins, and, as
[the blood] becomes warmer and finer, it gently swells all the parts of the
25   face, rendering its demeanor more smiling and cheerful.

414   ## Article 116.   How Sadness makes one turn pale.

Sadness, on the other hand, in contracting the heart's orifices, makes blood
5   flow more slowly into the veins, and, as it becomes colder and thicker,
obliges it to occupy less space there, so that, receding into the largest ones,
closest to the heart, it leaves the most remote ones. The most conspicuous of
10   these being those of the face, this makes it appear pale and gaunt, especially
when the Sadness is great or springs up suddenly, as we see in Terror, in
which surprise increases the action constricting the heart.

15   ## Article 117.   How one often flushes when sad.

But it often happens that one does not turn pale when sad—on the contrary,
one's color rises. This must be attributed to other passions joined to Sadness,
20   namely Love or Desire and sometimes also Hatred. For these passions,
heating or agitating the blood coming from the liver, intestines, and other
internal parts, drive it to the heart, and thence through the great artery to
25   the facial veins—the Sadness which constricts the heart's orifices on either
415   side not being able, except when quite extreme, to impede it. But though it
may be only moderate, it easily prevents the blood which has thus entered

the facial veins from descending to the heart as long as Love, Desire, or
Hatred is driving [blood] there from other internal parts. That is why this 5
blood, being held back around the face, turns it red, even redder than during
Joy: because the color of blood is all the more noticeable as it flows less
swiftly, and also because more of it can collect in this manner in the facial 10
veins than when the heart's orifices are open more. This is noticeable above
all in Shame, which is composed of Love of oneself and an urgent Desire to
avoid present infamy—which makes blood come from the internal parts to
the heart and then from there via the arteries to the face—and also a 15
moderate Sadness—which prevents this blood from returning to the heart.
The same thing is also commonly noticeable when one cries, for, as I shall
say below, it is Love joined to Sadness that causes most tears. And the same 20
thing is noticeable in anger, in which a sudden Desire for vengeance is often
mixed with Love, Hatred, and Sadness.

Article 118.   About Trembling.

Trembling has two different causes: first sometimes too few spirits, then 25
sometimes too many, come from the brain into the nerves for them to be
able to close very precisely the little muscle passages which, according to 416
what was said in article XI, must be closed in order for them to determine
the movements of the members. The first cause becomes apparent in sadness
and in fear, and likewise when one trembles with cold. For these Passions, as 5
well as the coldness of the air, may so thicken the blood that it does not
supply enough spirits to the brain to send any into the nerves. The other
cause often becomes apparent in those who ardently desire something and in
those who are strongly moved by anger, and likewise in those who are 10
drunk. For these two passions, as well as wine, sometimes introduce so
many spirits into the brain that they cannot be led out into the muscles with
regularity.

Article 119.   About Languor.[42]   15

Languor is a disposition, felt in all the members, to relax and be motionless.
Like trembling, it comes about because not enough spirits are entering the 20

---

42. Descartes changed his mind about whether languor is excusable: see two letters to
Elisabeth of May 1646: AT IV, 411: K 194; AT IV, 414–415. After his rare admission
of error, he disparaged languor for the same sort of reason he gives in a. 170 below for
his disdain of irresolution.

nerves, but in a different manner. For the cause of trembling is that there are
not enough of them in the brain to obey the determinations of the gland
when it drives them toward some muscle, whereas languor comes about
25   because the gland does not determine that they go toward some muscles
rather than others.

417   Article 120.   How it is caused by Love and by Desire.

And the Passion that most commonly causes this effect is Love, joined to the
5   Desire for a thing whose acquisition is not imagined as possible at the present
time. For Love so engrosses the soul with the consideration of the object
loved that [the soul] employs all the spirits in the brain to represent its image
10   to it,[43] and stops all movements of the gland not conducive to this effect.
And it must be noted in connection with desire that the property I have
attributed to it,[44] of rendering the body more mobile, is congenial to it only
when one is imagining the desired object to be such that one can, from that
15   very time, do something conducive to acquiring it. For if, on the contrary,
one imagines that it is impossible then to do anything useful to that end, all
the agitation of Desire remains in the brain, without passing into the nerves
at all, and being entirely employed in strengthening the idea of the desired
20   object there, it leaves the rest of the body languishing.

Article 121.   That it may also be caused by other Passions.

It is true that Hatred, Sadness, and even Joy may also cause some languor
25   when they are extremely vigorous, because they entirely engross the soul
418   with the consideration of their object, especially when there is joined with
it[45] Desire for a thing to whose acquisition one can contribute nothing at the
present time. But because one pauses to consider the objects one joins to
5   oneself in volition much more than those one separates, or any others, and
because languor does not depend upon surprise, but requires some time to be
formed, it is encountered much more in Love than in all the other passions.

10   Article 122.   About Fainting.

Fainting is not far removed from dying, for one dies when the fire in the
15   heart is extinguished altogether, and one merely faints when it is smothered

43. I.e. to represent the object's image to the soul, or conceivably to the brain.
44. In a. 101.
45. As at 417.8, Descartes occasionally bathes his pronominal antecedents in obscurity.

in such a way that some residue of heat still remains which can later rekindle it. Now there are many indispositions of the body that can make one thus fall into a faint, but among the passions only extreme Joy is observed to have this power. And the way I believe it causes this effect is as follows: opening the orifices of the heart extraordinarily wide, venous blood enters it in such a rush and in such great quantity that it cannot be rarefied by the heat there quickly enough to raise the little membranes that close the openings of these veins. By this means it smothers the fire it usually maintains when it only enters the heart in moderation.

Article 123.   Why no one faints from Sadness.

It might seem that a great Sadness which springs up unexpectedly ought so to constrict the heart's orifices that it could also extinguish its fire. Nevertheless this is never observed to happen; if it does happen, it is very rare. I believe the reason for this is that there can hardly ever be so little blood in the heart that it does not suffice to maintain the heat when its orifices are nearly closed.[46]

Article 124.   About Laughter.

Laughter consists in this: [1] blood coming from the right cavity of the heart through the arterial vein, suddenly and repeatedly swelling the lungs, compels the air they contain to come out forcefully through the windpipe, where it forms an inarticulate and explosive cry; and [2] the lungs as they swell and this air as it emerges each push against all the muscles of the diaphragm, chest, and throat, and thereby make the ones in the face that

---

46. Descartes argues against the physician Plempius in truly amazing style in favor of his thermodynamic explanation of the heartbeat (see notes 7 and 10 in Part I). Plempius had argued that the heartbeat is caused, not by the sudden heating of the blood, but by a faculty of the soul, since even the pieces of a dissected heart will continue to beat for some time. Descartes replied that a little heated blood always remains on the pieces, and then argued metaphysically: "Besides, this very objection seems to me to have much more strength against this common opinion of so many others who believe that the movement of the heart proceeds from a faculty of the soul: for how, I ask, can that [motion] depend on the human soul—that [motion], I repeat, which is even found in the divided parts of the heart? For it is a point of faith that the rational soul is indivisible and that it has no other soul, neither sensitive nor vegetative, to which it is joined" (15 February 1638: AT I, 523). Cf. *Description of the Human Body*: AT XI, 282.

have some connection with them move. And what we call Laughter is only this action of the face, together with that inarticulate and explosive cry.

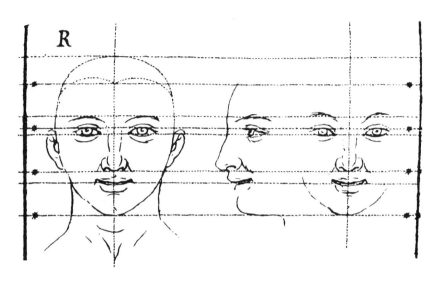

La Joye—Joy

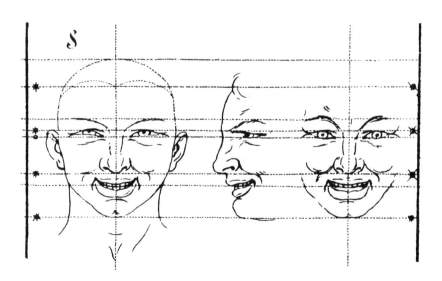

Le Ris—Laughter

Article 125.   Why it does not accompany the greatest Joys.[47]   420

Now although Laughter might seem to be one of the principal signs of Joy, the latter can nevertheless cause the former only when [joy] is merely *5* moderate and when there is some wonder or hatred mingled with it. For we find by experience that when we are extraordinarily joyful the subject of that joy never makes us break into laughter, and we cannot even be incited *10* to it by some other cause so easily as when we are sad. The reason for this is that, in great joys, the lungs are always so full of blood that they cannot be swelled by repeated bursts any more.

Article 126.   What its principal causes are.   *15*

And I can discover[48] only two causes that might thus make the lungs suddenly swell. The first is the surprise of Wonder, which, when joined to joy, can open the orifices of the heart so rapidly that a profusion of blood, *20* entering its right side all at once by the vena cava, is rarefied there and, passing on through the arterial vein, swells the lungs. The other is the mixture of some liquid which increases the rarefaction of the blood. I can *25* find nothing fit for doing that but the most free-flowing part of that which   421 comes from the spleen: this part of the blood, driven to the heart by some slight excitation of Hatred and helped along by the surprise of Wonder and mingling there with the blood from other parts of the body which joy sends *5* in abundance, is able to make this latter blood expand there much more than it usually does, just as we see a great many other liquids expand all at once on the fire when a little vinegar is thrown into the vessel they are in, for the *10* most free-flowing part of the blood that comes from the spleen is like vinegar in nature.[49] Experience also shows that in all the incidents capable of producing this explosive Laughter that comes from the lungs, there is always some small subject of Hatred, or at least Wonder. And those whose spleens *15* are not entirely healthy are apt to be not only more sad than others but also

47. On the relation of joy to love, see to Elisabeth, 15 September and 6 October 1645: AT IV, 292-294 and 308-309: K 172-173 and 176-177.
48. *Remarquer.* Since the contrast is with what experience shows (421.12), "observe" and the like are incorrect here. In response to the first draft of this article, Elisabeth asked (25 April 1646: AT IV, 405) how wonder, being cerebrally based, could affect the heart; Descartes replied in May 1646: AT IV, 409-410: K 193.
49. The reliance on a similarity between splenetic blood and vinegar looks ad hoc, but Descartes has previously conceived the heart's fire as a kind of fermentation: *Discourse,* Part 5: AT VI, 46: CSM I, 134; *Description of the Human Body:* AT XI, 228.

intermittently more cheerful and disposed to laugh, inasmuch as the spleen
sends the heart two sorts of blood—the one, which causes Sadness, extreme-
20   ly thick and coarse, the other, which causes Joy, extremely fluid and fine.
And often, after having laughed a lot, one feels naturally[50] inclined to
Sadness, because as the most fluid part of the blood from the spleen gets used
25   up, the other which is coarser follows it to the heart.

Article 127.   What its cause is in Indignation.

As for the Laughter that sometimes accompanies Indignation, it is com-
422   monly artificial and feigned. But, when it is natural, it seems to spring from
the Joy one gets from seeing that one cannot be injured by the evil one is
indignant about and, along with this, from finding oneself surprised by the
5   novelty of or the unexpected encounter with this evil—so that Joy, Hatred,
and Wonder contribute to it. Nevertheless I am willing to believe that it can
also be produced without any joy, solely by the movement of Aversion,
which sends blood from the spleen to the heart, where it is rarefied and
10   driven on into the lungs, which it easily swells when it finds them almost
empty. And in general anything that can suddenly swell the lungs in this
manner will cause the external action of Laughter, except when Sadness
15   changes it into that of the groans and cries which accompany tears. On this
subject, Vives writes of himself that when he had gone a long time without
eating, the first morsels he put in his mouth forced him to laugh:* this might
20   have come about from his lungs—devoid of blood for lack of sustenance—
being rapidly swelled by the first juice passing from his stomach to the heart,
which the mere imagination of eating could have led there even before [the
juice] from the food he was eating had arrived.[51]

Article 128.   About the origin of Tears.

423   As Laughter is never caused by the greatest Joys, so tears do not come from
extreme Sadness, but only from that which is moderate and accompanied or

---

*J. L. Vives, 3, *de Animâ*, chap. "de Risu."
50. I.e. by the institution of nature, even in the case of healthy people not suffering
from manic depression because of spleen disease.
51. Juan Luis Vives (1493-1540), Spanish philosopher. *De anima & vita* appeared in
1538. In Book III, chapter 10, Vives had reported, "And I cannot keep back a smile at
the first and second mouthful I take after a long fast, for the contracted midriff
becomes extended because of the food." On the relation between Vives's and Descartes's theories of the passions, see RL 24-29. The added touch here about imagination is due to Descartes. For more on laughter among the indignant, see a. 197.

followed by some sensation of Love, or Joy as well. To understand their origin rightly, one must note that, even though a great many vapors are 5 continually issuing from all parts of our body, there is nevertheless none from which so many issue as the eyes, because of the size of the optic nerves and the multiplicity of the little arteries by which they reach them; and that, 10 as sweat is only composed of vapors which, coming from the other parts, turn into water on their surfaces, so tears are made of vapors coming from the eyes.

Article 129.   About the manner in which vapors turn into 15 water.

Now as I wrote in the *Météores*, in explaining the manner in which the vapors of the air turn into rain—that it comes about because they are less agitated or more abundant than ordinary[52]—so I believe that when those 20 which come from the body are much less agitated than usual, though they may not be so abundant, they still turn into water; this causes the cold sweats that stem from weakness when one is sick. And I believe that when 25 they are much more abundant, provided they are not more agitated as well, they also turn into water; this causes the sweat that breaks out when one **424** does some exercise. The eyes do not sweat then, because, during the body's exercises, with the greater part of the spirits going into the muscles for 5 moving [the body], fewer go through the optic nerve to the eyes. And but a single stuff[53] composes blood, while in the veins or the arteries; spirits, when in the brain, nerves, or muscles; vapors, when issuing from them in the form 10 of air; and finally sweat or tears, when condensing into water on the surface of the body or eyes.

Article 130.   How what brings about pain in the eye excites 15 it to cry.

And I can discover only two causes that might make the vapors issuing from the eyes turn into tears. The first is when the shape of the pores they pass through is, by whatever accident, changed, for, by hindering the motion 20 of these vapors and changing their order, this can make them turn into

52. *Meteorology*, Discourses 2 and 6: AT VI, 239–248 and 308–311: Olscamp 269–274 and 319–321: nowhere in this essay, however, is the explanation of rain made so neat as it is here.
53. A case of the approach to physics recommended in to Morin, 13 July 1638: AT II, 199–200: K 58–59.

water. Thus it only takes a mote falling into the eye to draw some tears from
it, because, in exciting pain in it, it changes the disposition of its pores in
such a way that, as some become narrower, the vapors' little parts pass
through them less quickly, and, whereas they previously came forth at equal

25

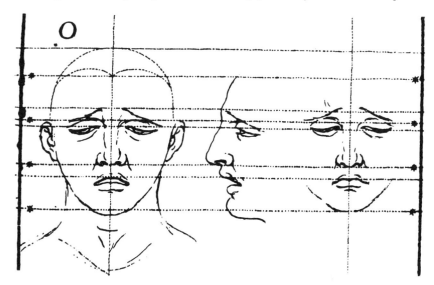

La Tristesse—Sadness

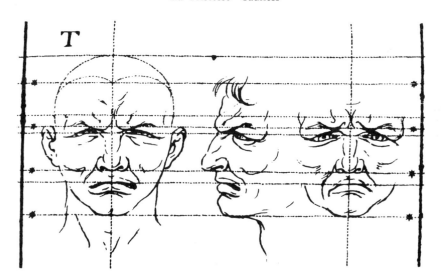

Le Pleurer—Tears

distances from one another, thus remaining separate, now, because the order   425
of these pores is disturbed, [the parts of the vapor] come into contact with
each other, thereby becoming joined together and so turning into tears.

Article 131.   How one cries from Sadness.   5

The other cause is Sadness, followed by Love or Joy or in general by some
cause that makes the heart drive a lot of blood through the arteries. Sadness   10
is needed, because in cooling all the blood it contracts the eyes' pores. But
because it also diminishes the quantity of vapors—which must pass through
them—in proportion as it contracts them, this does not suffice to produce
tears unless the quantity of these vapors is simultaneously increased by some   15
other cause. And there is nothing which increases it more than the blood
sent to the heart in the passion of Love. We see too that those who are sad
do not shed tears continually, but only intermittently, when they make some   20
new reflection upon the objects they are fond of.

Article 132.   About the groans that accompany tears.

And then the lungs are sometimes also swelled all at once by the abundance   25
of blood which enters them and expels the air they contained; [this air],   426
emerging through the windpipe, gives rise to the groans and cries that
usually accompany tears. These cries are commonly more shrill than the
ones that accompany laughter, even though they are produced in almost the   5
same manner. The reason for this is that the nerves used to expand or
contract the organs of the voice to render it more gruff or more shrill, being
joined with the ones that open the heart's orifices during Joy and contract   10
them during Sadness, make [the vocal] organs expand or contract at the same
time.

Article 133.   Why children and old people cry easily.

Children and old people are more inclined to cry than those of intermediate   15
age, but for different reasons. Old people often cry from affection and joy, for
these two passions joined together send lots of blood to their heart and a   20
great many vapors from there to their eyes, and the agitation of these vapors
is hindered by the coldness of their constitution in such a way that they
easily turn into tears, though no Sadness may have gone before. If some old
people also cry extremely easily from being upset, it is not so much the   25

temperament of their body as that of their mind which so disposes them; this only happens to those who are so weak that they let themselves be completely overcome by little causes of pain, fear, or pity.[54] The same thing happens to children, who cry very little from Joy but much more from Sadness, even when it is not accompanied by Love. For they always have enough blood to produce a great many vapors, which turn into tears as their motion is hindered by Sadness.

Article 134.   Why some children turn pale instead of crying.

Nevertheless there are some [children] who turn pale instead of crying when they are upset; this may indicate extraordinary courage and judgment in them, when it arises from their taking into consideration the magnitude of the evil and preparing themselves for a strong resistance, as in those who are older. But it is more commonly a mark of a bad constitution, when it arises from an inclination to Hatred or Fear in them, for these are passions that diminish the stuff of tears. And, on the other hand, we see that those who cry very easily are inclined to Love and Pity.[55]

Article 135.   About Sighs.[56]

The cause of Sighs is very different from that of tears, though the former, like the latter, presuppose Sadness. For whereas one is incited to cry when the lungs are full of blood, one is incited to sigh when they are almost empty and some imagination of hope or joy opens the orifice of the venous artery which Sadness had contracted. For then, as the small remnant of blood in the lungs falls all at once through the venous artery into the left side of the heart, driven there by the Desire to attain this Joy which is at the same time agitating all the diaphragm and chest muscles, air is suddenly driven through the mouth into the lungs to fill the space this blood is leaving there. And it is this that we call sighing.

Article 136.   Whence come the effects of Passions that are peculiar to certain men.

And now, to make do in a few words here for everything that could be added concerning the various effects or the various causes of the passions, I

---

54. A special case of the weakness of soul introduced in a. 48.
55. See the early *Observations*: AT X, 217: CSM I, 4; and a. 200 below.
56. On the cause of sighs, see to Elisabeth, May 1646: AT IV, 410–411: K 194.

shall content myself with repeating the principle on which everything I 20
have written about them is based:[57] namely, that there is such a connection
between our soul and our body that when we have once joined some bodily
action with some thought, one of the two is never present to us afterwards 25
without the other also being present to us; and that the same actions are not
always joined to the same thoughts. For this will suffice to provide an
account of everything anyone might notice that is peculiar to himself or to 429
others, along these lines, which has not been explained here. It is not
difficult, for example, to think that some people's unusual aversions, which 5
make them unable to tolerate the smell of roses or the presence of a cat or
similar things, come only from having been badly shocked by some such
objects at the beginning of life, or from having sympathetically felt the
sensation of their mother who was shocked by them while pregnant. For it 10
is certain that there is a relation between all the movements of a mother and
those of the child in her womb, which is such that what is adverse to the
one is harmful to the other.[58] The smell of roses may have given a child a
severe headache when he was still in the cradle, or a cat may have frightened 15
him badly, without anyone having been aware of it and without him having
had any memory of it afterwards, though the idea of the Aversion he had
then for the roses or the cat may remain imprinted in his brain to the end of 20
his life.

Article 137.   About the use of the five Passions explained here insofar as they have reference to the body.[59]

After having given the definitions of Love, Hatred, Desire, Joy, and Sadness, 25
and treated all the bodily movements which cause or accompany them, we

57. The Principle of Habituation, mentioned above at aa. 44, 50, and 107. Descartes
seeks elsewhere to explain psychological peculiarities in terms of traces left in the
brain by previous experience: to Mersenne, 18 March 1630: AT I, 133-134: K 7-8.
He regards this phenomenon as strictly analogous to bodily (as opposed to intellectual) memory, which he explains similarly.
58. Descartes tends to downplay this prenatal avenue of explanation, which exhibits a
tendency common in renaissance folk science. See Alquié I, 699, n. 1. Cf. to Mersenne, 27 May 1630: AT I, 153: K 16; *Treatise on Man*: AT XI, 177: Hall 87;
Dioptrics, Fifth Discourse: AT VI, 129: Olscamp 100; to Meyssonnier, 29 January
1640: AT III, 20-21: K 70.
59. Descartes concludes Part II (aa. 137-148) with a study of the use of the primitive
passions other than wonder, examining both their natural value to us and the
remedies for their disorders (see note 43 in Part I). He has opened the question of the
use of the passions in general at a. 74 and has already considered the use of wonder at

430 have nothing more to consider here but their use. In this connection it should be noted that, according to the institution of Nature, they all have reference to the body, and are given to the soul only insofar as it is joined

5 with [the body], so that their natural use is to incite the soul to consent and contribute to actions which can serve to preserve the body or render it more perfect in some way. And in this context,[60] Sadness and Joy are the first two

10 that are employed. For the soul is immediately informed of things that harm the body only by the sensation it has of pain, which produces in it first the passion of Sadness, next Hatred of what causes the pain, and in the third

15 place the Desire to get rid of it. So also the soul is immediately informed of things useful to the body only by some sort of titillation, which, exciting Joy in it, next arouses love of what one believes to be its cause, and finally the

20 desire to acquire what can make one continue having this Joy or enjoy one like it later on again. This shows that all five of them are very useful with respect to the body—and even that Sadness is in a way primary and more

25 necessary than Joy, and Hatred than Love, because it is more important to repel the things that harm and can destroy than to acquire those that add some perfection without which one can survive.[61]

---

aa. 75-78. He gives a sketch of his position in to Chanut, 1 February 1647: AT IV, 613-617: K 215-218.

Since the primitive passions other than wonder are normally aroused by thoughts of what is good or bad for us (a. 56), they are valuable to us because they can incline the will toward action useful to us (aa. 40, 52). Descartes's main technique in studying them is to analyze into cases (see note 1 in Part I for this aspect of the method). He considers first the value of the passions for the body (aa. 137-138) and then their value for the soul (aa. 139-148). In the latter case, he considers the intrinsic value of the passions, or their value unrelated to desire for action (aa. 139-142) (in effect amending a. 52, which appears to ignore this aspect of their value), and then their instrumental value to the soul, or their use in relation to desire for action (aa. 143-146). Here he considers the nature of desire in the light of the truth about divine Providence and chance or fortune, developing recommendations about which desires to encourage and what remedies to seek for the others. In examining the passions' instrumental value, he considers desire whose outcome depends only on us (a. 144), then only on other causes (a. 145), and finally on both (a. 146). Then, in aa. 147-148, Descartes turns to consider "inner excitations of the soul," which are distinct from the passions, but possess their own value and provide a further source for remediation of disordered passions.

60. *En ce sens*: when the question concerns the use of passions for the body, in their natural sequence the first passions to have any use are joy and sadness. The contrast is with the case in which the passions are useful to the soul; in this case (a. 139), love and hatred that are not first generated by joy and sadness are worth mentioning. Articles 137 and 138 amplify a. 40.

61. Descartes's hope for a mechanistic medicine that would prolong life indefinitely— for references see note 10 in the Preface—was gradually supplanted by increasing

Article 138.   About their defects and the means of correcting   **431**
them.

But, though this use of the passions is the most natural one they can have,
and though animals that lack reason all direct their lives entirely by bodily   *5*
movements like those which usually follow them in us, to which they incite
our souls to consent, it is nevertheless not always good, inasmuch as there
are many things harmful to the body that cause no Sadness at the beginning,   *10*
or even give Joy, and others that are useful to it though they are distressing
at first. Moreover they almost always make both the goods and the evils
they represent appear much greater and more important than they are, so   *15*
that they incite us to seek the former and flee the latter with more ardor and
more anxiety than is suitable—as, we likewise see, beasts are often deceived   *20*
by bait, and in order to avoid small evils rush into larger ones. This is why
we should make use of experience and reason to distinguish the good from
the evil and to discern their true worth, in order not to take one for the   *25*
other and not to tend toward anything immoderately.[62]

Article 139.   About the use of the same Passions insofar as[63]   **432**
they belong to the soul; and first about Love.

This would suffice if we only had the body in us or if it were the better part   *5*
of us, but inasmuch as it is the lesser, we must consider the Passions
principally insofar as they belong to the soul, with respect to which Love
and Hatred originate from knowledge and precede Joy and Sadness, except   *10*
when these latter two, which are species of knowledge, take its place.[64] And
when this knowledge is true—that is, when the things it inclines us to love

---

reliance upon the use of naturally instituted sensations in sustaining the body: to
Mersenne, 9 January 1639: AT II, 480; Sixth Meditation: AT VII, 82-90: CSM II,
56-62. See Alquié 1052, n. 2.

   While all the passions are generated by the body, usually in response to things that
matter to us, they are not all generated in response to things that matter for the *body*.
In a. 139 we see other possibilities concerning their genesis.

62. Although this defect of instinct is in a way natural, it is similar to the dropsy
discussed in Meditation 6: AT VII, 85-86: CSM II, 58-59, in disposing us to desires
harmful to the body. The defect helps clarify the value of the virtues mentioned in aa.
48 and 49. The advice offered here is developed more thoroughly in a. 211.

63. *Entant qu'*: not "to the extent that," but "when what is at issue is the fact that"—
qua, for short. The contrast is with the title of a. 137.

64. A dark saying. The hatred that concerns harm to the soul rather than to the body
need not be aroused by pain or sadness, but merely by the thought that a thing is not
good for me, together with the resulting motion of the spirits. Characteristically,

15 are truly good and those it inclines us to hate are truly bad—Love is
incomparably better than Hatred, it cannot be too great, and it never fails to
produce Joy. I say this Love is extremely good because, joining true goods to
20 us, it perfects us to that extent. I also say it cannot be too great, since the
only thing that the most immoderate [love] can do is join us so perfectly to
those goods that the Love we have for ourselves in particular makes no
25 distinction between us and them, which I believe can never be bad. And it is
necessarily followed by Joy because it represents to us what we love as a
good that belongs to us.[65]

433 ## Article 140.   About Hatred.

Hatred, on the other hand, cannot be so little that it fails to harm; and it is
5 never without Sadness. I say that it cannot be too little, because we are
incited to no action by Hatred of evil, to which we might not be still more

---

perhaps, what harms the body arouses pain and confused judgment, whereas what
harms the soul arouses clearer judgment—and "clearer knowledge" (a. 140). When
harm to soul and not to body is at issue, we can usually expect the judgment "this is
bad for me" to precede the judgment "this is not only bad for me; it belongs to me";
so we can usually expect hatred to precede sadness (see aa. 56, 61, 79, and 92). Of
course sometimes the reverse will be the case.

Descartes makes an analogous remark about what he calls "the love which is
purely intellectual or rational" in the letter to Chanut, 1 February 1647: AT IV, 601–
602: K 208–209: "When our soul perceives some present or absent good, which it
judges to be fitting for itself, it unites itself to it in volition, that is to say, it considers
itself and the good in question as forming two parts of a single whole. Then, if the
good is present, that is, if the soul possesses it or is possessed by it or is united to it not
only in volition but also in fact and reality in the appropriate manner, in that case the
movement of the will which accompanies the knowledge that this is good for it is
joy; if, on the other hand, the good is absent, then the movement of the will which
accompanies the knowledge of its lack is sadness, while the movement which
accompanies the knowledge that it would be a good thing to acquire it is desire."

On the parenthetical claim that joy and sadness are species of knowledge, recall
that a. 17 identifies the soul's passions in the general sense with *perceptions ou
connoissances*. And observe that while Meditation 4 makes error involve both
intellect and will, it treats knowledge as a simpler phenomenon, involving only
intellect, and in fact dubs intellect "the faculty of knowledge": AT VII, 56 (*facultate
cognoscendi*): IX, 45 (*la puissance de connoistre*): CSM II, 39.

65. This argument yields a constraint upon our interpretation of Descartes's account
of love in a. 79. If an object seems good for the soul and it joins itself in volition to
that object, then the passion must represent the beloved object to the soul as a good
that belongs to the soul.

by Love of the good to which [the evil] is opposed[66]—at least when the good
and the evil are sufficiently known. For I grant that Hatred of evil mani-   *10*
fested only by pain is necessary with respect to the body, but here I am only
speaking of that which originates from clearer knowledge, and I am only
referring it to the soul. I also say that it is never without Sadness, because   *15*
evil, being only a privation, cannot be conceived without some real subject
which it is in, and there is nothing real that does not have some goodness in
it; so the Hatred that estranges us from some evil estranges us by that very
means from the good it is joined to, and the privation of this good, being   *20*
represented to our soul as a defect belonging to it, excites Sadness in it. For
example, the Hatred that estranges us from someone's bad behavior estranges
us by that very means from his company, in which we would otherwise be   *25*
able to find some good—which we are upset at being deprived of. And so, in
every other Hatred, some cause of Sadness may be recognized.

Article 141.   About Desire, Joy, and Sadness.   **434**

As for Desire, it is plain that, when it proceeds from true knowledge, it
cannot be bad, provided that it is not immoderate, and this knowledge   *5*
regulates it. It is plain too that Joy cannot fail to be good or Sadness bad with
respect to the soul, because all the distress the soul receives from evil consists *10*
in the latter, and all the enjoyment of the good that belongs to it consists in
the former, so that, if we had no body, I should be so bold as to say that we
could not abandon ourselves too much to Love and Joy, or shun Hatred and
Sadness too much. But all of the bodily movements that accompany them   *15*
can be harmful to the health, when they are extremely vigorous, and can on
the other hand be useful to it, when they are only moderate.

Article 142.   About Joy and Love compared with Sadness   *20*
and Hatred.[67]

Furthermore, since Hatred and Sadness should be rejected by the soul even
when they proceed from true knowledge, they should be so all the more   *25*

---

66. *Contraire.* Recall note 26, to a. 87, although the opposition here is between hatred
of an evil and love of the opposed good, whereas there the opposition was between
two desires. Does Descartes think this opposition, like that one, is really an identity?
67. Descartes discusses similar questions in to Elisabeth, 6 October 1645: AT IV, 304-
307: K 174-176, and in to Chanut, 1 February 1647: AT IV, 613-617: K 215-218.

435 when they originate from some false opinion. Still, it may be doubted
whether or not Love and Joy are good when they are thus ill founded; and it
seems to me that if one considers in abstraction[68] only what they are in
themselves, with respect to the soul, it can be said that even though Joy is
5 less solid and Love less advantageous than when they have a better foundation, they remain preferable to Sadness and Hatred likewise ill founded. So
10 in life's contingencies, in which we cannot avoid the risk of being deceived,
we always do much better to incline toward the passions that tend to the
good than toward those that concern evil, though this be only to avoid it.
And often even a false Joy is worth more than a Sadness whose cause is true.
15 But I do not venture to say the same of Love in comparison with Hatred.
For when Hatred is just, it estranges us only from the subject containing the
evil it is good to be separated from; whereas Love that is unjust joins us to
20 things which may harm, or at least which deserve less consideration than we
pay them, which disgraces and debases us.

25 ## Article 143.   About the same Passions insofar as they have reference to Desire.

And it must be noted carefully that what I have just related[69] about these
four passions takes place only when they are considered in abstraction, in
436 themselves, and when they do not incline us to any action. For insofar as
they excite Desire in us, by whose mediation they regulate our behavior, it is
certain that all those whose cause is false may harm, and that on the other
5 hand all those whose cause is just may help—and even that, when they are
equally ill-founded, Joy is commonly more harmful than Sadness, because
the latter, bestowing caution and apprehension, disposes one in a way toward
10 Prudence, whereas the former renders those who abandon themselves to it
unthinking and rash.

68. *Precisement*: in abstraction—both from the question whether they benefit or
harm the body (that was considered in aa. 137–138) and from the question whether
their links with desire yield other kinds of benefit or harm (such effects on the soul
will be considered in aa. 143–146). The word also appears at 435.28. Descartes is no
ethical hedonist: aa. 139–142 make it clear that love and hate, as well as joy and
sadness, have intrinsic value to the soul; see also to Elisabeth, 6 October 1645: AT IV,
304–309: K 174–176.

For Descartes's theory of value, see to Elisabeth, 18 August 1645: AT IV, 271–278,
and to Christine, 20 November 1647: AT V, 81–86: K 225–226. The letter to
Christine is often known as "the letter on the Supreme Good."
69. In articles 139–142.

Article 144.   About Desires whose outcome depends only on us.

But because these Passions can incline us to any action only through the   *15*
mediation of the Desire they excite, it is that Desire in particular which we
should be concerned to regulate; and the principal utility of Moral Philosophy
consists in this. Now, as I have lately said that [desire] is always good when it
follows true knowledge, it similarly cannot fail to be bad when it is founded on   *20*
some error. And it seems to me that the error most commonly committed in
connection with Desires is to fail to distinguish sufficiently the things that
depend entirely on us from those that do not depend on us.[70] For as to those   *25*
that depend only on us—that is, on our free will—knowing they are good
excludes any possibility of desiring them too ardently, because to do good things   *437*
that depend on us is to follow virtue, and it is certain that one cannot have too
ardent a Desire for virtue. Besides, as what we desire in this way cannot fail to   *5*
turn out well for us, since it depends on us alone, we always receive from it all
the satisfaction we have expected from it.[71] In fact the error usually committed

70. Considering the value of passions to the soul insofar as they incline us to action,
Descartes begins, just as he had in to Elisabeth, 4 August 1645: AT IV, 264-265: K
164-165, with a distinction that is Stoic in inspiration. The task now, as then, is to
give a definitive restatement of the third maxim of his provisional moral philosophy:
"to try always to master myself rather than fortune, and change my desires rather
than the order of the world" (*Discourse*, Part 3: AT VI, 25-27: CSM I, 123-124).
     Nothing is absolutely in our power but our thoughts (see note 41 in Part I).
Commenting on the passage from the letter to Reneri for Pollot which we cited
there, Gilson says: "This conception, obviously Stoic in origin, receives in the
definitive moral philosophy an extremely rich development, one that is characteristically Cartesian. What we are given is essentially the following: (1) nothing is
completely in our power but our thoughts, but they are absolutely in our power
because they depend only on our free will. (2) Now this free will, as we know from
the metaphysics we already possess, is indivisible, and therefore so to speak infinite,
and the most immediate resemblance between God and ourselves [Meditation 4: AT
VII, 56.26-57.27]. (3) This consequence for the definitive moral philosophy follows:
the merit and dignity of man are measured by the use he can make of that faculty of
his which assimilates him most closely to God. (4) The esteem we have for ourselves, insofar as we are considering ourselves as making good use of this supreme
control given us over our volitions, is the virtue of Generosity; it is also one of the
essential components of perfect wisdom." (Étienne Gilson, *René Descartes: Discours
de la méthode: Texte et commentaire* [Third edition: Paris: J. Vrin, 1962], p. 248).
     Gilson concludes by referring us to aa. 152-153 of the *Passions*, for the solution to
the problem of aa. 143-146 is finally gained only in Part III, when the nature of the
passion of generosity is sufficiently understood.
71. How is satisfaction gained? An initial clarification appears in Descartes's account

10   here is only to desire too little; it is never to desire too much. And the supreme
      remedy for that is to free the mind as much as one can from all sorts of other
      less useful Desires, and then to try to understand very clearly and consider
15   attentively the goodness of what is to be desired.

Article 145.   About those which depend only on other causes; and what Fortune is.

20   As for things which in no way depend on us, no matter how good they may
      be, one should never desire them with Passion—not only because they may
      fail to come about and thereby afflict us all the more, the more we have
25   wished for them, but mainly because, in occupying our thought, they divert
      us from casting our affection upon other things whose acquisition does
438   depend on us. And there are two general remedies for these vain Desires.
      The first is Generosity, which I shall speak about later.[72] The second is that
      we should often reflect upon divine Providence, and represent to ourselves
5   that it is impossible that anything should happen otherwise than has been
      determined by this Providence from all eternity; thus it is like a fate or
      immutable necessity which must be opposed to Fortune, in order to destroy
10   it, as a chimera arising only from error in our understanding.[73] For we can
      desire only what we consider in some way to be possible,[74] and we can

---

of *beatitude*—the term is not used in the *Passions*—in his letter of 4 August 1645 to
Elisabeth: "*beatitude* consists, it seems to me, in a perfect contentment of the mind
and an inner satisfaction which those who are commonly most favored by fortune do
not have, and which the sages acquire without it. So *vivere beate*, to live in
beatitude, is just to have one's mind perfectly content and satisfied" (AT IV, 264: K
164).

   This account in the letter of 4 August introduces what has come to be known—I
think misleadingly—as Descartes's "definitive moral philosophy." Further conditions
for obtaining satisfaction are given in the three maxims in that letter (AT IV, 265-
266: K 165-166); in to Elisabeth, 18 August and 1 September 1645: AT IV, 276-277
and 281-287: the latter is at K 167-171; and in to Christine, 20 November 1647: AT
V, 84-85: K 227-228. In articles 143-153 here Descartes traces a similar but more fully
articulated path from his original third maxim to his final restatement.

72. On this use of generosity, see especially aa. 153, 156, and 161.

73. See the similar emphasis on knowledge of God's providence in to Elisabeth, 15
September 1645: AT IV, 291-292: K 171; and see note 47 in Part III below. In aa. 145
and 146 Descartes offers, as means for freeing the mind from incorrect desires,
understanding certain truths and attending reflectively to them. See note 51 in Part I
and notes 18 and 47 in Part III.

74. Articles 58 and 166 seem to entail a rule: believing that it is possible to acquire a
good is necessary and sufficient for having the desire to acquire it. Still, upon learning

consider possible things which do not depend on us only insofar as we think
they depend on Fortune—that is, insofar as we judge that they might   15
happen and that something like them has happened at other times. Now this
opinion is founded only on our failure to know all the causes that contribute
to each effect. For when something we have considered to depend on
Fortune does not happen, this shows that one of the causes necessary to   20
produce it was lacking, and consequently that it was absolutely impossible,
and that something like it has never happened—that is, something for the
production of which a similar cause was also lacking. So if we had not been   25
ignorant of that beforehand, we would never have considered it possible, nor
consequently have desired it.

Article 146.   About those which depend both on us and on others.   439

It is therefore necessary to reject completely the common opinion that there
is a Fortune outside of us which makes things happen or fail to happen at its   5
pleasure, and to understand that everything is directed by divine Providence,
whose eternal decree is infallible and immutable in such a way that, except
for the things which this same decree has willed to depend on our free will,
we ought to think that from our point of view nothing happens which is   10
not necessary and as it were fated, so that we cannot without error desire it
to happen otherwise. But because most of our Desires extend to things
which do not depend entirely on us or entirely on others, we should   15
distinguish carefully within [those things] that which depends only on us, in
order to limit our desire to that alone. As for what is left, even though we
ought to consider its outcome entirely fated and immutable, so that our
Desire may not be occupied therewith, we should not cease to attend to the   20
reasons that make it hope to a greater or lesser extent, so that they may be

---

that Huygens's wife had died, Descartes wrote to him that "it is certain that when
hope is entirely extinguished, desire ceases, *or at least relaxes and loses its force*": May
1637: AT I, 371-372. The amendment which I have italicized to the simple rule
relating desire to belief about what is possible perhaps allows room for the suggestion,
at 437.21, that it is possible to "desire without passion" (cf. a. 120, and see note 15 in
Part III). That suggestion is an attempt to resolve the strain between the second and
third maxims of Descartes's provisional moral philosophy: both to act decisively in a
world largely beyond our control and to limit desire to what is in our power. The
strain is still present in the *Passions*, encapsulated in the first sentence of a. 156;
"Descartes desires success and domination of nature, and counsels abstention and
resignation" (Alquié 1059, n. 1). Descartes also seeks a way out in to Elisabeth, May
1646: AT IV, 411: K 194— "I do not believe one ever sins by excess through desiring
the things necessary to life; it is only desires for those that are bad or superfluous that
must be regulated"—and in a. 146, at 439.18ff.

25 instrumental in regulating our actions. So, for example, if we have business somewhere we could reach by two different routes, of which one is usually much safer than the other, then even though the decree of Providence may perhaps be such that if we go by the route considered safer we shall

440 definitely be robbed there, while on the contrary we can take the other with no danger at all, we should not on that account be indifferent to choosing one or the other, or rest upon the immutable fatefulness of that decree;

5 reason dictates that we should choose the route that is usually safer. And our Desire regarding it must be fulfilled once we have taken it, whatever evil may thereby have befallen us, because, this evil having been inevitable from

10 our point of view, we had no reason to wish to be free from it but only to wish to do everything as well as our understanding could discern, as I am supposing we have done. And it is certain that when one applies oneself thus

15 to distinguishing Fate from Fortune, one will easily accustom oneself to regulating one's Desires in such a way that they can always give us complete satisfaction, since their fulfillment depends only on us.[75]

Article 147.   About the inner Excitations of the soul.[76]

20 I shall add but one further consideration here, which seems to me to be very good for keeping us from suffering any distress from the Passions: our good

25 and our ill depend principally on inner excitations, which are excited in the soul only by the soul itself—in which respect they differ from those passions that always depend on some motion of the spirits. And although these

441 excitations of the soul are often joined with the passions that are like them, they may also frequently be found with others, and may even originate from those that are in opposition to them. For example, when a husband mourns

5 his dead wife, whom (as sometimes happens) he would be upset to see resuscitated, it may be that his heart is constricted by the Sadness which funeral trappings and the absence of a person to whose company he was

10 accustomed excite in him; and it may be that some remnants of love or pity,

75. See to Hyperaspistes, August 1641: AT III, 422-423: K 110; to Elisabeth, 6 October 1645: AT IV, 307: K 176.

76. Although the inner excitations are not themselves passions, these two articles continue the discussion of how the primitive passions other than wonder are good and bad for the soul. Since our good and ill depend primarily on these excitations, the present passages moderate the conclusions of aa. 139-146.

Descartes appears to use the modifiers *interieur* (440.19) and *intellectuel* (441.23) in this context to pick out the same kinds of excitations (but inner satisfaction, mentioned in aa. 63 and 204, is evidently a passion). These excitations are discussed in *Principles* IV, a. 190: AT VIII, 317-318: CSM I, 281; to Elisabeth, 1 and 15 September 1645: AT IV, 284 and 294-295: K 169 and 173; to Chanut, 1 February 1647: AT IV, 601-604: K 208-210; and aa. 91-93 above.

presented to his imagination, draw genuine tears from his eyes—in spite of
the fact that at the same time he feels a secret Joy in the innermost depths of
his soul, whose excitation has so much power that the Sadness and tears
accompanying it can diminish none of its strength. And when we read of   *15*
unusual adventures in a book or see them represented on a stage, this
sometimes excites Sadness in us, sometimes Joy or Love or Hatred, and in
general all the Passions, according to the diversity of the objects offered to   *20*
our imagination; but along with this we have the pleasure of feeling them
excited in us, and this pleasure is an intellectual Joy, which can originate
from Sadness as well as from any of the other Passions.[77]

Article 148.   That the exercise of virtue is a supreme remedy   *25*
for the Passions.

Now, inasmuch as these inner excitations affect us more intimately and
consequently have much more power over us than the Passions from which   **442**
they differ but which are found with them, it is certain that, provided our
soul always has what it takes to be content in its interior,[78] none of the
disturbances that come from elsewhere have any power to harm it. On the   *5*
contrary, they serve to increase its joy, for in seeing that it cannot be injured
by them it comes to understand its perfection. And in order that our soul
may thus have what it takes to be content, it needs only to follow virtue   *10*
diligently. For anyone who has lived in such a way that his conscience
cannot reproach him for ever having failed to do anything he judged to be
best (which is what I call following virtue here) derives a satisfaction with   *15*
such power to make him happy that the most vigorous assaults of the
Passions never have enough power to disturb the tranquillity of his soul.

77. On the complex passions and excitations aroused by stage performances (a
perennial problem of philosophy), see to Elisabeth, 18 May 1645: AT IV, 202-203:
translated in note 25 in Part III; to Elisabeth, May or June 1645, 6 October 1645, and
January 1646: AT IV, 219-220, 309, and 354-356: K 161-162, 177, and 189-190; and
aa. 94 and 187.

78. Since the soul has no parts (aa. 30, 47, 68), it is hard to see how to distinguish
theoretically the *interieur* (470.9), let alone *le plus interieur* (441.13), of the soul
from the rest of it. As we intimated in note 27 in Part I, it is perhaps more reasonable
to see such passages as signs of Descartes's genuinely neo-Stoic attitude toward the
world. We have seen his focus successively narrow in this work: the body, the pineal
gland, the soul, and now its "interior." A similar itinerary can be traced in the First
Meditation: objects that are very small or far away, familiar nearby objects, the body
and its senses, the soul and its reason. And so can one more: examining "the great
book of the world" on military travels through several countries; Amsterdam, Ley-
den, and the isolated village of Egmond; and finally the palace in Stockholm. What
walled fastness can ever provide security?

THE
PASSIONS
OF THE SOUL

THIRD PART

About the Particular Passions

5 ### Article 149. About Esteem and Scorn.[1]

After having explained the six primitive Passions, which are as it were the genera of which all the others are species, I shall note briefly here what is 10 special about each of these others, keeping the same order according to which I enumerated them above. The first two are Esteem and Scorn. For although these names commonly signify only the opinion someone has, 15 without any passion, of a thing's worth, still, because from these opinions there often arise Passions, to which no particular names have been given, it seems to me that these [names] may be attributed to them. And Esteem, 444 insofar as it is a Passion, is an inclination the soul has to represent to itself the worth of the thing esteemed—an inclination caused by a particular movement of the spirits, guided into the brain in such a way that they strengthen 5 there the impressions which contribute to this subject. Similarly, on the other hand, the Passion of Scorn is an inclination the soul has to consider the lowliness or meanness of what it scorns, caused by the movement of spirits that strengthens the idea of that meanness.

1. Part III investigates in order (a. 52) the nature and use of the principal passions that are not primitive; these are all species of the primitives or composed of some of them (a. 69). Articles 149-164 consider passions that are species of wonder or that have it as a chief component. By far the most important are generosity and its inverse, meanness; as it turns out (a. 160), pride and humility are, respectively, not really distinct passions from them—a discovery for which the disjunctive language in the title of a. 54 has left room.

Article 150. That these two Passions are only species of   10
Wonder.

So these two Passions are only species of Wonder. For when we do not
wonder at the greatness or the meanness of an object, we take account of it
neither more nor less than reason tells us we ought to, so that we esteem or   15
scorn it without passion then. And although Esteem is often excited in us by
Love and Scorn by Hatred, that is not universal; it occurs only because one   20
is more or less inclined to consider the greatness or meanness of an object to
the extent that one has more or less affection for it.

Article 151. That one can esteem or scorn oneself.

Now these two Passions may generally have reference to all sorts of objects,   25
but they are especially noticeable when we refer[2] them to ourselves—that is,   **445**
when it is our own merit that we esteem or scorn. And the movement of
the spirits which causes them is so obvious then that it even alters the   5
countenance, the gestures, the walk, and in general all the actions of those
who contrive a better or a worse opinion of themselves than the usual.

Article 152. For what cause one may esteem oneself.   10

And because one of the principal parts of Wisdom is to know in what
manner and for what cause anyone should esteem or scorn himself, I shall
attempt to give my opinion about it here. I observe but a single thing in us   15
which could give us just cause to esteem ourselves, namely the use of our
free will and the dominion we have over our volitions. For it is only the
actions that depend on that free will for which we could rightly be praised   20
or blamed; and in making us masters of ourselves, it renders us like God in a
way, provided we do not lose by laziness the rights it gives us.[3]

2. *se . . . rapporter, rapportons*: two clear examples in support of the suggestion (note
23, Part I) that Descartes uses each of these verbs to specify an intentional object of a
passion, by reference to the thought that normally causes it.
3. Descartes has argued (to Christine, 20 November 1647: AT V, 81-85: K 225-228)
both that good use of one's free will is the individual's supreme good and that it
produces an individual's greatest contentment (see notes 70 and 71 in Part II). Now,
given the new context of esteem and scorn, he argues that it is the only just cause for
esteeming oneself. It is possible that *lascheté*, at 445.23, means cowardice, as it does
elsewhere in the treatise, and not laziness.

25   ## Article 153.   What Generosity consists in.[4]

446   So I believe that true Generosity, which makes a man esteem himself as
        highly as he can legitimately esteem himself, consists only in this: partly in
        his understanding that there is nothing which truly belongs to him but this
        free control of his volitions, and no reason why he ought to be praised or
5   blamed except that he uses it well or badly; and partly in his feeling within
        himself a firm and constant resolution to use it well, that is, never to lack the
        volition to undertake and execute all the things he judges to be best—which
10   is to follow virtue perfectly.

        ## Article 154.   That it keeps one from scorning others.

        Those who have this understanding and this feeling[5] about themselves are
15   easily convinced that every other man can also have them about himself,
        because there is nothing therein that depends on others. That is why they
        never scorn anyone. And though they often see that others commit errors
20   that show up their weakness, they are nevertheless more inclined to excuse
        than to blame them, and to believe that they commit [those errors] through
        lack of understanding rather than lack of good will.[6] And as they do not
        think themselves to be greatly inferior to those who have more goods or
25   honors, or even those who have more intelligence, knowledge, or beauty, or
        in general surpass them in other perfections, neither do they esteem them-
447   selves greatly above those they surpass, because all these things seem to them
        to be extremely insignificant in comparison with the good will for which
        alone they esteem themselves, and which they suppose also to be—or at least
5   to be capable of being—in every other man.

4. Descartes completes a line of thought begun in a. 143, and keeps a promise made in
a. 145. As he had with *pensée* in Meditation 2 (note 18, Part I), Descartes takes an
ordinary word, *generosité*, whose sense was much what it is now, and consciously
extends its use for his own philosophical purposes. In this case, though, the word was
already freighted with the French moralists' ideal of nobility, but it retained both the
ordinary meaning of the English word "generosity" and the etymological association
with the genetic. See notes 12 and 41 to aa. 161 and 204 below.
5. Given *sentir* ("to feel") at 446.5, "feeling" rather than the usual "sensation" is
dictated for *sentiment* here.
6. The generous are inclined more to magnanimity than to rigorous Cartesian good
sense here, as well as in this article's final sentence, where they apparently blur the
disjuncts. For Descartes's views on weakness of will, see note 11 on a. 160 below.

Article 155.   What virtuous Humility consists in.

Thus the most Generous are usually the most humble. And virtuous
Humility just consists in this: our reflection on the infirmity of our nature   *10*
and on the errors we may previously have committed or are capable of
committing—which are no less than those which may be committed by
others—causes us not to prefer ourselves to anyone, but to think that since   *15*
others have their own free will just as we do, they can use it too.

Article 156.   What the properties of Generosity are, and
how it serves as a remedy for all the disorders   *20*
of the Passions.

Those who are Generous in this way are naturally inclined to do great
things, and yet to undertake nothing they do not feel themselves capable of.   *25*
And because they esteem nothing more highly than doing good to other   **448**
men and for this reason scorning their own interest, they are always perfectly courteous, affable, and of service to everyone. And along with this,
they are entirely masters of their Passions[7]—particularly Desires, Jealousy,   *5*
and Envy, because there is nothing whose acquisition does not depend on
them which they think is worth enough to deserve being greatly wished for;
and Hatred of men, because they esteem them all; and Fear, because their   *10*
confidence in their virtue reassures them; and finally Anger, because, esteeming only very little all things that depend on others, they never give their
enemies such an advantage as to acknowledge being injured by them.   *15*

Article 157.   About Pride.

All those who contrive a good opinion of themselves for some other cause,
whatever it may be, have no true Generosity, but only a Pride which is   *20*
always extremely unvirtuous[8]—although it is the more so, the more unjust
the cause is for which one esteems oneself. And the most unjust of all occurs
when someone is proud without any reason—that is, when he gets that way   *25*

7. *Maistres.* A special case of the goal of science which Descartes proclaims in the
Discourse—"to make ourselves, as it were, masters and possessors of Nature": Part 5:
AT VI, 62: CSM I, 142-143. See aa. 152 and 212.
8. *Vitieux.* The contrast is with article 153. See to Elisabeth, 6 October 1645: AT IV,
307-308: K 176.

without thinking he has any merit for which he should be appreciated, but only because he takes no account of merit, and, imagining that glory is nothing but usurpation, believes that those who attribute the most of it to themselves actually have the most. This vice is so unreasonable and so absurd that I would hardly have believed there were men who gave themselves up to it, if no one were ever praised unjustly. But flattery is everywhere so common that there is no man so deficient that he does not often see himself esteemed for things that deserve no praise, or even deserve blame—which gives the most ignorant and stupid occasion to fall into this species of Pride.

Article 158. That its effects are opposite to those of Generosity.

But whatever may be the cause for which we esteem ourselves, if it is anything other than the volition we feel within ourselves always to make good use of our free will, from which I have said Generosity arises, it always produces a most blameworthy Pride, which is so different from that true Generosity that it has completely opposite effects.[9] For since all other goods, such as intelligence, beauty, riches, honors, etc., are usually esteemed more the fewer people they are found in, and are even, for the most part, of such a nature that they cannot be communicated to very many, the Proud try to abase all other men, and, as they are slaves of their Desires, their souls are incessantly agitated by Hatred, Envy, Jealousy, or Anger.

Article 159. About unvirtuous Humility.

As for Servility or unvirtuous Humility, it consists mainly in feeling weak or not very resolute, and in being unable to keep from doing things we know we will later repent of, as though we did not have full use of our free will, and also in believing we cannot survive by ourselves or do without many things whose acquisition depends on others. So it is directly opposed to Generosity, and those whose minds are most servile often turn out to be the most arrogant and haughty, just as the most generous are the most modest

---

9. The contrast in aa. 156 and 158 between the effects of generosity and those of pride constitutes a precedent for many later moralists, such as Spinoza and Rousseau, who also distinguish emotions that are competitive from those that are not, by distinguishing, among the objects of emotions, goods that can be shared from those that cannot. See also a. 183 and to Chanut, 6 June 1647: AT V, 55-56: K 223-224.

and humble. And whereas those whose minds are strong and generous do   *15*
not alter their temper over strokes of prosperity or adversity which befall
them, those whose [minds] are weak and abject are guided by fortune alone,
and prosperity puffs them up no less than adversity renders them humble. In   *20*
fact we often see them abase themselves shamefacedly around those from
whom they expect some profit or fear some evil, and at the same time vaunt
themselves insolently over those from whom they neither hope nor fear
anything.   *25*

Article 160.   What the movement of the spirits is in these   *451*
Passions.[10]

Furthermore, it is easy to understand that Pride and Servility are not only
vices but also Passions, because their excitation is very noticeable externally   *5*
in those who are suddenly puffed up or cast down by some new occasion.
But it may be doubted whether Generosity and Humility, which are virtues,
can also be Passions, because their movements are less noticeable and because   *10*
virtue does not seem to partake of the nature of Passion as much as vice does.
Still, I see no reason at all why the same movement of spirits that serves to
strengthen a thought when it has a foundation that is bad could not also   *15*
strengthen it when it has one that is just. And because Pride and Generosity
consist only in the good opinion we have of ourselves, and differ only in that
this opinion is unjust in one and just in the other, it seems to me that they   *20*
can be referred to a single Passion—excited by a movement composed of
those of Wonder, Joy, and Love, both that which we have for ourselves and
that which we have for the thing making us esteem ourselves. Similarly, on
the other hand, the movement which excites Humility, whether virtuous or   *25*
unvirtuous, is composed of those of Wonder, Sadness, and Love for ourselves, mingled with Hatred for the defects making us scorn ourselves. The   *452*
only difference I observe between these movements is that the [movement]
of Wonder has two properties, the first being that surprise renders it strong
from its inception, the other that it is even in its continuation—that is, that   *5*

---

10. The next two articles examine moral dispositions—virtues and vices—which are
specific cases of the dispositions (*habitudes*) examined in the final articles of Part I.
Descartes agrees with the scholastic tradition that virtues and vices are generated by
repetitions of the same occurrences to which they dispose us (though he makes a
special exception for wonder, as opposed to its excess, astonishment, in a. 78). The
characteristic Cartesian advice—to make good use of reason and attention (see aa. 145
and 146, and note 73 in Part II)—yields in the end "a general remedy for the disorders
of the Passions" (454.7-8).

the spirits keep moving with the same tendency in the brain. The first of
these properties is found much more in Pride and Servility than in Generos-
10   ity and virtuous Humility; the second, on the other hand, is observed more
in the latter ones than in the former two. The reason for this is that vice
commonly springs from ignorance,[11] and that it is those who know themselves least who are most apt to take pride in themselves and humble
15   themselves more than they ought, because whatever happens to them newly
surprises them and, as they attribute it to themselves, makes them wonder at
themselves and esteem or scorn themselves, according as they judge that
20   what is happening to them is to their advantage or not. But because a thing
which has made them proud is often succeeded by another which humbles
them, the movement of their Passion is variable. On the other hand, there is
nothing in Generosity which is not compatible with virtuous humility, nor
25   anything else which can alter them; this makes their movements firm,
constant, and always quite similar to one another. But [these movements] do
not spring so much from surprise, because those who esteem themselves in
30   this way know well enough what causes make them esteem themselves.
453   Still, it can be said that those causes (namely the power of using our free
will, which makes us appreciate ourselves, and the infirmities of the subject
this power is in, which keep us from esteeming ourselves too much) are so
marvelous that whenever we represent them newly to ourselves, they
5   always give off a new Wonder.

Article 161.   How Generosity may be acquired.

And it must be noted that what are commonly named virtues are disposi-
10   tions in the soul which dispose it to certain thoughts, so that they are
different from these thoughts but can produce them and conversely be
produced by them. It must also be noted that these thoughts can be pro-
15   duced by the soul alone, but that often some movement of the spirits
happens to strengthen them, and that then they are actions of virtue and at

11. Descartes frequently flirts, as here and in a. 154, with Plato's doctrine that
knowledge is virtue; but, given a. 48, it would be surprising to see him deny the
possibility of weakness of will. See *Discourse*, Part 3: the fourth maxim of the
provisional moral code contains the famous dictum *il suffit de bien juger, pour bien
faire* ("to do well it suffices to judge well"): AT VI, 27–28: CSM I, 124–125. And see
to Mersenne, end of May 1637: AT I, 366: K 32–33, where Descartes cites the
scholastic slogan *omnis peccans est ignorans* ("all sin is ignorance") but seems to
allow for the moderate position that although we always act for an apparent good,
we sometimes act in defiance of what appears better.

the same time Passions of the soul. So, although there is no virtue to which good birth seems to contribute so much as that which makes one esteem oneself only at his true worth, and although it is easy to believe that all the souls God puts in our bodies are not equally noble and strong (which is the reason I have named this virtue Generosity, following the usage of our language, rather than Magnanimity, following the usage of the Schools, where [this virtue] is not well understood), it is certain nevertheless that good education is very useful for correcting deficiencies of birth, and that if one frequently occupies oneself in considering what free will is and how great the advantages are that come from a firm resolution to use it well and also, on the other hand, how vain and useless all the cares are that trouble the ambitious, one may excite in oneself the Passion and then acquire the virtue of Generosity.[12] And since this is, as it were, the key to all the other virtues, and a general remedy for all the disorders of the Passions, it seems to me that this consideration is well worth noting.

20

25

454

5

10

Article 162.   About Veneration.

Veneration, or Respect, is an inclination of the soul not only to esteem the object it reveres but also to submit to it with a certain apprehension, in order to try to render it propitious. So we have Veneration only for free causes which we judge capable of doing us good or evil, without our knowing which of the two they will do. For we have Love and Devotion, rather than a simple Veneration, for those from which we expect only good, and we have Hatred for those from which we expect only evil; and if we do not judge that the cause of this good or evil is free, we do not submit to it to try to make it propitious. So when Pagans had Veneration for forests, springs, or mountains, it was not properly those lifeless things which they revered, but the divinities they thought presided over them. And the movement of spirits which excites this Passion is composed of the one that excites Wonder and the one that excites Apprehension, of which I shall speak below.

15

20

25

455

5

12. French usage here is rooted in the etymological link between *générosité, généatique,* and *généalogie,* and is imbued with the ideal of noble birth; Descartes thinks it provides a better model than the use of *magnanimité* by the current schools, which do not sufficiently understand the traditional doctrine of this virtue. But while "good birth" (453.18) is a natural source of generosity, anyone can be trained in its acquisition (collate aa. 50 and 154): no one is barred from the Cartesian artificial aristocracy. See note 4 above.

Article 163.   About Disdain.

10   Likewise, what I name Disdain is the inclination the soul has to scorn a free
cause, judging that, even though by its nature it is capable of doing good or
evil, it is nevertheless so far beneath us that it can do us neither. And the
15   movement of spirits which excites it is composed of those which excite
Wonder and Confidence or Boldness.

Article 164.   About the use of these two Passions.

20   And it is Generosity and Weakness of mind, or Servility, which determine
whether these two Passions have a good or a bad use. For the more noble
and generous one's soul is, the greater one's inclination is to render everyone
25   his own; thus one does not merely have a very profound Humility with
respect to God, but also without reluctance renders all of the Honor and
456   Respect that is due to men, to each according to his rank and authority in
the world, and scorns nothing but vices. On the other hand, those whose
5   minds are servile and weak are apt to sin by excess, sometimes in revering
and fearing things worthy only of scorn and sometimes in insolently disdain-
ing those which deserve most to be revered. And they often pass quite
10   suddenly from extreme impiety to superstition and from superstition back to
impiety, so that there is no vice or disorder of the mind they are not capable
of.

Article 165.   About Hope and Apprehension.[13]

15   Hope is a disposition of the soul to be convinced that what it desires will
come to pass, caused by a particular movement of the spirits, namely by that
of Joy and Desire mingled together.[14] And Apprehension is another disposi-
20   tion of the soul, convincing it that it will not come to pass. And it is to be
noted that, although these two Passions are opposites, we can nevertheless
have both of them at once, namely when we simultaneously represent

13. In aa. 165-176, Descartes treats passions that are species of desire or in which
desire is a main component. But see note 15 below.
14. A problem for the psychophysical theory of composite passions must be raised:
On what grounds should it be expected that the *mechanical* combination of the
movements of spirits that separately produce joy and desire will yield a passion that is
phenomenologically or introspectively similar to both of them?

different reasons to ourselves, some making us judge that the fulfillment of 25
the Desire is easy, the others making it appear difficult.

Article 166.   About Confidence and Despair.

And neither of these Passions ever accompanies Desire without leaving
room for the other. For when Hope is so strong that it drives Apprehension 5
out completely, it changes its nature and is named Confidence or Assurance.
And when we are sure that what we desire will come to pass, though we
continue to will that it should come to pass, we nevertheless cease to be
agitated by the passion of Desire, which made us restlessly seek its fulfill- 10
ment.[15] Likewise, when Apprehension is so extreme that it entirely displaces
Hope, it turns into Despair; and this Despair, representing the thing as
impossible, completely extinguishes Desire, which[16] inclines itself only to 15
things that are possible.

Article 167.   About Jealousy.

Jealousy is a species of Apprehension which has reference to our Desire to
retain possession of some good.[17] It arises not so much from the strength of 20
the reasons making us judge that we might lose it as from our great esteem
for it, which causes us to examine even the slightest grounds for suspicion,
and regard them as reasons worth serious consideration.

Article 168.   Wherein this Passion may be honorable.

And since one should be concerned to preserve goods which are very great
more than those which are lesser, this Passion can on some occasions be just 5

15. This may be a case of volition without desire, but it is more likely to be a case of
volition without impassioned or agitated desire—or volition with "desire without
passion," in the words of a. 145.
   How do confidence and despair fit under the rubric of a. 69? On the one hand, a.
166 implies that they cannot be species of desire or contain desire as a component. On
the other hand, it seems that, as a conceptual matter, if you do not desire a thing, then
your conviction that it is unobtainable cannot lead to despair (despair over what?).
Analogously for confidence. Conceivably Descartes will reply that these passions
contain "desire without passion," as note 74 in Part II suggests in a similar case.
16. According to a. 145.
17. Given the suggestion in note 23 in Part I about Descartes's use of *se rapporter*,
jealousy will evidently possess an iterated intentional object.

and honorable. So, for example, a captain guarding a fortress of great importance has a right to be jealous of it—that is, to be suspicious of every means
by which it might be taken by surprise; and an honorable woman is not
blamed for being jealous of her honor—that is, not only abstaining from
doing evil but also avoiding even the slightest causes for slander.

Article 169.   Wherein it is blameworthy.

But an avaricious person is mocked when he is jealous of his treasure, that is,
when he devours it with his eyes and is never willing to leave it for fear he
will be robbed of it; for money is not worth being watched over with such
solicitude. And a man who is jealous of his wife is scorned, because this is a
sign that he does not love her as he should, and has a bad opinion of himself
or her. I say he does not love her as he should, for, if he had a true Love for
her, he would have no inclination to distrust her. It is not even she that he
loves, properly speaking; it is only the good he imagines to consist in having
sole possession of her, and he would not be apprehensive about losing this
good if he did not judge that he was unworthy of it or that his wife was
unfaithful. Finally, this Passion has reference only to suspicions and distrust-
ings, for it is not, properly speaking, being jealous to try to avoid some evil
when one has just cause to be apprehensive about it.

Article 170.   About Irresolution.[18]

Irresolution is also a species of Apprehension, which, keeping the soul
balanced as it were among many actions it is able to do, causes it to execute

18. Every passion has its use, but Descartes's emphasis is on the dangers in the abuse
of this one. Within his provisional ethics, Descartes reported, "my second maxim was
to be as firm and decisive in my actions as I could, and to follow even the most
doubtful opinions, once I had adopted them, with no less constancy than if they had
been quite certain" (*Discourse*, Part 3: AT VI, 24: CSM I, 123). By the time he had
begun to draft the *Passions*, his aim was no longer to live so as to sustain the scientific
enterprise, but to use the scientific knowledge he had gained so as to live well. Facing
the fact that science cannot give certain knowledge about which actions are best, he
concludes the "definitive moral code" with these words: "I have only this to add, that
one must also examine minutely all the customs of one's place of abode to see how far
they should be followed. Though we cannot have certain proofs of everything, still
we must take sides, and in matters of custom embrace the opinions that seem the
most probable, so that we may never be irresolute when we need to act. For nothing
causes regret and remorse except irresolution" (to Elisabeth, 15 September 1645: AT
IV, 295: K 173). See Alquié 1079–1080, n. 1.

none of them, and thus to have time for choosing before deciding. In this,   *15*
truly, it has some beneficial use. But when it lasts longer than necessary and
causes the time needed for acting to be spent deliberating, it is extremely
bad. Now I say it is a species of Apprehension, in spite of the fact that it   *20*
may happen, when someone has a choice of many things whose goodness
appears quite equal, that he remains uncertain and irresolute without on that
account having any Apprehension. For this latter sort of irresolution arises
only from the subject presented and not from any excitation of the spirits;   *25*
that is why it is not a Passion unless one's Apprehension about choosing
badly increases its uncertainty. But this Apprehension is so common and so
strong in some that often, even though they do not have to choose, and see   **460**
only a single thing to take or leave, it holds them back and makes them pause
uselessly to look for others. And then it is an excess of Irresolution, arising   *5*
from too great a desire to do well, and from a weakness of the understanding, which only has a lot of confused notions and none that are clear and
distinct. That is why the remedy for this excess is to accustom ourselves to
form certain and decisive judgments about whatever is presented, and to   *10*
believe that we always discharge our duty when we do what we judge to be
best, even though perhaps we judge very poorly.

Article 171.   About Courage and Boldness.   *15*

Courage, when it is a Passion and not a disposition or natural inclination, is a
certain fervor or agitation which disposes the soul to be exceedingly inclined   *20*
to the execution of the things it wills to do, whatever their nature may be.
And Boldness is a species of Courage, which disposes the soul to the
execution of the things that are most dangerous.

Article 172.   About Emulation.   *25*

And Emulation is also a species of it, but in another sense. For Courage may
be regarded as a genus which is divided into as many species as there are   **461**

To Pierre Mesnard this article "seems to amount to a psychological confession. We
see in its conclusion the psychological reasons that drive Cartesian philosophy to seek
above all a secure and certain Method: Descartes seemed always to require obvious-
ness for his peace of mind, and rules for his own self-restraint. It is worthy of notice
that he returns to the same subject three times, with *Irresolution, Remorse* [a. 177],
and *Repentance* [a. 191]" *(Les Passions de l'âme* [Paris: Boivin et Cie., 1937], p. 154, n.
54). For one explanation why, see note 78 in Part II.

different objects, and into as many others as it has causes. In the first way
Boldness is a species of it; in the other, Emulation. And the latter is nothing
but a fervor which disposes the soul to undertake things it hopes it may
succeed at because it sees others succeed at them; thus it is a species of
Courage, of which the external cause sets the example. I say the external
cause, because there must always be an internal one in addition, which
consists in having one's body disposed in such a way that Desire and Hope
have more power to propel a great quantity of blood to the heart than
Apprehension or Despair has to hinder it.

Article 173.   How Boldness depends on Hope.

For it is to be noted that although the object of Boldness is difficulty—from
which Apprehension or even Despair commonly follows—so that it is in the
most dangerous and desperate matters that the greatest Boldness and Courage is employed, one must nevertheless hope, or even be sure, that the end
one intends will come about, in order to set oneself vigorously against the
difficulties one encounters. But the end is different from the object, for one
cannot be sure and despairing concerning the same thing at the same time.
Thus, when the Decii threw themselves into the midst of the enemy and
flew to certain death, the object of their Boldness was the difficulty of
preserving their life during that action, over which difficulty they had only
Despair, as they were certain to die. But their end was to enliven their
soldiers by their example and cause them to win the victory, of which they
had Hope; perhaps their end was also to have glory after their death, of
which they were sure.[19]

Article 174.   About Cowardice and Fear.

Cowardice is in direct opposition to Courage, and is a languor or coldness
which keeps the soul from being inclined to the execution of the things it

19. Given their normal cognitive causes (aa. 58, 165, 166), hope and apprehension can
coexist, but it would appear that confidence cannot coexist with apprehension or
despair, nor despair with hope. Here Descartes explains that despair can coexist with
both hope and confidence provided they have different ends: preserving my life is
impossible (hence despair); rallying my soldiers is possible though perhaps unlikely
(hence hope mingled with apprehension); and gaining glory is certain (hence confidence).
   The Roman consul Decius Mus sacrificially threw himself into enemy ranks at
Veseris in 344 B.C., out of devotion to the gods, as did his son at Sentinum in 295 and
his grandson at Asculum in 279. See note 24 in Part II: this is a good example of the
kind of devotion discussed in a. 83.

would do if it were free of this Passion. And Fear or Terror, which is   15
opposed to Boldness, is not merely a coldness, but also a disturbance and an
astonishment of the soul, which takes away its power to resist the evils it
thinks are near.

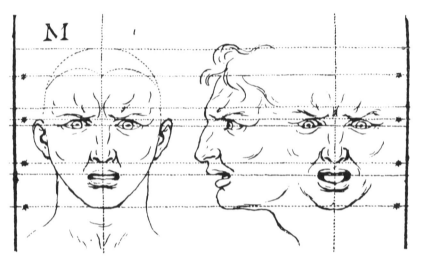

La Crainte—Fear

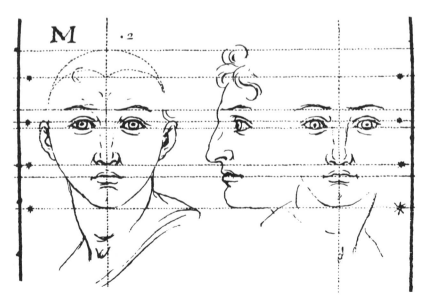

La Hardiesse—Boldness

20   Article 175.   About the use of Cowardice.

25   Now although I cannot convince myself that nature has given men any
        Passion which is always unvirtuous and has no good and praiseworthy use, I
        nevertheless have a lot of trouble divining what these two may be good for.
463   It only seems to me that Cowardice has some use when it frees us from the
        pains we might be incited by probable reasons to take, if other, more certain
5   reasons that have made us judge them useless had not excited this Passion.
        For besides freeing the soul from these pains, it is useful to the body then
        too: hindering the spirits' motion, it keeps us from dissipating our powers.
10   But ordinarily it is very harmful, because it diverts the will from useful
        actions. And because it only arises from not having enough Hope or Desire,
        it is only necessary to increase these two Passions in ourselves in order to
        correct it.

15   Article 176.   About the use of Fear.

        As for Fear or Terror, I cannot see that it can ever be praiseworthy or useful;
        consequently it is not a particular Passion[20]—it is only an excess of Coward-
20   ice, Astonishment, and Apprehension, which is always unvirtuous, just as
        Boldness is an excess of Courage which is always good, provided our intend-
        ed end is good. And because the principal cause of Fear is surprise, there is
25   no better way to free ourselves of it than to make use of forethought and
        prepare ourselves for every eventuality the apprehension of which may
        cause it.

464   Article 177.   About Remorse.[21]

        Remorse of conscience is a species of Sadness which springs from our doubt
5   that something we are doing or have done is good. And it necessarily
        presupposes doubt. For if we were entirely sure that what we were doing

---

20. Descartes gives two grounds for concluding that something is not a passion: it has
no good use (as in this article), and it is not caused by any particular movement of
the animal spirits (as in aa. 170, 194, and 207): see note 30 to a. 194 below and note 39
in Part I. What might appear to be a passion is often an excess of a passion or a vice.
On excesses of the passions, see to Elisabeth, 3 November 1645: AT IV, 331-332: K
184-185; and elsewhere in this treatise aa. 73, 76, 78, 170, 203, and 211.
21. In aa. 177-210 Descartes treats passions that are species of joy or sadness and
passions of which joy or sadness is a prominent component. However, see note 28
below.

was bad, we would abstain from doing it, inasmuch as the will is inclined only to things which have some appearance of goodness. And if we were sure that what we had already done was bad, we would have repentance over it, and not just Remorse. Now the use of this Passion is to make us investigate whether the thing we have doubts about is good or not, and to keep us from doing it another time, so long as we are not sure it is good. But because it presupposes evil, it would be better never to have had reason to feel it; and we can prevent it by the same means as those by which we can free ourselves from Irresolution.

Article 178.   About Mockery.

Derision or Mockery is a species of Joy mingled with Hatred which arises from perceiving some small misfortune in a person we think to be deserving of it. We have Hatred for this misfortune, and Joy in seeing it in someone who deserves it. And when it springs up unexpectedly, the surprise of Wonder causes us to break into laughter, in accordance with what was said above[22] about the nature of laughter. But the misfortune must be small, for if it is great we will not be able to believe that he who has it deserves it, unless we have a very bad constitution or bear a great deal of Hatred toward him.

Article 179.   Why the most imperfect are usually the greatest mockers.

And we see that those who have very obvious defects—for example, those who are lame, one-eyed, or hunchbacked, or those who have received some public affront—are particularly inclined to mockery. For, desiring to see everyone else in as much disgrace as they are in, they are very much pleased by the misfortunes that happen to them, and deem them deserving thereof.

Article 180.   About the use of Bantering.

As for moderate Bantering, which constructively admonishes vices by making them appear ridiculous, but in which one does not laugh at them oneself or express any hatred against anyone, it is not a Passion but a quality of a cultivated man, which shows off the cheerfulness of his temper and the tranquillity of his soul, which are marks of virtue, and often also the

22. Article 126.

ingenuity of his mind, in that he is able to impart a pleasing appearance to the things he mocks.

Article 181.   About the use of Laughter in bantering

And it is not unseemly[23] to laugh upon hearing another's bantering; it may even be such that it would be peevish not to laugh at it. But when one is bantering oneself, it is more fitting to abstain from it, in order not to seem either to be surprised by the things one is saying or to wonder at one's ingenuity in making them up. This makes them surprise those who hear them all the more.

Article 182.   About Envy.

What is commonly named Envy is a vice consisting in a perversity of nature which makes certain people get upset at the good they see happening to other men. But I use the word here to signify a Passion which is not always unvirtuous. Envy, therefore, insofar as it is a Passion, is a species of Sadness mingled with Hatred which comes from seeing good happen to those one thinks to be unworthy of it. This can be rightly thought only of goods of fortune. For as for [goods] of the soul, or even the body, insofar as they originate from birth, the fact that someone has received them from God before he was capable of committing any evil is sufficient for him to be worthy of them.

Article 183.   How it may be just or unjust.

But when fortune sends someone goods he is truly unworthy of and Envy is excited in us just because, naturally loving justice, we are upset that it is not observed in the distribution of those goods, it is a zeal which may be excusable—especially when the good one envies others is of such a nature that it may turn to evil in their hands, as when it is some post or office in whose exercise they may comport themselves badly. Even when one desires the same good for oneself and is kept from having it because others less worthy of it possess it, that renders this passion more vigorous, but it

23. *Deshonneste*: contrary to good manners; lacking decency or modesty. This word's only occurrence in the treatise.

remains excusable, provided that the hatred it contains has reference only to the faulty distribution of the good one envies and not to the people who possess or distribute it. But there are few so just and so generous as to have *25* no Hatred for those who anticipate them in the acquisition of a good not communicable to many, which they have desired for themselves, even though those who have acquired it may be just as worthy of it or more so. **468** And what is commonly envied the most is glory. For although that which others have does not keep us from being able to aspire to it, it nevertheless renders access to it more difficult and raises its cost. *5*

Article 184.   Why the Envious are apt to have leaden complexions.

Furthermore, there is no vice so harmful to human felicity as that of envy. *10* For not only do those who are tainted by it afflict themselves, they also do everything in their power to disturb the pleasure of others. And they usually have leaden complexions—that is, pale, mingled with yellow and black, as though bruised. That is why Envy is named *livor* in Latin. This *15* squares quite well with what was said above[24] about the blood's movements in Sadness and in Hatred. For [hatred] makes the yellow bile which comes from the lower part of the liver and the black which comes from the spleen *20* spread from the heart through the arteries into all the veins, and [sadness] causes the venous blood to have less heat and to flow more slowly than usual, which suffices to render the color livid. But because bile, both yellow and black, can also be sent into the veins through many other causes, and *25* because Envy does not drive it there in large enough quantities to change the color of the complexion unless it is great and of long duration, it should **469** not be thought that all those in whom this color is seen are inclined to it.

Article 185.   About Pity.

Pity is a species of Sadness, mingled with Love or good will toward those we *5* see suffer some misfortune of which we deem them undeserving. So it is opposed to Envy in respect of its object, and to Mockery because it considers it in a different way. *10*

24. In aa. 103 and 105. At 468.15: bruised (*de sang meurtri*)—literally, ecchymotic; *livor*—paleness.

Article 186.   Who are the most subject to pity.

15 Those who feel very weak and very much subject to fortune's adversities seem to be more inclined to this Passion than others are, because they represent the misfortune of others to themselves as possibly happening to them; thus they are moved to Pity by the Love they bear to themselves rather than by that which they have for others.

20 ## Article 187.   How the most generous are affected by this Passion.

Nevertheless, those who are most generous and whose minds are strongest, *470* so that they are apprehensive of no misfortune for themselves and consider themselves beyond the power of fortune, are not free from Compassion when they see the infirmity of other men and hear their lamentations. For *5* one part of Generosity is to have good will for everyone. But the Sadness in this Pity is not bitter; like that caused by the fateful actions we see represented on a stage, it is more on the outside and in the senses than in the *10* inside of the soul[25]—which all the while has the satisfaction of thinking it is

25. Cf. to Elisabeth, 18 May 1645: AT IV, 202-203 (and recall the related texts cited in note 77 in Part II): "But it seems to me that the difference between the greatest souls and those who are servile and common consists mainly in the fact that common souls give in to their passions, and are happy or unhappy only according as things that befall them are pleasing or displeasing; whereas the reasonings of the former [souls] are so strong and powerful that even though they also have passions, often even more forceful than the usual, their reason always remains mistress [over them], making even afflictions serve them and contribute to the perfect felicity they enjoy in this life. For, on the one hand, considering themselves as immortals and as capable of receiving profound contentment, and, on the other hand, considering that they are joined to mortal and fragile bodies, subject to many infirmities and inevitably perishing in a few years, they do everything in their power to render Fortune favorable in this life, but they nevertheless esteem it so little in relation to Eternity that they come close to considering the events of [this life] as we do those of a Play. And just as the sad and lamentable Stories we see represented on a stage often give us as much recreation as cheerful ones do, even though they bring tears to our eyes, so the greatest souls I speak of derive satisfaction within themselves from everything that happens to them, no matter how upsetting and unbearable; and thus, feeling pain in their bodies, they apply themselves to bear it patiently, and the proof of their strength which they get in this way is pleasant to them; and thus, seeing their friends greatly afflicted, they are compassionate over their misfortunes and do everything they can to deliver them from them and do not even fear to risk death on that account if necessary. But nevertheless the witness their conscience bears that they have done

doing its duty in being compassionate to the afflicted. Now there is a difference present here: whereas the common person has compassion for those who lament because he thinks the misfortunes they suffer are extreme- 15
ly grievous, the main object of the Pity of the greatest men is the weakness of those they see lamenting, because they consider that no possible accident could be so great a misfortune as the Cowardice of those unable to suffer it 20
with steadfastness. And even though they hate vices, they do not on that account hate those they see subject to them; for these they have only Pity.

Article 188.   Who is not affected by it.   25

But it is only malicious and envious minds, who naturally hate all men, or those who are so brutish and are made so blind by good fortune or so 471
despairing by bad as to think no further misfortune can befall them, who are insensible to Pity.

Article 189.   Why this Passion provokes one to cry.   5

Finally, in this Passion one cries very easily because Love, sending a lot of blood to the heart, makes many vapors come forth through the eyes, and because the coldness of Sadness, hindering the agitation of these vapors, 10
makes them turn into tears, in accordance with what has been said above.[26]

Article 190.   About Self-satisfaction.

The Satisfaction which those who constantly follow virtue always have is a 15
disposition in their soul which is called tranquillity and repose of conscience. But that which one acquires afresh when one has just done some action one thinks good is a Passion, namely a species of Joy, which I believe to be the 20
sweetest of all, because its cause depends only on ourselves. Nevertheless, when this cause is not just, that is, when the actions from which one draws great satisfaction are not of great importance or are even unvirtuous, it is 472

---

their duty and performed a praiseworthy and virtuous action bestows a happiness on them that is greater than all the sadness with which their compassion afflicts them. Finally, as the greatest prosperities of Fortune never make them conceited and do not make them more insolent, so the greatest adversities cannot cast them down, or render them so sad that the health of the body to which they are joined is harmed."
26. Article 131.

ridiculous and serves only to produce a pride and an impertinent arrogance. This may be observed in particular in those who, believing they are Devout,
5   are merely Bigoted and superstitious—that is, under cover of frequenting the Church, reciting plenty of prayers, wearing their hair short, fasting, and giving alms, think they are entirely perfect, and imagine that they are such
10   great friends of God that they can do nothing which would displease him, and that everything their Passion dictates to them is righteous zeal, even though it sometimes dictates to them the greatest crimes man can commit,
15   such as betraying cities, killing Princes, and exterminating whole peoples just because they do not accept their opinions.

Article 191.   About Repentance.

Repentance is directly opposed to Self-satisfaction; it is a species of Sadness
20   which comes from believing oneself to have done some bad action; it is very bitter, because its cause comes from us alone. Still, this does not keep it from being extremely useful, when it is true that the action we repent of is bad,
25   and we have certain knowledge of that, because it incites us to do better another time. But it often happens that weak minds repent of things they
473 have done without knowing for sure that [those things] are bad; they are convinced of this only because they are apprehensive that it is so, and if they had done the opposite they would repent in the same way. This is an
5   imperfection in them deserving of Pity. And the remedies for this defect are the same ones that serve to get rid of Irresolution.[27]

27. Repentance, unlike irresolution and remorse (aa. 170, 177), need not involve uncertainty. However, in the case of weak minds (as described in a. 48), repentance comes to resemble these passions and to require a similar remedy. According to the provisional moral code, we can avoid both remorse and repentance by following the second maxim (*Discourse*, Part 3: AT VI, 25: CSM I, 123). Elucidating his "definitive moral code," Descartes says that repentance is inappropriate when we have followed our conscience and have done what we judged best at the time (to Elisabeth, 6 October 1645: AT IV, 307: K 176; cf. to Elisabeth, 4 August 1645: AT IV, 265-266: K 165-166). A month later he tells her more specifically that, in effect, repentance is useful just when one has committed one of the errors to be mentioned in aa. 48 and 49 of his work in progress—"repentance . . . is a Christian virtue which is useful for self-correction, not only from errors committed voluntarily but also from those done in ignorance, when some passion has kept one from knowing the truth" (3 November 1645: AT IV, 331). Since, as a. 63 also suggested, repentance is directly opposed to self-satisfaction, a good deal may be inferred about Descartes's opinion of its nature and use from his considerable comments about contentment or self-satisfaction (see note 71 in Part II).

Article 192.   About Approval.[28]

Approval is properly a Desire to see good come to someone for whom one   *10*
has good will, but I use the word here to signify that will, insofar as it is
excited in us by some good action on the part of the one for whom we have
it. For we are naturally inclined to love those who do things we consider   *15*
good, even though no good may accrue to us from them.[29] Approval in this
sense is a species of Love, not of Desire, though the Desire to see good come
to the one whom one approves always accompanies it. And it is commonly   *20*
joined to Pity, because the disgraces we see befalling the unfortunate cause us
to reflect more on their merits.

Article 193.   About Gratitude.   *25*

Gratitude is also a species of Love excited in us by some action on the part of
the one for whom we have it, by which we believe he has done us some   **474**
good or at least had that intention. So it contains everything Approval does,
and this in addition: it is founded on an action that affects us, which we have   *5*
the Desire to reciprocate. This is why it has much more strength, especially
in souls that are even a little noble and Generous.

Article 194.   About Ingratitude.   *10*

As for Ingratitude, it is not a Passion, for nature has put within us no
movement of the spirits which excites it.[30] It is only a vice directly opposed
to gratitude, to the extent that this latter is always virtuous and one of the   *15*

28. The next four passions—approval, gratitude, indignation, and anger—are
described here as containing, not joy or sadness, but rather love or hate mingled with
desire. This appears to violate the spirit of the enumeration which opens Part II.
29. Possibly the people, probably the things they do. A philosophical problem: how
does this sentence square with the thesis of a. 56, that love is aroused by an opinion
that the beloved is beneficial to us? An analogous problem arises in the case of
indignation (aa. 65, 195), when judged against the more general thesis of a. 52 that
every passion is normally aroused by an opinion that its object somehow matters to
us. Solutions must observe the points made in notes 39 and 40 below.
30. The principle Descartes appeals to, in denying that ingratitude is a passion, is the
one set out in a. 37, but, since he surely lacked the physiological data that would
make reliance on that principle possible, he probably relies instead upon the principle
he explicitly rests on in a. 176: that any true passion must have some beneficial use.
See note 20 above.

principal bonds of human society. That is why this vice is present only in
brutish, foolishly arrogant men, who think all things are due them; in stupid
20 ones, who fail to reflect on the benefits they receive; or in weak and abject
ones, who, feeling their infirmity and need, in a servile manner seek the help
of others, and after they have received it hate them, because—lacking the
25 volition to render them in kind or despairing of being able to, and imagining
that everyone is mercenary like them and that no one does good but with
the hope of being recompensed—they think they have deceived them.[31]

475 ## Article 195. About Indignation.

Indignation is a species of Hatred or aversion which one naturally has for
5 those who do some evil, whatever its nature. And it is often mingled with
envy or with pity, but it has nevertheless an altogether different object. For
one is indignant only with those who do good or evil to people who do not
10 deserve it, but one bears envy against those who receive the good, and takes
Pity upon those who receive the evil. It is true that it is, in a way, doing evil
to possess a good one does not deserve. This may be the reason why
15 Aristotle and his followers, supposing that Envy is always a vice, called that
which is not unvirtuous by the name of Indignation.[32]

Article 196. Why it is sometimes joined to Pity and sometimes to Mockery.

20 It is also, in a way, receiving evil to do it, whence some join Pity to their
Indignation and others Mockery, according to whether they incline to good
476 or bad will for those they see committing errors. And thus it is that the
laughter of Democritus and the tears of Heraclitus might have proceeded
from the same cause.[33]

31. Who do the weak and abject think have deceived whom? Either reading is
possible, and neither makes much sense. Another dark saying.
32. In other words, Aristotelians use the label "indignation" for what Descartes calls
virtuous envy, because those who are envied on these grounds do evil "in a way,"
namely in possessing undeserved good, and we are indignant against those who do
evil. See Aristotle *Nicomachean Ethics* II, 7: 1108a30-1108b10; and *Rhetoric* II, 9 and
10: 1386b9-1388a28.
33. See aa. 178 and 185 for the relation of mockery to pity: we have mockery for
those who receive evil fairly, pity for those who receive it unfairly. This picture of
the opposed characters of Democritus and Heraclitus was traditional; Descartes had
read at least two writers who repeat it—Montaigne and Vives. Heraclitus flourished

Article 197. That it is often accompanied by Wonder, and is not incompatible with Joy.

Indignation is also often accompanied by Wonder. For we customarily suppose that everything will be done in the way we judge it ought to be— that is, in the way we deem good; this is why, when things go otherwise, it surprises us, and we wonder at it. Neither is it incompatible with Joy, even though it is more commonly joined to Sadness. For when the evil we are indignant about cannot harm us, and we take into consideration that we would not be willing to do likewise, this gives us some pleasure. Perhaps this is one of the causes of the laughter that sometimes accompanies this Passion.[34]

Article 198. About its use.

Finally, Indignation is observed much more in those who will to appear virtuous than in those who truly are so. For although those who love virtue cannot see the vices of others without some aversion, they become impassioned only over the greatest and most extraordinary. To have great indignation over things of little importance is to be difficult and peevish; to have it over those which are not blameworthy is to be unjust; and to fail to restrict this Passion to the actions of men and extend it to the works of God or of Nature is to be impertinent and absurd—as is done by those who, never content with their circumstances or their fortune, are so bold as to find fault with the governance[35] of the world and the secrets of Providence.

Article 199. About Anger.

Anger is also a species of Hatred or aversion which we have for those who have done some evil or tried to do harm, not just to anyone indifferently but

---

about 500 B.C. and wrote about the ubiquity of impermanence; Democritus lived about 460–370 and proclaimed materialism.

34. An amplification of the explanation given in a. 127.

35. *Conduite*: the only occurrence of this word in the treatise. Descartes probably intends many of the passions he enumerates to rest upon a belief that their object is a "free cause" in the sense specified in aa. 162 and 163. While it is clear why a person who is indignant over the works of God would be impertinent, the intention just alluded to probably helps explain why Descartes would hold that a person who is indignant over the works of Nature is being absurd.

to us in particular. So it contains everything Indignation does, and this in
addition: it is founded on an action which affects us and of which we have
the Desire to avenge ourselves, for this Desire almost always accompanies
it.[36] [Anger] is directly opposed to Gratitude, as Indignation is to Approval.
But is it incomparably more vigorous than these other three Passions,
because the Desire to repel harmful things and avenge oneself is the most
urgent of all. It is Desire joined with Love for oneself that supplies Anger
with just as much agitation of the blood as Courage and Boldness can cause.
And Hatred brings it about that bilious[37] blood in particular, coming from
the spleen and the little veins of the liver, acquires this agitation and enters
the heart, where, because of its abundance and the nature of the bile it is
mixed with, it excites a heat more sharp and burning than that which can be
excited there by Love or by Joy.[38]

Article 200.   Why those it makes flush are less to be feared than those it makes turn pale.

And the external signs of this Passion differ according to the differing
temperaments of people and the diversity of the other Passions which
compose it or are joined to it. So we see some who turn pale or tremble
when they become angry, and we see others who flush or even cry. And we
commonly judge that the Anger of those who turn pale is more to be feared
than the Anger of those who flush. The reason for this is that when
someone is either not willing or not able to avenge himself otherwise than
by looks and words, he employs all his fervor and all his strength as soon as
he is moved, causing him to turn red. In addition, sometimes regret and self-
pity over not being able to avenge himself otherwise cause him to cry. On
the other hand, those who contain themselves and decide to exact a greater
vengeance grow sad from thinking themselves bound to do so by the action
that angers them, and sometimes too they are apprehensive about the evils

36. See to Elisabeth, 1 September 1645: AT IV, 285: K 169.
37. London: "colericke." Not surprisingly, Descartes incorporated some of the traditional wisdom about the four humors into his derivation en physicien of various
temperaments.
38. In to Chanut, 1 February 1647, Descartes derives anger primarily from self-love
and only secondarily from hatred: "Anger can indeed make a man bold, but it
borrows its strength from love of self, which always provides its foundation, and not
from the hatred which is merely an accompaniment of it" (AT IV, 616: K 217).
Descartes speaks of self-love elsewhere at aa. 117, 160, 186, 199, 204, and 205, but he
does not mention it under the head of love in this work. It is probably a disposition,
instituted by nature, rather than a particular passion.

which may follow upon the resolution they have made; this immediately   5
renders them pale, cold, and trembling. But when they chance afterwards to
execute their vengeance, they warm up all the more for having been cooler

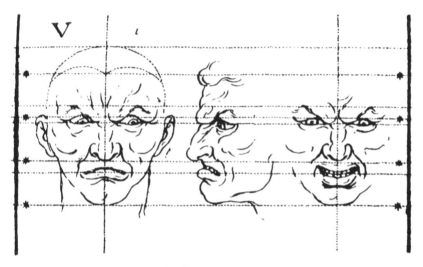

La Colere—Anger

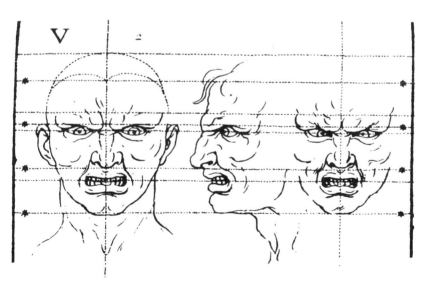

La Colere—Anger

10   at first, just as we see that fevers that begin with chills are usually the most severe.

Article 201.   That there are two sorts of Anger, and that those who have the most goodness are the most subject to the first.

15   This tells us that two species of Anger may be distinguished: one which is very sudden and very obvious externally, but yet has little effect and can easily be calmed, and another which is not immediately so conspicuous, but *20*   gnaws at the heart more and has more dangerous effects. Those with much goodness and Love are the most subject to the first. For it does not spring from a profound Hatred, but from a sudden aversion which takes them by surprise, because, being inclined to imagine that everything must go as they *25*   judge best, as soon as something happens otherwise, they wonder at it and take offense at it—often without the thing affecting them in particular, **480**   because, possessing a great deal of affection, they are concerned about those they love in the same way as they are about themselves. So what would only be a subject of Indignation for someone else is a subject of Anger for *5*   them.[39] And because their inclination to love provides their heart with much heat and much blood, the aversion which takes them by surprise cannot drive so little bile there that it does not immediately cause a great excitation in this blood. But this excitation hardly lasts at all, because the strength of *10*   the surprise does not continue, and because as soon as they perceive that the subject which has upset them ought not to have moved them so much, they repent of it.

Article 202.   That it is weak and servile souls who let *15*   themselves get carried away most by the other.

The other species of Anger, in which Hatred and Sadness predominate, is not immediately so noticeable, except perhaps in making the face turn pale.

---

39. Because the tendency of love is to make us feel for the beloved everything we naturally feel for ourselves (aa. 82, 83; to Elisabeth, 15 September 1645: AT IV, 292-294: K 172-173; to Chanut, 1 February 1647: AT IV, 611-613: K 214-215), it is capable of altering other passions; for example, it transforms mere indignation into anger, as we come to take evil done to our beloved personally. (On the relation of anger to indignation, see aa. 195 and 199.) Cf. a. 203, concerning the similar effect that generosity can have on other passions.

But its strength is increased little by little by the agitation which an ardent 20
Desire for vengeance excites in the blood, which, upon mingling with the
bile being driven to the heart from the lower part of the liver and the spleen,
excites a very sharp and very prickling heat there. And as it is the most
generous souls who have the most gratitude, so it is those with the most 25
pride and those who are the most servile and infirm who let themselves get
carried away most by this species of Anger. For wrongs seem all the greater, 481
the more pride makes one esteem oneself and the more one esteems the
goods they remove; and one esteems them all the more, the weaker and 5
more servile one's soul is, because they depend on others.

Article 203.   That Generosity serves as a remedy for its
excesses.

Finally, although this Passion is useful in giving us the vigor to repulse 10
wrongs, there is nevertheless none whose excesses should be more assiduously avoided, because, disturbing the judgment, they often make one commit errors which are afterwards repented, and sometimes they even keep 15
one from repulsing those wrongs as well as could be done with less excitation. But, as nothing renders it more excessive than pride, just so I believe
that Generosity is the best remedy to be found for its excesses, because, 20
making us esteem very little any goods that can be taken away, and on the
other hand making us greatly esteem liberty and absolute dominion over
ourselves, which we cease to have when we can be injured by anyone, it
limits us to having scorn or at most indignation for the wrongs at which 25
others usually take offense.[40]

Article 204.   About Vainglory.[41] 482

What I call by the name of Vainglory here is a species of Joy founded on
Love of ourselves, arising from our opinion that others praise us or our hope 5

---

40. On a much larger scale than love was observed in a. 201 to accomplish, generosity
alters our passions; here it replaces anger by an impersonal indignation. See to
Chanut, 1 November 1646: "It is true that I consider anger one [passion] that one
must protect oneself against, insofar as it has as its object an injury received. In order
to do that, we must try to elevate our minds so high that the injuries others may do
to us never affect us. But I believe it is just to have indignation in place of anger, and I
confess that I have often borne it against the ignorance of those who wish to be
regarded as learned, when I see it joined to malice" (AT IV, 538).
41. In articles 204-207, Descartes offers his own account of the passions behind the

that they will. So it differs from inner satisfaction, which arises from our opinion that we have done some good action. For we are sometimes praised
10   for things we do not believe to be good, and blamed for those we believe to be better. But both of them are species of self-esteem, as well as species of Joy. For seeing that we are esteemed by others is a reason for esteeming ourselves.

15   Article 205.   About Shame.

Shame, on the other hand, is a species of Sadness, also founded on Love of ourselves, arising from our opinion that we are being blamed or our appre-
20   hension that we will be. It is in addition a species of modesty or Humility, and of diffidence. For when we esteem ourselves so highly that we cannot imagine being scorned by anyone, we cannot easily be ashamed.

25   Article 206.   About the use of these two Passions.

483   Now Vainglory and Shame have the same use, in that they incite us to virtue—the one by hope and the other by apprehension. One merely needs to instruct the judgment about what truly deserves blame or praise, in order
5   not to be ashamed of doing good or grow vain over one's vices, as takes place with many. But it is not good to divest oneself entirely of these Passions, as the Cynics used to do.[42] For though the people[43] may judge very badly, still

---

classical French conception of glory and honor, which, together with generosity (see note 12), helped constitute the ideal of the hero. Though his account is characteristic-ally moderate, he thinks it worth his time to express an opinion about the ideal—by contrast with the last three passions he discusses (a. 210).

42. The Cynics were a philosophical school originating with Diogenes of Sinope (ca. 410-320 B.C.) and lasting into the sixth century A.D. Living a life of asceticism and inspired by an ideal of self-sufficiency, they advocated in particular a disregard for social and political conventions—"Change the currency!" was Diogenes' slogan. In Descartes's France, they were conceived as an extreme version of the Stoics. Both early and late, however, Descartes counsels a degree of regard for custom and the opinions of others: *Discourse*, Part 3, the first rule: AT VI, 23-24: CSM I, 122-123; to Elisabeth, 15 September 1645: AT IV, 295: K 173. And that counsel places a limit on his more famous dictum "To do well it suffices to judge well" (*Discourse*, Part 3: AT VI, 28: CSM I, 125): at least for the "external aspect of our actions," we should sometimes follow those who judge badly.

43. *Le peuple*. Elsewhere in the treatise, this word is used in the plural—at 308.11, 309.8 and 20, 321.31, and 472.14—always to refer to cultural or national conglomer-

because we cannot live without them and because it matters to us to be   *10*
esteemed by them, we should often follow their opinions rather than our
own concerning the external aspect of our actions.

Article 207.   About Impudence.

Impudence or Effrontery, which is a scorn of shame and often of vainglory   *15*
too, is not a Passion, because there is no particular movement of the spirits in
us that excites it; it is rather a vice opposed to Shame and also to Vainglory,
insofar as both are good, as Ingratitude is opposed to Gratitude and Cruelty   *20*
to Pity. And the main cause of effrontery comes from having received great
affronts many times. For there is no one who does not imagine, when he is
young, that praise is a good and infamy an evil much more important in life   *25*
than he finds them to be by experience, when, having received a few
conspicuous affronts, he discovers himself entirely deprived of honor and
scorned by everyone. This accounts for the effrontery of those who, mea-   **484**
suring good and evil only in terms of bodily comforts, see that they enjoy
them after these affronts just as much as before or sometimes even much   *5*
more, because they are discharged from many constraints to which honor
had bound them; and that, if loss of goods is joined to their disgrace,
charitable people may be found who will give them some.

Article 208.   About Distaste.   *10*

Distaste is a species of Sadness, which arises from the same cause from which
Joy has previously arisen. For we are so composed that most of the things
we enjoy are good from our point of view only for a time, and afterwards   *15*
become irksome. This is noticeable above all in drinking and eating, which
are useful only while one has an appetite and are harmful when one no

---

ates of people, with no suggestion of class distinctions. But Boyer's 1700 French-
English dictionary gives, as one meaning of the term in the singular, "the People, the
meaner sort, the mobile, the Vulgar." The present article may therefore provide the
treatise's clearest hint of Descartes's attitudes about the opinions of the lower classes.
That interpretation is fortified by Descartes's use of the word in the *Discourse*: see
the plural occurrences, at AT VI, 6.22, 10.21, 12.09, and 61.14; and contrast the
singular uses, at 16.26 and 31.08. The following article, 207, is reasonably convoluted
and discusses effrontery, which finally turns out not to be a passion at all. At such
places (a. 183 is another), we may fairly suspect Descartes of transcending the bounds
of the official agenda for reasons of politics or controversy.

20   longer does. Because they cease then to be pleasing to the taste, this Passion
has been named Distaste.

Article 209.   About Regret.

25
485   Regret is also a species of Sadness, which has a particular bitterness in that it
is always joined to some Despair, and to the memory of the pleasure Enjoyment has given us. For we never have regret over anything but the goods
we have enjoyed that are lost in such a way that we have no hope of
5   recovering them at the time and in the manner which our regret over them
concerns.[44]

Article 210.   About Lightheartedness.

To conclude, what I name Lightheartedness is a species of Joy with this
10   particular feature: its sweetness is increased by the remembrance of evils we
have suffered of which we feel relieved—just as we would feel unburdened
of some heavy load we had carried on our shoulders for a long time. And I
15   see nothing very noteworthy in these three passions; I have only put them
here to follow the order of the enumeration I made above. But it seems to
me that this enumeration has been useful in showing that we have omitted
none that deserved special consideration.

Article 211.   A general remedy for the Passions.[45]

And now that we understand them all, we have much less reason to fear
25   them than we had before. For we see that they are all in their nature good,
486   and that we have nothing to avoid but misuses or excesses of them, for
which the remedies I have explained could suffice if everyone had enough

44. This time cannot be the time at which the original pleasure occurred, for every
past good is "lost" in that sense. It cannot be the time of the regretting, since a person
who has regret does not necessarily regret not having the goods at that time. It must
be the time at which we want to enjoy those goods again or would want to if we
thought such enjoyment possible. The translation attempts to convey this last interpretation. The verb *regreter*, here "have regret over," occurs elsewhere only at 304.25
in the Preface, where it means "to mourn."
45. The nature of all the enumerated passions having been considered (a. 210), it is
now possible to generalize in the final two articles about their value in human life and
about the remedies for their disorders.

interest in putting them into practice.[46] But because I have included among
these remedies the forethought and skill by which we can correct our   5
constitutional deficiencies, in applying ourselves to separate within us the
movements of the blood and spirits from the thoughts to which they are
usually joined, I grant that there are few people who are sufficiently pre-   10
pared in this way against all sorts of contingencies, and that these movements, excited in the blood by the objects of the Passions, immediately
follow so swiftly from mere impressions formed in the brain and from the

46. On 1 November 1646 Descartes wrote to Chanut: "You seem to infer from the
fact that I have studied the passions that I ought no longer to have any; but I tell
you, quite to the contrary, that in examining them I have found almost all of them
good, and so useful to this life that our soul would have no reason to want to remain
joined to its body for a single moment if it could not feel [*ressentir*] them" (AT IV,
538). And see to Elisabeth, 18 May and 1 September 1645: AT IV, 201-202 and 286-
287: the latter at K 170-171; and to Silhon, March or April 1648: AT V, 135.

The goodness of the passions is a consequence of the perfection of their author.
According to the Sixth Meditation, the perceptions we refer to external objects or to
our body are given to us by God "to inform the mind of what is beneficial or
harmful for the composite of which the mind is a part; and to this extent they are
sufficiently clear and distinct" (AT VII, 83: CSM II, 57). *Mutatis mutandis*, the
same is true of the perceptions we refer to the soul alone—the passions of the soul.

Not only are they by nature good; their misuses and excesses are remediable. The
first remedy Descartes mentions requires long-term preparation: forethought and
skill at altering the connection between bodily movements and thoughts. The
feasibility of this remedy rests on the Principle of Habituation: "although each
movement of the gland seems to have been joined by nature to each of our thoughts
from the beginning of our life, one can nevertheless join them to others by habituation" (a. 50).

The easiest and most generally accessible remedy is to attend skilfully to other
thoughts. That will either distract one from action—the "morals of disengagement"
advised in to Elisabeth, May or June and 15 September 1645: AT IV, 218-222 and
294-295: K 161-163 and 173—or call up reasons for acting otherwise than as passion
suggests—the analogue, for passion and action, of Descartes's way with habitual belief
in the First Meditation.

The propriety of the advice rests on the intrinsic deceptiveness of thoughts
generated by the soul's union with the body (see the passages cited in note 29 in Part
I). The feasibility of the advice rests on our ability (a. 43) to divert our minds at will
and, again, on the Principle of Habituation (in the style exemplified in a. 45).

The capacity to attend to different thoughts is a special case of the capacity to use
free will, guided by reason, in order to discipline one's passions. Like the first remedy
that Descartes mentions in this article, this remedy requires the enlightened and
resolute use of the understanding (which is partially within our control) and the will
(which is absolutely in our control). See to Elisabeth, 4 August and 6 October 1645,
and May 1646: AT IV, 265-266, 306-307, and 411: K 165-166, 175-176, and 194.

15   disposition of the organs, even though the soul may in no way contribute to them, that there is no human wisdom capable of withstanding them when one is insufficiently prepared for them. Thus many cannot abstain from laughing when tickled, even though they derive no pleasure from it. For, in

20   spite of themselves, the impression of Joy and surprise which previously made them laugh for the same reason, being awakened in their fantasy, makes their lungs suddenly swell with the blood that the heart sends there.

25   And so those who are strongly inclined by their constitution to the excitations of Joy, Pity, Fear, or Anger cannot keep from fainting, crying, trembling, or having their blood all stirred up just as though they had a fever,

30   when their fantasy is greatly affected by the object of one of these Passions.

487   But what can always be done on such an occasion, and what I think I can set down here as the most general remedy for all the excesses of the Passions and the easiest to put into practice, is this: when one feels the blood stirred

5   up like that, one should take warning, and recall that everything presented to the imagination tends to deceive the soul, and to make the reasons for favoring the object of its Passion appear to it much stronger than they are,

10   and those for opposing it much weaker. And when the Passion favors only things whose execution admits of some delay, one must abstain from making any immediate judgment about them, and distract oneself by other thoughts

15   until time and rest have completely calmed the excitation in the blood. Finally, when it incites one to actions requiring one to reach some resolution at once, the will must be inclined above all to take into consideration and to

20   follow the reasons opposed to those the Passion represents, even though they appear less strong. As is the case when one is unexpectedly attacked by some enemy, the situation does not allow one to spend any time deliberating. But what it seems to me that those who are accustomed to reflecting on their

25   actions can always do is this: when they feel seized by Fear, try to divert their thought from considering the danger, by representing to themselves the reasons why there is much more security and honor in resistance than in

30   flight; on the other hand, when they feel both the Desire for vengeance and

488   anger inciting them to rashly pursue those attacking them, recall that it is imprudence to lose oneself when one can save oneself without dishonor, and

5   that if the contest is very unequal, it is better to make an honorable retreat or beg for mercy than to expose oneself senselessly to certain death.

Article 212.   That all the good and evil of this life depend on them alone.

10   Finally, the soul may have pleasures by itself. But as for those that are common to it and the body, they depend entirely on the Passions, so that the

men they can move the most are capable of tasting the most sweetness in this life. It is true that [these men] may also find the most bitterness in it, when they do not know how to employ them well and fortune is opposed to them. But Wisdom is useful here above all: it teaches us to render ourselves such masters of them, and to manage them with such ingenuity, that the evils they cause can be easily borne, and we even derive Joy from them all.[47]

15

20

47. The primary use of Wisdom is to teach us mastery over our passions. What is distinctive about "the greatest souls," as we saw in note 25, is that their reasonings "are so strong and powerful that even though they also have passions, often even more forceful than the usual, their reason always remains mistress [over them], making even afflictions serve them and contribute to the perfect felicity they enjoy even in this life" (to Elisabeth, 18 May 1645: AT IV, 202). That mastery is one aspect, indeed the central aspect, of the ideal of dominion over the external world, body, and soul which gives direction to Cartesian science—"to make ourselves, as it were, masters and possessors of Nature."

LEXICON

The Lexicon records the translation of certain French terms. Some are central theoretically; some are ambiguous or for other reasons have more than one English rendering; some are translated similarly as other terms; some have possibly controversial renderings, about which my cards should be laid on the table; and some have a usage in this treatise significantly different from that in twentieth-century French. The Lexicon gives some rules used in this translation but not all the exceptions to them. Terms are given in their present-day spelling. The Lexicon supplements RL's *Lexique*, which should also be consulted. More lexical information occurs in the Preface, notes 20 and 24; Part I, notes 4, 6, 17, 19, and 20; Part II, notes 41 and 68; and Part III, notes 23, 43, and 44.

Terms are typically located by article number (the treatise contains 212 articles), thus: "*empire.* dominion: 50, 152, 203." When a more precise location is wanted, the page and line in AT's Volume XI are added in *italics* (the treatise runs from pages 301 to 488 there), thus: "*répugner.* oppose: 47 *(365.3* and *22–23)*." Terms appearing in the treatise's Preface are located by italicized AT XI page number (the Preface runs from pages 301 to 326), thus: "*modestie.* modesty: *305, 307, 310–312,* . . ." The markers "(A)," "(B)," etc., within entries indicate different *concepts* expressed by the French term; otherwise English *phrases* used to translate that term are given.

admiration. wonder: *passim.*

adresse. ingenuity: *320,* 180, 181, 212.

agrément. delight: 85, 88–90. A species of love. See entries *chatouillement, jouissance, plaisir.*

apercevoir. (1) perceive: 19, 20, 26, 33, 38, 47, 56, 73, 76, 113, 178. (2) see: *314.* Cognate to *perception;* see entries *perception, sentir.*

apprendre. learn: *317, 319,* 44, 75.

bassesse. (1) servility: *305,* 54, 159, 160, 164. (2) lowliness: 149. Theoretically important.

bête. beast: 16, 50, 138. The focus is on the irrationality of beasts.

bruit. (1) fuss: *305, 307, 313, 317.* (2) noise: 46, 50. "Rustling" (of a leaf) at 89 records the same usage.

brutal. brutish: 82, 188, 194. Pertaining to the animal, rather than to the violent, crude, or savage.

cause. Usually, cause. See entries *force, raison.*

chatouillement. titillation: 94, 137. Refers to physical pleasure, primarily tickling. See next entry, and entries *agrément, jouissance, plaisir.*

chatouiller. (1) tickle: 72, 211. (2) titillate: 94. Cognate with previous entry; used metonymously.

concevoir. (1) understand: *308.25, 309.4, 310.14,* 319, 324, 11, 13, 32, 34. (2) apprehend: *317,* 50. (3) conceive: 3, 4, 30, 47, 51, 140. (4) contrive: 151, 157. A theoretical term. The divergence among (1)-(4) is due to context and nuance rather than significant ambiguity. See entries *connaître, entendre, savoir.*

connaître. (1) understand: *308.22, 310.10–11, 314,* 2, 17, 42, 74, 78, 88, 97, 148, 153, 160, 161, 211. Used in this way, the term suggests a more thorough awareness than mere knowledge of a fact. (2) know: *307.16, 316,* 25, 28, 32, 49, 51, 53, 83, 112, 140, 145, 160. A couple of variants: (3) tell: 48. (4) discern: 68, 138, 146. No sharp ambiguity between (1) and (2); often either would do. Many occurrences here are nontheoretical. See entries *concevoir, entendre, savoir.*

content. content: 148, 198. This usage turns on having one's wishes or desires satisfied. Similarly for *contentement* (contentment: 95) and *se contenter* (be content: *302, 309, 311,* 136, 148).

convenable. suitable: 53, 56, 79, 81, 85, 86. 107, 109, 111, 138. Not: decent, acceptable. Theoretically important.

convenir. (1) agree: 82. (2) be congenial: 120. See preceding entry.

crainte. (1) apprehension: 36, 58, 143, 162, 165, 176, 200, 205, 206. N. K. Smith's rendering, at 36, as "anxious apprehension," is just right; the term is used technically to refer to a principal passion, and all uppercase occurrences are translated in this way. (2) fear: *326,* 133. Use (2) is nontheoretical. The same bifurcation occurs with *craindre.* See entry *peur.*

défaut. (1) deficiency: *310,* 76, 161, 211—à la Aristotle, by contrast with "excess." (2) defect: 92, 93, 138, 140, 160, 179, 191—sometimes explicitly broader than "deficiency," and inclusive of "excess." (3) failing: *303.* Apart from the Preface, generally used theoretically. See entries *erreur, faute.*

désir. desire: throughout. Often used technically to speak of the passion. Similarly: *désirable* (desirable: *310*), *désirer* (desire: throughout). See entries *souhaiter, vouloir.*

dessein. Used nontechnically and only in the Preface, to speak teleologically; translated to fit the context: intention: *301;* ambition: *304;* design: *307;* enterprise: *310, 311;* plan: *318, 323, 324;* project: *321, 322;* purpose: *326.*

dévotion. devotion: 83, 162. See note 24 in Part II.

digne. (1) deserving: 62, 178, 179, 191, 195, 206, 210. (2) worthy: 70, 164, 182, 183. An important evaluative term, requiring distinct renderings, since one is normally "worthy" of a good but "deserving" of either good or evil; thus contexts (1) tend to be more general. See entries *mériter* and *valoir.*

disposition. Used to express three distinguishable notions: (A) control, (B) arrangement, (C) tendency. They are rendered, respectively, in these ways: (1) control: 153. (2) disposition: 15, 30, 38, 47 *(366.6)*, 50 *(369.22)*, 94, 130, 211 *(486.14)*. (3) disposition: 119, 165. The use of the same word in contexts (2) and (3) suggests that the notions of arrangement and tendency are connected for Descartes: things' tendencies are grounded in the arrangements of their parts. See entry *habitude.*

douleur. pain: 13, 24, 29, 33, 46, 94, 130, 133, 137, 140. Opposed to *chatouillement* (see entry); distinguished from *tristesse.*

effort. (1) mission: 322. (2) *faire* ——. make a difference: 47 *(365.14, 15)*. (3) impetus: 47 *(365.23)*. (4) assault: 148. Contexts (2)-(4) are important theoretically; only (1) involves something like the present-day notion of attempt or endeavor. What is in question is a "blow" or "impact" made upon the soul—or the soul's reaction to repel such an action.

égard. (1) regard: 1. (2) point of view: 56, 146, 208. Both uses of this particle are theoretically important.

émotion. excitation: throughout. The only term so translated. Cognate with *émouvoir,* which (see entry below) is very close to *exciter.* "Emotion" is never right: Descartes maintains a clear distinction between *émotion* and *passion*—for example, in 27-29, using *émotion* to speak of the genus and *passion* to speak of the species, and in 79, 91, 147, and 148 avoiding the use of *passion* to speak of the *émotions interieures* mentioned there. Descartes uses *émotion* extremely broadly, to refer to a disturbance or commotion or excitation, in soul or body. Thus it refers to physical excitations of the heart, blood, or spirits at 46, 170, 201, and 211 *(487.14)*; to disturbances of the soul—thoughts—in general at 27-29; to judgments at 79; to passions at 79, 89, 91, and 203; and to internal excitations or intellectual analogues of the passions at 79, 91, 147, and 148. At 126, 160, and 211 *(486.24)*, it can be read as referring either to a disturbance in the soul or to the associated disturbance in the body, again suggesting that Descartes uses the term so broadly that he can see its propriety without having to focus first on the mental or the physical. The same holds for his use of *exciter* (see entry). Curiously, the word appears accented only in Part I and at *421.2-3*, and unaccented only in Parts II and III. Uppercase is used only at 147.

émouvoir. (1) move: 26, 53, 94, 118, 186, 200, 201, 212. (2) stir up: 65, 211. The notion is that of stirring up or exciting—see entry *exciter*—and the verb occurs in these contexts: a disturbance stirs someone up; a disturbance is stirred up; something stirs up a disturbance.

empire. dominion: 50, 152, 203. Descartes has in mind the notion of absolute authority, sovereignty, or power (over our passions, our volitions, ourselves). Theoretically important.

entendement. understanding: 75, 76, 91, 94, 102, 145, 146, 170. The only term so translated. Theoretically significant. See entries *esprit, raison.*

entendre. (1) understand: *303, 307, 317,* 30, 112, 128. (2) hear: 181, 187. (3) intend: 80. Hence ambiguous. None of these uses is especially important for theory. See entries *concevoir, connaître, savoir.*

erreur. error: *305, 309, 313,* 5, 6, 47, 49, 144 *(436.21, 22),* 145, 146. See entries *défaut* and *faute.*

esprit. (1) [animal] spirits: 7-9 and *passim.* Appears only in plural form in this usage. (2) intelligence: *311, 320, 322,* 77, 154, 158. (3) mind: *309, 316, 317, 319, 324,* 83, 133, 144, 164, 180, 187, 188, 191. Thus heavily ambiguous and dated in its usage. See entries *entendement, raison.*

estimer. (1) esteem: 55, 150, 151, etc.—the technical use: to have the passion of esteem. (2) consider: *301,* 5, 145, 146, 187, 192. (3) deem: 62, 79, 179, 185, 197. *Considerer* is also often rendered by "consider." While the notion involved in contexts (2) and (3) is not technical, some occurrences there also have theoretical importance. *S'estimer* calls for similarly varied renderings.

évident. plain: *310,* 28, 50, 57, 89, 93, 141.

exactement. (1) carefully: 143, 146. (2) diligently: 148. Not: without error.

exciter. excite: throughout. The verb has a stronger sense than it does today, sometimes tantamount to "create" and not just "heighten" or "sharpen." Used of both the mental and the physical. Very similar to *emouvoir;* see that entry.

exemple. (1) example: at most occurrences. (2) precedent: 45; this rendering is also possible at 172 and 173.

experimenter. find by experience: 3, 17. In Descartes's use, not standard today, the verb marks a form of learning or knowing; it has the implication of success. Its two occurrences have theoretical import. See note 19 in Part I.

fatal. fated: 146. Not necessarily bad. See following entry.

fatalité. (1) fate: 145, 146. (2) fatefulness: 146. As with *fatal,* simply the idea of necessity, with either a good or a bad outcome.

faute. (1) fault: *304,* 6. (2) lack: 110, 127. (3) error: 144 *(437.8),* 154, 155, 196, 203. In (3) the notion is that of mistake, error in judgment, lapse of will, and the like, with no implication of injustice or moral wrong. See entries *défaut, erreur.*

fonction. function: 2, 7, 8, 17, 31, 32, 33, 47, 94. Of fundamental importance here. See entries *usage, utilité.*

force (noun, not adverb). (1) power: *312,* 43, 89, 172, 175. (2) strength:

302, 317, 36, 47–49, 72, 94, 147, 167, 193, 200, 201.   (3) force: 11, 14, 16, 70, 96, 102, 172.   In addition, there are some idiomatic renderings. A single notion, very widely applied—in (1) to the power of a volition, a passion, or a soul; in (2) to the strength of a person, soul, mind, passion, or nerves; and in (3) to bodily force. See entries *cause, pouvoir, puissance.*

    générosité.   generosity: 54, 145, 153, 156–161, 164, 187, 203. Similarly for *généreux:* generous: *322,* 83, 155, 156, 159, 164, 183, 187, 193, 202. Theoretically central. See notes 4 and 12 in Part III.

    habitude.   (1) habituation: 44 *(361.19* and *23),* 50 *(368.27–369.1, 369.15–16).*   (2) disposition: 44 *(362.16),* 50 *(369.6* and *17),* 54, 161, 171, 190.   (3) habit: 78.   A single basic notion; nuances and context dictate varying renderings. Extremely important for the theory. See entry *disposition.*

    homme.   man. Descartes sometimes has the species in mind (as at 36 and 153), sometimes the male of the species (as at 82)—much like English-speaking people who use "man" for both purposes. Hence this uniform rendering of *homme.* I may wish that Descartes had used two different words for these two situations, but the translator's task is not to improve on his use but to document it, in part to supply his critics the correct target. Descartes uses masculine pronouns in both ways too.

    horreur.   abhorrence: 50, 85, 88, 89. Opposed to *agrément* (see entry).

    humeur.   (1) temper: *305, 307, 310, 322, 323,* 159, 180.   (2) humor: 98.   In contexts (1) Descartes employs an old use of the term, to mean temperament, something that most people (and Descartes is no exception) thought to be a reflection of the varying balance of bodily fluids or humors referred to in context (2).

    industrie.   (1) artifice: **44,** 47.   (2) skill: 50, 211.   Old uses of this term, extremely important in this treatise; the notion is of activity that is conscious and skilful, perhaps even cunning.

    instituer.   (1) construct: 6.   (2) institute: *314,* 36, 89, 90, 94.   In the second use, cognate with *institution* in the second use noted in that entry.

    institution.   (1) education: 161.   (2) institution: 50, 137.   The latter is an older use, important here: Descartes uses it to speak of a primitive or innate disposition, one not subject to variation, as an *humeur* would be, or amenable to *industrie,* as an *habitude* would be.

    jouissance.   enjoyment: 90, 91, 141, 209. See entries *agrément, chatouillement, plaisir.*

    libre.   free: 12, 41; also, in "free cause," at 55, 162, 163; in "free control," at 153. See next entry.

    libre arbitre.   free will: *144,* 146, 152, 155, 158–161. See entry *libre. Volonté* is not used in this context (see entry).

    mal.   (1) misfortune: 48, 178–179, 185–188.   (2) illness: *310* (and "headache" at 136).   (3) ill: 147.   (4) evil: 48, 55, and all other occurrences save a few idiomatic constructions.

mérite.   merit: 151, 157, 192.

mériter.   (1) deserve: *304, 305,* 142, 156, 157, 164.   (2) be worth: 76, 161.   Very similar to *être digne;* see entries *digne* and *valoir.*

modeste.   (1) moderate: 180.   (2) modest: 159.   The first is an older use—the notion of the moderate or temperate; the second is reflected in Descartes's use of *modestie* (see entry).

modestie.   modesty: *305, 307, 310–312,* 205.

naturel (noun, not adjective).   (1) constitution: 133, 134, 178, 211.   (2) (with *de*) constitutional: 77, 211.   Not: spontaneity or naturalness.

objet de dehors.   object outside us: 12, 13, 22.

objet extérieur.   external object: 29. Same notion as with previous entry.

obliger.   (1) obligate: *303, 306, 310.30, 323, 326;* related idiomatic rendering at *322.*   (2) oblige: 1.   (3) bind: 76, 200, 207.   (4) compel: *310.21,* 102.   (5) force: 127.   In contexts (1) the verb expresses moral obligation; in (2)–(5) it expresses the notion of forcing, binding.

offenser.   (1) injure: 94, 127, 148, 156, 203.   (2) shock: 136.   These are older uses of this verb.

s'offenser.   take offense: *311,* 201, 203.

paraître.   Used in two distinct ways, each somewhat different from the present ones: (A) become evident.   (1) be discernible: *308, 318.*   (2) be apparent: *310,* 1, 51.   (3) become apparent: 30, 37, 83, 118.   (4) become noticeable: 47.   (5) be noticeable: 117, 160, 208.   (6) be conspicuous: 201.   (7) appear: 211.   In the context *faire* ——, rendered idiomatically— show up: 154; show off: 180.   (B) seem.   (1) appear: 75, 78, 79, 116, 138, 165, 170, 180, 198.   (2) seem: 202, 211 *(487.20).* ("Seem" normally renders *sembler.*)

perception.   perception: 17, 19–28, 34, 41. Theoretically central. See entries *apercevoir, sentiment.*

peur.   fear: throughout. Used technically as the name of the excess of a passion. See entry *crainte.*

plaisir.   pleasure: 50, 94, 95, 146, 147, 184, 197, 209, 211, 212. Used non-theoretically. See entries *agrément, chatouillement, jouissance.*

pouvoir.   power: *319.10, 321, 323, 325,* 41, 45, 47 *(365.28),* 50, 73, 122, 147, 148, 174, 184, 187. Sometimes used technically. See entries *force* and *puissance.*

prétendre.   (1) maintain: *303, 305.21, 306, 311.*   (2) claim: *304, 305.11.*   (3) aim for: *326.*

puissance.   power: *319.12–13,* 47 *(366.10),* 160. Theoretically significant. See note 47 in Part I, and entries *force* and *pouvoir.*

raison. Three notions: (A) ground. Usually, reason; sometimes various related terms, like explanation or ground. cause: only at *309*, 72, 125, 152. See entry *cause*.   (B) intellect. reason: 47, 50, 76, 85, 90, 138, 146, 150. See entries *entendement, esprit.*   (C) proportion, in the idiom *à —— de.*   (1) in accordance with: 1.   (2) in proportion to: 30, 52.   (3) to the extent that: 49, 150.   (4) in respect of: 185. See note 32 in Part I.

rapporter.   refer: 1, 22-25, 27, 29, 62, 65, 66, 68, 140, 151, 160. Theoretically important. See next entry and note 23 in Part I.

rapporter, se.   (1) have reference: 25, 26, 29, 62, 80, 82, 85, 87, 137, 143, 151, 167, 169, 183. (2) be related: 30, 31. (3) correspond: 36, 41. See above entry.

répugnance.   (1) opposition: 47.   (2) reluctance: 164.   Only the second use is common today.

répugner.   oppose: 47 *(365.3* and *22-23).* See the preceding entry.

savoir.   (1) know: *304, 306, 307* (except for *307.16), 309, 310, 312, 313, 315, 317, 320, 323, 325*, 7, 8, 11, 13, 30, 31, 50, 68, 75, 87, 88, 94, 98, 113, 144, 152, 159, 162.   (2) understand: *305, 309.30,* 12, 146.   (3) be aware: *314.*   No sharp ambiguity behind these three uses. The verb is also rendered (now ambiguously) by "be able," throughout, and sometimes by idiomatic constructions. See entries *concevoir, connaître, entendre.*

science.   science: *306, 309, 310, 313-317, 319, 322*, 1, 76. The classical sense was of learning or intellectual acquaintance with a field. The writer uses the word in its *present* sense, hinting only once (76) at the older use.

sens.   Three different notions: (A) the physiological variety: part of the sensory apparatus, e.g. one of the five senses; never "sensation," for which *sentiment* (see entry) is used. sense: 7, 8, 12, 13, 16, 22, 23, 31, 32, 46, 47, 51, 52, 70-72, 75, 85, 89, 94, 101, 106, 111.   (B) the linguistic variety. Here "meaning" is preferred; *sens* used in this way seems interchangeable with *signification* (see entry).   (1) meaning: 44.   (2) context: 137 (see note 60 in Part II).   (3) sense: 172.   Also in the construction *en vrai ——,* at face value: *307.*   (C) the construction *commun ——,* common sense: 77.

sensible.   capable of being sensed: *316*, 34, 46.

sensitif.   sensitive: 47, 68.

sentiment.   (1) sensation: 13, 23, 25, 27-29, 40, 94, 128, 136, 137.   (2) feeling: *322*, 154 (see note 5 in Part III).   Here (1) is fundamental; cf. our readings of *sens* (A), *sensible, sensitif.* Descartes maintains a clear contrast with *perception* (see entry), which stands to *sentiment* as genus to species.

sentir.   feel: 1, 23-26, 31, 33, 36, 46, 72, 89, 90, 97-100, 110, 119, 147, 153, 158, 177, 194, 211. The subject-terms that Descartes uses with this verb refer to us, to men, and to souls. The accusatives refer to a wide variety of items: external things or contact with them, movements, conditions of or alterations in the body, imagined bodily alterations, pains and the like, passions, the "effects" of the passions, inner excitations of the soul, volitions, resolve, and the like, one's inclinations and dispositions. Sometimes the accusatives are "internal," referring to the feeling itself. In each case, the English verb "feel" will do; not so with *apercevoir* (see entry) and the like: cf. 33, where both occur. See note 28 in Part I.

signification. (1) sense: 21, 25, 41, 44, 192. The preferred rendering. (2) meaning: 50. See entry *sens.*

soin. interest: *303*, 211; care: *307*, *326*, 31, 161; assiduity: *308*, 203; diligence: *308;* mission: *322;* solicitude: 82, 169; anxiety: 138; concern: 144, 168. Sometimes these nouns are collapsed into cognate words. A much wider use of this word than is common today. While not used technically, the word has mild theoretical import.

souhaiter. wish: *passim.* A nontechnical variant on *désirer.* See entry *désir.*

souverain. supreme. Used to qualify *divinité* at 83 and *remède* at 144, 148. Not: infallible or politically supreme.

succès. outcome: 48, 146, etc., with no implication of favorableness.

symboliser avec. partake of the nature of: 160 *(451.11).* Pierre Mesnard's gloss is "use the dynamism of"; Rodis-Lewis's is "agree with." Boyer's 1700 dictionary gives "to Symbolize, concur." A fragment from the O.E.D. entry for "to symbolize" is instructive:

> *intr.* To agree or harmonize in qualities or nature (or in some quality); *s.with,* to partake of the qualities or nature of; hence often = to be like, resemble. (A technical term of early physics, said of elements or other substances having qualities in common; hence in general use.) *Obs.*

Some uses given there:

> Sylvester, 1591: But Aire turne Water, Earth may Fierize, Because in one part they do symbolize. Jackson, 1613: Thrice happie is that Land . . . where civill pollicie and spiritual wisedome . . . doe rightly symbolize. H. More, 1687: It is as much Spiritual as before, and does not herein symbolize with Matter, but approves itself contrary thereto.

usage. Three notions are expressed by this word, each theoretically central: (A) practice or custom. (1) practice: *304*, *314*, 50. (2) use: 78. (B) de facto use or employment, whether beneficial or harmful. use: for example *431.3–9*, *455.20.* (C) benefit. use: 52, 137, 139, etc. This last is no longer common. See entries *fonction, utilité.*

utilité. (1) profit: *303*. (2) utility: *305*, 74, 144. See entries *fonction, usage.*

valoir. be worth: *305*, *306*, 142, 156. Also rendered idiomatically. An older use, very similar to Descartes's use of *mériter.* See entries *mériter, digne.*

vicieux. unvirtuous: *306*, 157, 159, 160, 175, 176, 182, 190, 195. What is needed is the opposite of "virtuous," and "vicious" will no longer do.

volonté. (1) volition. (2) will. The first rendering is generally used for the act of the soul, the second for the capacity or faculty to exercise it—or occasionally for the soul itself which possesses that capacity. Nearly always used in a consciously theoretical way. See note 19 in Part II and entries *libre arbitre, vouloir.*

vouloir. (1) will. (2) want. (3) be willing. More often than not used theoretically, to correspond with *volonté.* Descartes always maintains a sharp contrast with *désirer,* which corresponds with *désir*—a passion rather than an action of the soul. See entries *désir, volonté.*

Index to Lexicon

To locate Lexicon entries which shed light on terms appearing in the book, use this index and the Lexicon's cross-references.

abhorrence	*horreur*	experience	*experimenter*
apparent	*paraître*	fate	*fatalité*
appear	*paraître*	fear	*peur*
apprehend	*concevoir*	feel	*sentir*
apprehension	*crainte*	feeling	*sentiment*
artifice	*industrie*	force	*force*
beast	*bête*	free	*libre*
brutish	*brutal*	function	*fonction*
cause	*cause*	generosity	*générosité*
conceive	*concevoir*	habit	*habitude*
constitution	*constitution*	habituation	*habitude*
content	*content*	humor	*humeur*
defect	*défaut*	ingenuity	*adresse*
deficiency	*défaut*	injure	*offenser*
delight	*agrément*	institute	*instituer*
deserve	*mériter*	institution	*institution*
deserving	*digne*	intelligence	*esprit*
desire	*désir*	know	*savoir*
devotion	*dévotion*	learn	*apprendre*
disposition	*disposition*	man	*homme*
dominion	*empire*	meaning	*sens*
education	*institution*	merit	*mérite*
enjoyment	*jouissance*	mind	*esprit*
error	*erreur*	modesty	*modestie*
esteem	*estimer*	move	*émouvoir*
evil	*mal*	noticeable	*paraître*
example	*exemple*	obligate	*obliger*
excitation	*émotion*	oppose	*répugner*
excite	*exciter*	outcome	*succès*

pain	*douleur*	strength	*force*
perceive	*apercevoir*	suitable	*convenable*
perception	*perception*	supreme	*souverain*
plain	*évident*	temper	*humeur*
pleasure	*plaisir*	titillation	*chatouillement*
power	*pouvoir*	understand	*connaître*
practice	*usage*	understanding	*entendement*
precedent	*exemple*	unvirtuous	*vicieux*
reason	*raison*	use	*usage*
refer	*rapporter*	utility	*utilité*
reference	*rapporter, se*	volition	*volonté*
science	*science*	want	*vouloir*
seem	*paraître*	will (noun)	*volonté*
sensation	*sentiment*	will (verb)	*vouloir*
sense	*sens*	willing	*vouloir*
servility	*bassesse*	wish	*souhaiter*
skill	*industrie*	wonder	*admiration*
spirit	*esprit*	worth	*valoir*
stir up	*émouvoir*	worthy	*digne*

BIBLIOGRAPHY

This bibliography lists important editions, partial and complete English translations, selected foreign-language works, and English-language works. Multiple publication dates indicate successive editions of books. I have personally confirmed the information about each work. I am greatly indebted to compilers of previous bibliographies, and I am particularly grateful to Vere Chappell and Willis Doney, who generously shared, before its publication, results from their work *Twenty-Five Years of Descartes Scholarship, 1960–1984* (New York: Garland Publishing Company, Inc., 1987).

1. EDITIONS OF DESCARTES'S TREATISE.

Many editions of *Les passions de l'âme* exist. Those listed are particularly worthy of notice for one reason or another. They are in chronological order.

Les Passions de l'ame. Par René Des Cartes. Amsterdam: Louys Elzevier, and Paris: Henry le Gras, 1649 and 1650.

Oeuvres de Descartes. Edited by Victor Cousin. Eleven volumes. Paris: F. G. Levrault, 1824–1826. The treatise appears in Volume 4.

Oeuvres de Descartes. Edited by Charles Adam and Paul Tannery. Twelve volumes. Paris: Cerf, 1897–1913; J. Vrin, 1957–1968. The treatise appears in Volume XI, along with Adam's Introduction and an Appendix on the 1650 Latin translation.

Les passions de l'âme. Edited by Pierre Mesnard. Paris: Boivin & Cie, Éditeurs, 1937.

Les passions de l'âme. Illustrated [with art deco watercolored line drawings] by J. Touchet. Paris, 1940. A coffee-table book.

Les passions de l'âme. Edited, with Introduction and notes, by Geneviève Rodis-Lewis. Paris: J. Vrin, 1955, 1964; 1966 and 1970 (revisions of second edition).

Oeuvres philosophiques de Descartes. Edited by Ferdinand Alquié. Three volumes. Paris: Éditions Garnier Frères, 1963 (Vol. I), 1967 (Vol. II), 1973 (Vol. III). *Les Passions de l'âme* appears in Volume III, with the editor's Introduction and notes.

Die Leidenschaften der Seele. French text with German translation and introduction by Klaus Hammacher. Hamburg: F. Meiner, 1984.

Les passions de l'âme, précédé de "La pathétique cartésienne." Edited, with a 150-page essay, by J[ean]-M[aurice] Monnoyer. Paris: Gallimard, 1988.

2. ENGLISH TRANSLATIONS.

Complete and partial English translations of the *Passions*, in chronological order. Unless otherwise noted, "complete" translations include all of Parts I–III but not the Preface.

The passions of the soule in three books . . . . By R. Des Cartes. And translated out of French into English. London, Printed for A. C. and are to be sold by J. Martin, and J. Ridley . . . , 1650. Translator anonymous. Contains a complete translation, including the only English version of the Preface other than the present one.

The Philosophy of Descartes in Extracts from his Writings. Selected and translated by Henry A.P. Torrey. New York: Henry Holt and Company, 1892. Translated from the Cousin French edition. From articles 1–8, 16, 30–34, 40–44, 47, 51–53, 68–69, 74, 79–80, 86, 91–92, 96, 137, 144–156, 185–187, 212.

The Philosophical Works of Descartes. Translated by Elizabeth S. Haldane and G.R.T. Ross. Two volumes. Cambridge: Cambridge University Press, 1912, 1931. Volume I contains a complete translation of *Passions* by Haldane.

Descartes. Selections. Edited by Ralph M. Eaton. New York: Charles Scribner's Sons, 1927. Contains selections from Haldane and Ross's translation of articles 1–11, 16–19, 30–36, 40–43, 51–52, 69–71, 74, 79, 82, 86, 91–92, 96–101, 112–113, 124–128, 132, 145–146, 148–149, 167, 171, 174, 178–181, 184, 199–200, 211–212.

Descartes' Philosophical Writings. Selected and translated by Norman Kemp Smith. London: Macmillan & Co. Ltd., 1952. Articles 1–6, 17–50, 52–53, 69–78.

Essential Works of Descartes. Translated by Lowell Bair. Introduction by Daniel J. Bronstein. New York: Bantam Books, 1961. Complete translation of *Passions*.

The Essential Descartes. Edited with Introduction by Margaret D. Wilson. New York: The New American Library of World Literature, 1969. Contains the Haldane and Ross translation of unnumbered selections from articles 1–7, 11–13, 16–32, 34–36, 38, 41, 44–45, 47–48, 50, with the editor's improvements of articles 12 and 30.

The Philosophical Writings of Descartes. Edited by John Cottingham, Robert Stoothoff, and Dugald Murdoch. Two volumes. Cambridge: Cambridge University Press, 1985. Volume I contains a complete translation of *Passions* by Stoothoff.

3. FOREIGN-LANGUAGE BOOKS, PARTS OF BOOKS, AND ARTICLES.

What follows is a selection, from a vast literature, of the works I judge to be most valuable. Where only certain chapters or essays in books have such value, they are mentioned explicitly.

Adam, Charles. *Vie et Oeuvres de Descartes: Étude Historique. Supplement à l'édition de Descartes*. Volume XII of AT. Paris: Cerf, 1910; J. Vrin, 1964. Book V, Chapters I and IV.

Alain (pseudonym of Emile Chartier). *Idées*. Paris: Paul Hartmann Éditeur, 1932. The essay "Étude sur Descartes."

Alquié, Ferdinand. *La découverte métaphysique de l'homme chez Descartes*. Paris: P.U.F., 1950, 1966. Chapters II, XV, XVI.

————— *Descartes. L'homme et l'oeuvre*. Paris: Hatier, 1950, 1960, 1969. Chapter 5.

Beyssade, Jean-Marie. "La classification cartésienne des passions." *Revue internationale de philosophie* 37 (1983) 278–287.

Cahné, Pierre Alain. *Un autre Descartes: Le philosophe et son langage*. Paris: J. Vrin, 1980.

Cassirer, Ernst. *Descartes, Corneille, Christine de Suede.* Translated by Madeline Frances and Paul Schrecker. Paris: J. Vrin, 1942. Part I, Chapter I, and Part II, Chapter IV.

Combès, Joseph. *Le dessein de la sagesse cartésienne.* Lyon: Emmanuel Vitte, Éditeur, 1960.

Descartes. Cahiers de Royaumont, Philosophie No. II. Paris: Les Éditions de Minuit, 1957. Two essays: (1) Lefebvre, H[enri]. "De la morale provisoire à la générosité." (2) Rodis-Lewis, Geneviève. "Maîtrise des passions et sagesse chez Descartes."

Espinas, Alfred. *Descartes et la morale.* Two volumes. Paris: Éditions Bossard, 1925. Particularly Volume II, Chapter III.

Gouhier, Henri. *Essais sur Descartes.* Paris: J. Vrin, 1937, 1949, 1973. Essay 6: "La philosophie de l'homme concret."

Guenancia, Pierre. *Descartes et l'ordre politique.* Paris: P.U.F., 1983.

Hammacher, Klaus. "La Raison dans la vie affective et sociale selon Descartes et Spinoza." *Études philosophiques de la France et de l'étranger* (1984) 73-81.

Lanson, Gustave. "Le Héros cornélien et le 'généreux' selon Descartes." *Revue d'histoire litteraire de la France* 1 (1984) 397-411. Also in his *Hommes et livres.* Paris: Lecène, Oudin et Cie., 1885.

Laporte, Jean. *Le rationalisme de Descartes.* Paris: P.U.F., 1945, 1950.

Lefèvre, Roger. *L'humanisme de Descartes.* Paris: P.U.F., 1957. Book One.

Matheron, Alexandre. "Amour, digestion et puissance selon Descartes." *Revue philosophique de la France et de l'étranger* (1988) 433-445.

———. "Psychologie et politique: Descartes: la noblesse du chatouillement." *Dialectiques* 6 (1974) 79-98.

Mesnard, Pierre. *Essai sur la morale de Descartes.* Paris: Boivin & Cie, Éditeurs, 1936.

Philipse, H. *Zekerheid in wetenschap en leven: een analyse van het begrip zekerheid in de ethiek van Descartes.* Delft: Eburon, 1986.

Plessner, Paul. *Die Lehre von den Leidenschaften bei Descartes: Ein Beitrag zur Beurteilung seiner praktischen Philosophie.* Leipzig: Gustav Fock, 1888.

Quercy, P[ierre]. "Remarques sur le traité des passions de Descartes." *Journal de psychologie normale et pathologique* 21 (1924) 670–693.

Röd, Wolfgang. *Descartes: Die Genese des Cartesianischen Rationalismus.* München: Verlag C.H. Beck, 1964 (under the title *Descartes: Die innere Genesis des cartesianischen Systems*), 1982. Chapter VII.

Rodis-Lewis, Geneviève. *L'Individualité selon Descartes.* Paris: J. Vrin, 1950. Published under surname Lewis.

———— *La morale de Descartes.* Paris: P.U.F., 1957, 1962, 1970.

———— *L'Oeuvre de Descartes.* Two volumes. Paris: J. Vrin, 1971. Chapter VII and Conclusion, with notes.

Segond, J[oseph]. *La sagesse cartésienne et la doctrine de la science.* Paris: J. Vrin, 1932. Chapter XI.

Serrurier, Cornelia. *Descartes: l'homme et le penseur.* Paris: P.U.F., 1951. Chapter ix.

Vuillemin, Jules. "Le Bonheur selon Descartes." *Tijdschrift voor Filosofie* 49 (1987) 230–240.

———— "L'intuitionnisme moral de Descartes." *Kant-Studien* 79 (1988) 17–32.

4. ENGLISH BOOKS AND PARTS OF BOOKS.

Deplorably few works in English have a substantial concern with Descartes's treatise. I encourage the reader to help create such a literature. In the meantime, sections 4 and 5 are, to my knowledge, exhaustive.

Alain (pseudonym of Emile Chartier). *Alain on Happiness.* Translated by Robert D. and Jane E. Cottrell. New York: Frederick Ungar Publishing Company, 1973. *Passim,* but especially essays 6, 11, 15, 72, 76, and 78.

Balz, Albert G.A. *Descartes and the Modern Mind.* New Haven: Yale University Press, 1952. Chapter 33.

Carter, Richard B. *Descartes' Medical Philosophy: The Organic Solution to the Mind-Body Problem.* Baltimore: The Johns Hopkins University Press, 1983.

Caton, Hiram. *The Origin of Subjectivity: An Essay on Descartes.* New Haven: Yale University Press, 1973. Chapter 6.

Cottingham, John. *Descartes.* Oxford: Basil Blackwell Ltd, 1986. Chapter 6.

Curley, Edwin. *Behind the Geometrical Method: A Reading of Spinoza's "Ethics."* Princeton: Princeton University Press, 1988. Chapter III.

Gibson, A[lexander] Boyce. *The Philosophy of Descartes.* London: Methuen & Co. Ltd., 1932. Chapter X.

Grene, Marjorie. *Descartes.* Minneapolis: University of Minnesota Press, 1985. Chapter 2.

Gueroult, Martial. *Descartes' Philosophy Interpreted According to the Order of Reasons.* Translated by Roger Ariew. Two volumes. Minneapolis: University of Minnesota Press, 1984. Volume Two.

Horowitz, Louise K. *Love and Language: A Study of the Classical French Moralist Writers.* Columbus: Ohio State University Press, 1977.

Keeling, S[tanley] V[ictor] *Descartes.* New York: Oxford University Press, 1934, 1968. Chapter VIII.

Kenny, Anthony. *Action, Emotion and Will.* New York: Humanities Press, 1963. Chapter 1.

Keohane, Nannerl O. *Philosophy and the State in France: The Renaissance to the Enlightenment.* Princeton: Princeton University Press, 1980. Chapter 6.

Levi, Anthony, S.J. *French Moralists: The Theory of the Passions, 1585 to 1649.* Oxford: Clarendon Press, 1964. Chapter 10.

Magnus, Bernd, and James B. Wilbur, editors. *Cartesian Essays: A Collection of Critical Essays.* The Hague: Martinus Nijhoff, 1969. An essay: Bertocci, Peter A. "The Person and his Body: Critique of Existentialist Responses to Descartes."

Marks, Joel, editor. *The Ways of Desire.* Chicago: Precedent Publishing, Inc., 1986. An essay: Baier, Annette. "The Ambiguous Limits of Desire."

Paulson, Michael G. *The Possible Influence of Montaigne's "Essays" on Descartes' "Treatise on the Passions."* Lanham, MD: University Press of America, Inc., 1988.

Rorty, Amélie Oksenberg, editor. *Essays on Descartes' "Meditations".* Berkeley: University of California Press, 1986. An essay: Rorty, Amélie Oksenberg. "Cartesian Passions and the Union of Mind and Body."

Saisselin, Rémy G. *The Rule of Reason and the Ruses of the Heart.* Cleveland: The Press of Case Western University, 1970.

Smith, Norman Kemp. *New Studies in the Philosophy of Descartes: Descartes as Pioneer.* New York: Russell & Russell, Inc., 1952, 1966. Chapter 6.

Strauss, Leo, and Joseph Cropsey, editors. *A History of Political Philosophy.* Chicago: University of Chicago Press, 1963, 1972, 1987. An essay: Kennington, Richard. "Descartes."

Williams, Bernard. *Descartes: The Project of Pure Enquiry.* New Jersey: Humanities Press, 1978. Chapter 10.

5. ENGLISH ARTICLES.

Articles that concern the *Passions of the Soul* in a substantial way and that are themselves substantial (thus, no brief discussion notes or reviews).

Aldrich, Virgil C. "The Pineal Gland Up-dated." *Journal of Philosophy* 67 (1970) 700-710.

Beavers, Anthony F. "Passion and Sexual Desire in Descartes." *Philosophy and Theology* (Disk Supplement 1) 2 (1988) 4-21.

Bertocci, Peter A. "Descartes and Marcel on the Person and his Body: A Critique." *Proceedings of the Aristotelian Society* 68 n.s. (1967-68) 207-226.

Burnett, Richard L. "Descartes' 'Les passions de l'âme': The Stylistics of Cartesian Rhetoric." *The USF Language Quarterly* 16 (1977-78) Nos. 1-2, 41-46; Nos. 3-4, 49-55. (Published at the University of South Florida, Tampa.)

Caton, Hiram. "Descartes' Anonymous Writings: A Recapitulation." *Southern Journal of Philosophy* 20 (1982) 299–311.

Comarnesco, Petru. "The Social and Ethical Conceptions of Descartes." *Ethics* 52 (1942) 493–503.

Davidson, Hugh M. "Descartes and the Utility of the Passions." *Romanic Review* 51 (1960) 15–26.

Galdston, Iago. "Descartes and Modern Psychiatric Thought." *Isis* 35 (1944) 118–128.

Gray, Philip H. "The Problem of Free Will in a Scientific Universe: René Descartes to John Tyndall." *Journal of General Psychology* 80 (1969) 57–72.

Han, Pierre. "The *Passions* in Descartes and Racine's *Phèdre*." *Romance Notes* 11 (1969–70) 107–109.

Heidsieck, François (translated by James M. Somerville). "Honor and Nobility of Soul: Descartes to Sartre." *International Philosophical Quarterly* 1 (1961) 569–592.

Irons, David. "Descartes and Modern Theories of Emotion." *Philosophical Review* 4 (1895) 291–302.

Jefferson, Geoffrey. "René Descartes on the Localisation of the Soul." *Irish Journal of Medical Science* 6 (1949) 691–706.

Keefe, T. "Descartes's 'Morale Définitive' and the Autonomy of Ethics." *Romanic Review* 64 (1973) 85–98.

Kennington, Richard. "The 'Teaching of Nature' in Descartes' Soul Doctrine." *Review of Metaphysics* 26 (1972–73) 86–117.

Lapp, J.C. "The *Traité des Passions* and Racine." *Modern Language Quarterly* 3 (1942) 611–619.

MacKenzie, Ann Wilbur. "A Word about Descartes' Mechanistic Conception of Life." *Journal of the History of Biology* 8 (1975) 1–13.

Matsuo, Yukitoshi. "'A Digression of the Animal Spirits': the Changes of the Concept of 'Spirit' in the Seventeenth-Century Science (I)." *Historia Scientiarum* 25 (1983) 1–15.

Millet, Louis. "Man and Risk." *International Philosophical Quarterly* 2 (1962) 417-427.

Rather, L.J. "Old and New Views of the Emotions and Bodily Changes: Wright and Harvey versus Descartes, James and Cannon." *Clio Medica* 1 (1965-66) 1-25.

Reed, Edward S. "Descartes' Corporeal Ideas Hypothesis and the Origin of Scientific Psychology." *Review of Metaphysics* 35 (1981-82) 731-752.

Remnant, Peter. "Descartes: Body and Soul." *Canadian Journal of Philosophy* 9 (1979) 377-386.

Riese, Walther. "Descartes as a Psychotherapist: The Uses of Rational Philosophy in the Treatment of Discomfort and Disease; its Limitations." *Medical History* 10 (1966) 237-244.

Rorty, Amélie Oksenberg. "Formal Traces in Cartesian Functional Explanation." *Canadian Journal of Philosophy* 14 (1984) 545-560.

———— "From Passions to Emotions and Sentiments." *Philosophy* 57 (1982) 159-172.

Ross, Stephanie. "Painting the Passions: Charles LeBrun's *Conférence sur l'expression*." *Journal of the History of Ideas* 45 (1984) 25-47.

Saveson, J.E. "Descartes' Influence on John Smith, Cambridge Platonist." *Journal of the History of Ideas* 20 (1959) 258-263.

Stempel, Daniel. "*The Garden*: Marvell's Cartesian Ecstasy." *Journal of the History of Ideas* 28 (1967) 99-114.

Stone, M.H. "Modern Concepts of Emotion as Prefigured in Descartes' 'Passions of the Soul'." *Journal of the American Academy of Psychoanalysis* 8 (1980) 473-495.

Voss, Stephen H. "How Spinoza Enumerated the Affects." *Archiv für Geschichte der Philosophie* 63 (1981) 167-179.

Watson, Robert I. "A Prescriptive Analysis of Descartes' Psychological Views." *Journal of the History of the Behavioral Sciences* 7 (1971) 223-248.

White, Howard. "Rembrandt and the Human Condition." *Interpretation* 4 (1974) 17–37.

Wright, John P. "Hysteria and Mechanical Man." *Journal of the History of Ideas* 41 (1980) 233–247.

INDEX

abhorrence, 48, 65, 67. *See also* aversion; hatred

absurdity, 106, 125

action
  and passion, 18-19
  of the eyes and face, 79
  of the soul, 25-26, 28-29, 34, 41-49. *See also* cause; free will; volition

affection, 64-65, 89-90, 103, 128

air (atmosphere), 12-13

ambition, 46-47, 63, 109

America, 6

ancients, 6-7, 18-19, 22. *See also* Aristotle, etc.

anger, 32, 44, 55-56, 79, 81, 125-129

animals, 5, 14, 27, 47-49, 67-69, 93. *See also* cats; partridges; setters

animal spirits. *See* spirits, animal

appetites, 25-26, 32, 44-46

apprehension, 39, 53, 109-113, 116. *See also* cowardice; fear

approval, 55, 123, 125-126

Archimedes, 12

architects, 12

Aristotle, 8-9, 12, 124. *See also* ancients; scholasticism

astonishment, 58-61, 114-116

astronomy, 11. *See also* stars

attention, 12, 42, 44, 56-57, 59-61, 97-100

automata, 21, 27. *See also* body (human)

aversion
  desire or a species of desire, 66, 67. *See also* desire
  hatred or a species of hatred, 62, 65, 74, 76, 86, 91, 124-125, 128. *See also* abhorrence; hatred

Bacon, Francis, 14

bantering, 117-118

beauty and ugliness, 13, 65, 67-69

benevolence, 62-63

birth, 5, 108-109, 118. *See also* life

blood
  circulation of, 22-23

movement of in passions, 72-78. *See also* entries for primitive passions

bodily sensations, 32 and *passim*

body (human)
  as a machine, 21-22, 26-27, 37-38. *See also* automata
  functions of, 19-27

boldness, 39-40, 43, 54, 113-116. *See also* courage

cats, 90-91

cause
  first, 5, 50-51
  free, 53, 109-110. *See also* action; free will; volition
  proximate, 32, 34-35, 50-51

chemistry, 13

children, 63-64, 89-91

chimeras, 13, 29, 98-99

clarity, 6, 10-12, 39, 94-95, 97-98, 112-113

concupiscence, 55-56, 62-63. *See also* delight; sex

confidence, 53, 111

contentment, 71-72, 101, 125. *See also* satisfaction

courage, 40, 54, 90, 113-116. *See also* boldness

cowardice, 54, 114-116. *See also* apprehension; fear

Cynics, 130-131

death, 20-21, 64-65, 67, 82-83, 114, 134. *See also* life

deception, 4-5, 33, 65, 93-96, 123-124, 134

Decii, 114

deficiency of passions. *See* excess and deficiency of passions

definition
  of passions of the soul, 32-35, 39, 44
  of primitive passions, 56, 62, 66, 69-70

delight, 65, 67-69. *See also* love; sex

Democritus, 124

derision. *See* mockery

desire, 82, 110-116. *See also* aversion
  definition, 66-69

enumerated, 53–54
movement of blood in, 73–76, 78
use of, 95–100
despair, 53, 111, 114, 132
devotion, 64–65, 109
Dinet, Père Pierre, 8
Dioptrique, 8–9, 25–26. *See also Essays*
disdain, 53, 110
dissimulation of passion, 79
distaste, 55, 131–132
distinctness and distinctions, 19, 28–30, 34,
    41, 44–45, 50–51, 55–56, 62–65, 71, 79,
    93–94, 97–100, 112–113, 128
doubt, 116–117
dreaming, 29–30, 33
duty, 2–7, 112–113, 120–121, 131
earth, 12, 14–15
Elisabeth, Princess, 16
emulation, 54, 113–114
enumeration, 8–9, 14–15
    of the principal passions, 51–56, 102, 132
envy, 54, 118–119, 124
Essays, 8–9. *See also Dioptrique; Météores*
esteem, 52–53, 64–65, 102–109, 111, 128–131.
    See also self-esteem
excess and deficiency of passions, 58–61, 93,
    112–113, 116, 122, 129, 132–134. *See also*
    vice
external signs of passions, 78–91. *See also*
    entries for particular passions
fainting, 82–83
fate, 98–100. *See also* fortune; providence
fathers, 63–64
fear, 39–40, 44, 46–47, 54, 81, 114–116. *See*
    also apprehension; cowardice
fire, 12–13, 20, 23–24, 32, 44, 82–83, 85–86.
    See also heart, heat of
flushing, 80–81, 126–129
fortune, 98–100, 106–107, 118–121, 125,
    134–135. *See also* fate; providence
France, 8, 15
free will, 41, 43–44, 97–100, 103–109. *See*
    also action; cause; volition
friendship, 63–65
funerals, 100–101
Galileo Galilei, 12
generosity, 52, 98, 104–110, 120–121, 128–129.
    See also humility, virtuous; pride;
    self-esteem; servility
geometry, 10

Gilbert, William, 12, 14
glory, 114, 119. *See also* honor; vainglory
God, 6, 7, 13, 15, 28, 64–65, 108–110, 118,
    121–122, 125. *See also* nature
    our likeness to, 103
gratitude, 55, 123–126, 131
groaning, 89
habit and habituation, 39, 42–43, 47–49, 52,
    61, 108–109, 113, 121–122
habituation, principle of, 42–43, 47–49,
    76–77, 90–91, 132–134
Harvey, William, 12, 22
hatred, 82–83. *See also* abhorrence; aversion
    definition, 62–65
    enumerated, 53
    movement of blood in, 73–75, 77
    use of, 94–96
heart, heat of, 23–24, 27, 73–74, 76–77, 82–83,
    85–86, 126, 128–129. *See also* fire
heavens. *See* sky
Heraclitus, 124
Holland, 2
honor, 63–64, 110–112, 131. *See also* glory
hope, 53, 99–100, 110–111, 114
humility, virtuous, 52, 105, 107–108, 110. *See*
    also generosity; pride; scorn; servility
husbands and wives, 100–101, 112
ideas, 13, 59, 74–76, 82, 90–91, 102
imagination, 12, 29–30, 33, 42, 62, 67–70, 79,
    82, 86, 90, 100–101, 133–134
impudence, 131
indignation, 55, 79, 86, 124–126, 129
ingratitude, 123–124, 131
inner excitations, 100–101. *See also* joy;
    sadness
Instauratio Magna (Bacon), 14
institution. *See* nature (origin of things)
irresolution, 46–47, 54, 112–113, 116–117, 122
jealousy, 53, 111–112
Jesuits, 8–9
joy, 80, 82–83, 85–87, 116–132, 134–135
    definition and causes, 69–72
    enumerated, 54–55
    intellectual, 69–70, 100–101. *See also* inner
        excitations
    movement of blood in, 73, 75, 77–78
    use of, 95–96
Kepler, Johannes, 12
knowledge of good and evil, 46–47
language. *See* meaning

languor, 70, 81-82, 114-115

laughter, 54, 83-86, 117-118, 125

life, 20-21, 23, 95-96, 101, 130-131, 134-135.
See also death
beginning of, 47, 76-78, 90-91. *See also* birth

light, 31, 37-38

lightheartedness, 55, 132

love, 82, 86-87, 89. *See also* benevolence; concupiscence; delight
definition, 62-65
enumerated, 53
movement of blood in, 73-74, 76-77
use of, 93-96

machines. *See* automata; body (human)

magnanimity. *See* generosity

magnets, 12-14

mathematics, 10-12

meaning, 42-43, 47-48.

medicine and sickness, 3, 5-7, 21-22, 76-77, 87

memory, 41-42, 59, 90-91, 132, 134

Météores, 8-9, 87. *See also* Essays

method, 10, 12-14

mockery, 54, 79, 117-119, 124

moral philosophy, 17, 97. *See also* duty; vice; virtue

mothers, 90-91

nature (origin of things), 42-43, 51-52, 116, 118, 123-125. *See also* God
institution of, 39, 47-48, 67-69, 71, 91-92

nourishment, 22, 27, 48, 73-78, 86, 131-132

Novus Atlas (Bacon), 14

order, 87-88
of passions, 50-53, 55-56, 102, 132

pain, 32, 34, 37, 44, 71, 87-89, 91-92, 94-95

paleness, 80, 90, 126-129

Paris, 1

particular passions, 102 and Part III, *passim*

partridges, 48

passions. *See* blood; definition; dissimulation of passion; enumeration; excess and deficiency of passions; external signs of passions; order; particular passions; primitive passions; remedies for defects of the passions; uses of the passions

perception, 28-35 and *passim*

perfection, 67-69, 91-94, 101, 104

philosophy, 2, 7-10, 12
scholastic, 7-10, 12

physics, 16-17
Descartes's prospects in, 7-12
necessity for experiments, 12-15
scholastic, 9-10
usefulness of, 6-7

pineal gland, 36-46, 50, 81-82 and *passim*

pity, 54, 119-121, 124, 131

pride, 4, 52, 105-108. *See also* generosity; humility, virtuous; servility

primitive passions, 56, 102 and Part II, *passim*

Principles of Philosophy, 2, 10, 12, 14

privation, 66, 94-95

providence, 98-100, 125. *See also* fate; fortune

Pythagoras, 12

regret, 47, 55, 132

religion, 64-65, 109-110, 121-122

remedies for defects of the passions, 59-61, 93, 97-99, 101, 105, 108-109, 112-113, 116-117, 122, 132-135

remorse, 54, 116-117

repentance, 47, 55, 116-117, 122

respect. *See* veneration

roses, 90-91

sadness, 80-81, 83, 86-87, 89-90, 116-132
definition and causes, 70-72
enumerated, 54-55
intellectual, 70. *See also* inner excitations
movement of blood in, 73, 75, 78
use of, 95-96

satisfaction, 97-101, 120-121. *See also* contentment; self-satisfaction

scholasticism, 66, 109. *See also* Aristotle; philosophy; physics

scorn, 52-53, 102-108, 110. *See also* humility, virtuous; servility

self-esteem, 52, 103-109, 128-130. *See also* esteem; generosity; pride

self-satisfaction, 55, 121-122, 129-130. *See also* contentment; satisfaction

sense perception, 25-26, 31, 38 and *passim*

servility, 4, 52, 106-108, 110, 123-124, 128-129. *See also* generosity; humility, virtuous; pride

setters, 48-49

sex, 67-69. *See also* concupiscence; delight

sexual violence, 63-64

shame, 55, 81, 130-131

sighing, 90

sky, 12-15, 37

soul
faculties of, 55-56. *See also* soul, simplicity of
functions of, 19-21, 28-35
rational, 44-46
simplicity of, 35, 44-46, 55-56. *See also* soul, faculties of
union with body, 34-49

spirits, animal, 22-27, 44-46, 107-108 and *passim*

stars, 37. *See also* astronomy

strength and weakness of the soul, 4, 12-13, 39, 46-49, 104, 110, 112-113, 120-122

struggles imagined within soul, 44-46

tears, 81, 86-90, 100-101, 121

terror. *See* fear

Thales, 12

theater, 71, 100-101, 120-121

theologians, 7-9

tickling, 58, 133-134

titillation, 71, 91-92

trembling, 81

ugliness. *See* beauty and ugliness

uses of the passions, 40-41, 51-52, 59. *See also* entries for the primitive passions

vainglory, 55, 129-131. *See also* glory

value. *See* glory; honor; moral philosophy; uses of the passions; vice; virtue

veneration, 53, 109-110

vice, 105-108, 110, 116-119, 123-125. *See also* excess and deficiency of passions

virtue, 97-98, 101, 103-109, 117-118, 121-122, 125, 130-131

Vives, Juan Luis, 86

volition, 28-30, 41-49 and *passim. See also* action; cause; free will

water, 12-13, 86-89

weakness of the soul. *See* strength and weakness of the soul

weapons, 46-47

wisdom, 6, 103, 132-135

women, 63-64, 111-112. *See also* husbands and wives

wonder, 82-83, 85, 102-110, 125
definition and cause, 56-58
enumerated, 52-53
movement of blood absent in, 57-58
use of, 59-61

INDEX LOCORUM

The Index Locorum records references to passages in Descartes's works which appear in footnotes to *The Passions of the Soul*. *P* identifies footnotes to the Preface and roman numerals identify footnotes to Parts I-III of the text.

Correspondence
April 1622–February 1638: AT I

132–133	II 25
133–134	I 54; II 57
153	II 58
366	III 11
371–372	II 74
414–416	I 53
416	I 12
422	P 15
523	I 34; II 46
562–564	P 19

Correspondence
March 1638–December 1639: AT II

36–37	I 41; II 70
38	I 2
39–41	I 53
197–200	P 19
199–202	II 53
480	II 61
485	I 7

Correspondence
January 1640–June 1643: AT III

19–20	I 35
20–21	II 58
47–49	I 35
123–124	I 34, 35
248–249	I 41
263–265	I 34, 35
265–266	I 34
295	I 19, 21
361–362	I 35
369–370	I 53

371	I 47
372	I 19, 21
373	I 36
383	II 36
392–397	II 36
422–423	II 75
428	I 3
432	I 19
566	I 5
665–666	I 1
690–695	I 29

Correspondence
July 1643–April 1647: AT IV

64–65	I 53
166–167	I 32
188–192	I 8
201–202	III 46
202	III 47
202–203	II 77; III 25
218–222	III 46
219–220	II 77
264	II 71
264–265	II 70
265–266	II 71; III 27, 46
266–267	I 51
271–278	II 68
276–277	II 71
281–282	I 41
281–287	II 71
283–287	I 29
284	II 76
285	III 36
286–287	III 46
290–296	I 51
291–292	II 73
292–294	II 20, 47; III 39

294	II 13
294–295	I 29; II 76; III 46
295	III 18, 42
304–307	II 67
304–309	II 68
306–307	III 46
307	II 75; III 27
307–308	III 8
308–309	II 20, 47
309	II 77
309–313	I 26
310–311	I 18
311	I 23, 30, 36, 39
313	II 1
329	P 10
331	III 27
331–332	III 20
332	II 1
346	I 32
354–356	II 77
407–409	I 43; II 32
409–410	II 48
410–411	II 56
411	II 42, 74; III 46
414–415	II 42
441–442	P 10
538	III 40, 46
573–576	I 53
600–617	II 20
601–602	II 64
601–604	II 76
602–603	I 29
603–606	I 43
604–606	II 37
606	II 21
611–613	III 39
613–617	II 59, 67
616	III 38

Correspondence
May 1647–February 1650: AT V

51–52	P 15
55–56	III 9
55–58	II 20
65–66	I 43
81–85	III 3
81–86	II 68
82–83	I 41
84–85	I 29; II 71

135	III 46
221–222	I 44
274–275	P 15
275–279	I 5, 53
355–356	P 15

Discourse on Method: AT VI

2	I 53
3	I 2
6	III 43
10	III 43
12	III 43
16	III 43
18	I 1
19	II 1, 12
23–24	III 42
24	III 18
25	III 27
25–27	I 27, 41; II 70
27–28	III 11
28	I 2; III 42
31	III 43
45–60	P 19
46	II 49
46–55	I 10
49–55	I 11
55	II 36
56–59	I 53
61	P 7; III 43
61–63	P 10
62	III 7
63–65	P 19
66	P 7
74–75	P 5
76	P 19

Dioptrics: AT VI

105–108	I 44
109–114	I 11, 15
112–113	I 52
112–114	I 24
114–129	I 38
128–147	I 16
129	II 58

Meteorology: AT VI

231	II 17
235–236	I 7

239–248   II 52
308–311   II 52

Meditations on
First Philosophy: AT VII

12–14   I 34
18   I 27
25–29   I 18, 23
26   I 5
28–29   I 28
37   I 27, 28
56   II 64
56–57   II 70
57   II 17
64   P 16
74   I 40
78   I 18, 23
78–83   I 24
78–84   I 29
82–90   II 61
83   III 46
84–85   I 7
85–86   I 18, 23; II 62
85–89   I 34
86   I 43
86–88   I 35

Objections and Replies: AT VII

112–113   P 15
153–154   I 34
160–161   II 36
173–175   I 21
181   II 36
188   II 36
191   I 19
229–231   I 53
356   I 53
366   II 36
377–378   I 19
426   I 53

Letter to Dinet: AT VII

579–580   P 12

Principles of Philosophy: AT VIII

3–4   P 25
14–15   P 15

19–20   I 19
23   I 1
32   I 29
59–60   P 15
249   I 7
255–256   I 7
315   P 22
316–318   II 1
317–318   I 29, 47; II 76
318   II 31
321–323   I 7

Meditations,
French translation: AT IX

45   II 64

Principles,
French translation: AT IXB

1–3   P 8
14–15   P 10
17   P 4
18–19   P 14
20   P 18

Cogitationes Privatae: AT X

217   II 55
218   II 17

Rules for the Direction
of the Mind: AT X

379–387   I 1
379–392   II 1, 12
400–403   II 17
414–415   I 35
414–417   II 36
438–452   P 16
447–452   I 33

The World: AT XI

4   I 52
7–10   I 7

Treatise on Man: AT XI

119–120   I 1, 31
120   I 7

124–125	I 12
130–132	I 7
143–144	II 31
163–167	II 1
174–177	I 30; II 36
177	II 58
177–179	I 42

Description of
the Human Body: AT XI

223–226	I 1
224–226	I 5
228	II 49
231–244	I 10
242	P 19
282	II 46

Passions of the Soul: AT XI

Preface

302	P 20
303	P 20
304	P 20; III 44
308	P 20; III 43
308–310	P 3
309	III 43
310–318	P 3
318–321	P 3
319	II 36
320	P 9, 20
321	III 43
324	P 8
325	P 5
326	P 5; I 5, 13, 43; II 13

Part I: articles 1–50 [Parts I–III indexed by article number]

1	I 2, 27; II 26
1–6	I 1
2	I 2, 8, 31; II 36
3–6	I 4
4–6	I 5, 47
5	I 5
6	I 7
7	I 7
7–10	I 8
7–16	I 1, 8; II 39
8	I 7
10	I 48
12	I 30

12–16	I 37
13	I 7, 47
15	I 13
16	I 7
17	I 29; II 14, 64
17–29	I 1, 18
18	I 14, 44
19–20	I 41
21	I 26; II 3, 30, 41
22	I 23
22–25	I 22
23	I 23, 24, 30
24	I 23, 24, 30, 47
25	I 23, 29, 36
26	I 22, 26, 29; II 3, 30, 41
27	I 23, 39, 45
27–29	I 18
29	I 5, 23, 39; II 2
30	II 11, 78
30–50	I 1, 31
31	I 14, 36
32	I 30, 35
33–39	II 2
34	I 7, 14
35	I 30
36	I 36, 40
37	I 45; III 30
40	II 15, 59, 60
41	I 44
43	I 14; II 16; III 46
44	I 52, 54; II 32, 37, 57
45	I 49; II 3, 40; III 46
47	I 34, 47; II 11, 78
48	I 40, 47; II 14, 54, 62; III 11, 27
49	I 40; II 62; III 27
50	I 40, 43; II 32, 37, 57; III 12, 46

Part II: articles 51–148

51	I 26, 40; II 30
51–52	II 1, 3
51–69	II 1
52	I 23, 36; II 15, 59; III 1, 29
53	I 23
53–67	II 1
54	III 1
56	I 23; II 59, 64; III 29
57	I 23; II 4
58	II 8, 74; III 19
59	II 8
61	I 23; II 30, 64
63	II 76; III 27

65	III 29
68	I 34, 47; II 5, 13, 78
68–69	II 1
69	II 13; III 1, 15
70–73	II 13, 39
70–95	II 13
71	II 32
73	III 20
74	II 59
74–78	II 13
75	II 36
75–78	II 59
76	III 20
78	III 10, 20
79	II 19, 21, 29, 64, 65
79–136	II 13
80	II 19, 29
81	II 21
82	III 39
83	II 14, 24; III 19, 39
84	II 28
85	II 14, 27, 29
89	II 14
90	II 14, 23, 27
91–93	I 41; II 76
92	II 64
93	I 26; II 30
94	I 26; II 30, 77
96	II 32
96–111	II 13, 32, 39
97–101	II 32
98	II 35
101	II 44
102	II 14
102–106	II 32, 37
103	II 36; III 24
105	III 24
106	II 36
107	I 43; II 57
107–110	II 37
107–111	II 32. 37
112 136	II 13, 39
117	III 38
120	II 36, 45, 74
126	I 12; II 33, 48; III 22
127	III 34
131	III 26
133	I 40
136	I 40, 43; II 36
137	II 27, 60, 63

137–138	II 59, 68
137–148	II 13
138	I 29, 53; II 14, 60
139	II 14, 60, 61
139–142	II 59, 68, 69
139–146	II 76
140	II 14, 64
143	II 68; III 4
143–146	II 59, 68, 70
143–148	II 71
145	II 73, 74; III 4, 10, 15, 16
146	II 73, 74; III 10
147	II 76, 78
147–148	I 27, 41; II 59

Part III: articles 149–212

149	II 36
149–153	II 71
149–164	III 1
152	II 17; III 3, 7
152–153	II 70
153	I 19; II 72; III 5, 8
154	III 11, 12
156	II 72, 74; III 9
158	I 19; III 9
159	I 19
160	III 1, 38
161	I 40; II 7, 72; III 10, 12
162	III 35
163	III 35
164	I 40
165	III 19
165–176	III 13
166	II 14, 74; III 15, 19
170	I 39, 40; II 42; III 20, 27
173	II 14, 24
176	III 30
177	II 10; III 18, 27
177–210	III 21
178	III 33
183	III 9, 43
184	III 24
185	III 33
186	III 38
187	II 77, 78
190	III 43
191	III 18
194	I 39; III 20
195	III 29, 39
197	II 51

199	II 35; III 38, 39	204–207	III 41
200	II 55	205	III 38
201	III 40	207	I 39; III 20, 43
202	II 35	210	II 1; III 41, 45
203	III 20, 39	211	I 29, 43, 46; II 14, 40, 62; III 20
204	II 76; III 38	212	III 7

This book was set in
Jansen
by
Chief City Graphics

Jansen
is a modern typeface
based on designs
once thought to be
the work of
the Dutch typefounder
Anton Jansen.
The original typeface
is now believed
to have been designed by
Miklos Kis
in about 1690.